GREAT AMERICAN AIR BATTLES
OF WORLD WAR II

GREAT AMERICAN AIR BATTLES
OF WORLD WAR II

Martin W. Bowman

BARNES
&NOBLE
BOOKS
NEW YORK

Books by the author:
Fields of Little America
Encyclopedia of American Military Aircraft
The B-24 Liberator 1939–45
Castles In The Air
Home by Christmas?
The Bedford Triangle
Wellington: The Geodetic Giant
The World's Fastest Aircraft
Famous Bombers
Classic Fighter Aircraft
Modern Military Aircraft
Flying to Glory
Spirits in the Sky (with Patrick Bunce)
Four Miles High
Great American Air Battles 1942–1992
Eighth Air Force At War
Thunder In The Heavens (with Patrick Bunce)
Cavalry In The Clouds
The Men Who Flew the Mosquito (in preparation)
Low Level From Swanton (in preparation)

This edition published by Barnes & Noble Inc.,
by arrangement with Airlife Publishing Ltd.

Copyright © 1994 by Martin W. Bowman.

First published in the UK in 1994
by Airlife Publishing Ltd.

ISBN 1-56619-904-2

Printed in England.

CONTENTS

ACKNOWLEDGEMENTS

Material for this book came from many diverse sources and the following contributors supplied the 'icing on the cake' with much needed photographs, research material and, in some cases, very valuable assistance. I would particularly like to thank Larry Goldstein for 'doing the rounds' in various archive sections in Washington DC and unearthing much needed material. I am grateful too for Robert M. Foose's inspired suggestion to feature the 357th Fighter Group's momentous day in January 1945; he then provided me with very valuable encounter reports. I am most grateful to the 357th historian, Merle C. Olmsted, who came up with the necessary photographs and additional information. Frank J. Bertram, George M. Collar and William R. Dewey of the Kassel Memorial Association were equally forthcoming with information and photographs pertaining to the events of 27 September 1944.

Many interesting and entertaining Sunday mornings were spent with Ken Everett, Mike Harvey, Mike Nice and Richard Wilson at the Thorpe Abbotts Memorial Museum. I am extremely grateful for their input, help and assistance with much needed photographs and data on the Schweinfurt missions and for access to information contained in *Century Bombers*, the museum's own publication on the events surrounding the 100th Bomb Group in World War Two.

I would like to reiterate my thanks to Roland H. Baker for his account of the events of 29 March 1945 and for kindly providing photographs. Thanks too go to J. Hunter Reinburg, USMC (retd), for kindly allowing me to quote passages from his book, *Aerial Combat Escapades*. Captain Paul F. Stevens USN (Retd) and Cdr Ralph Tallmadge Briggs, USN, (Retd) kindly permitted me to adapt their original compilations, USN Intelligence reports, and submissions from Mihoko Yamagata, granddaughter of Admiral Yamagata; which were submitted to the US Naval Institute Proceedings and published in their *Naval History Quarterly*, Spring 1989 issue.

I would also like to thank the following for their valuable contributions of time and energy and for providing me with much sought after photographs: Mike Bailey; Col William R. Cameron; Claude Campbell; F.C. 'Hap' Chandler, 491st BG Assn; Henry C. Cordery; Roy G. Davidson; Don E. Ferguson; Robert M. Foose; Harry Gann, McDonnell Douglas; James F. Gerrits; Carl W. Groshell; the late Howard E. Hernan; Lloyd D. Hubbard; Robert Hughes; Virgil H. Jeffries; Myron H. Keilman, Col USAF (retd); Harold E. Lanning; Henry Latimore; Lois Lovisolo, Grumman Corporation; Ian McLachlan; Gus Mencow, Joseph Metcalf; Lloyd Murff; the late Heinz Nowarra; John Page; the late Budd J. Peaslee; the late Richard H. Perry; the late General Maurice 'Mo' Preston; Connie and Gordon Richards; Bill Rose; Ernst Schröeder; Edwin L. Smith; David Williams; Earl Zimmerman.

CHAPTER 1

Battle of the Coral Sea

On 7 December 1941 the United States suffered a massive blow with the Japanese air attack on Pearl Harbor in the Hawaiian islands. Eight battleships and three cruisers were among the damaged and sunken ships of the US Pacific Fleet and more than 2,000 sailors, soldiers and airmen perished. America entered the Second World War and Admiral Chester W. Nimitz, who took command of the Pacific Fleet, began rebuilding his forces for the strike back across the Pacific.

Nimitz could immediately call upon three aircraft carriers, the USS *Lexington* (CV 2), USS *Saratoga* (CV 3), and USS *Enterprise* (CV 6), which had been at sea during the Pearl Harbor attack (in US Navy nomenclature, 'CV' was the designator for a fleet carrier and the aviation squadrons on each carrier were numbered accordingly). These three carriers, or 'flat-tops' as they are known in Navy parlance, together with five others, USS *Langley* (CV 1), USS *Ranger* (CV 4), USS *Wasp* (CV 7), USS *Hornet* (CV 8) and USS *Yorktown* (CV 5), would form the backbone of the Pacific Fleet from 1941 to 1945. Almost twenty naval battles involving the US Navy and the Imperial Japanese Navy would be fought during this period and five of them would be fought between aircraft carriers. Critically, four of these battles would occur within a six month period during 1942 and their outcome would affect the whole course of the war. But for six months following Pearl Harbor America and her allies were powerless to stop the Japanese advance, which overran critical islands like the Philippines, East Indies, Guam and Wake. To turn the tide, the United States needed to recapture these islands and others under Japanese control.

By mid-April 1942 the Japanese were well on the way to total domination in the New Guinea/New Britain/Solomon Islands area of the South Pacific. The decision was taken to send a Japanese seaborne task force to take Tulagi in the Solomons and Port Moresby in New Guinea with the intention of cutting the America–Australia supply route and at the same time establishing a base for the invasion of Australia itself. The main Japanese task force assembled at Truk in the Carolines and on 30 April sailed south towards Rabaul at the northernmost tip of New Britain, where Vice-Admiral Shigeyoshi Inouye was assembling five separate naval forces to carry out his invasion plans. In addition, he could call upon over 140 land-based fighters and bombers. To repel the invasion Admiral Nimitz despatched Task Force 17 to the Coral Sea under the command

Armourers work on the wings of VF-6's F4F-3 Wildcats clustered on the deck of the USS *Enterprise* on 13 April 1942 (Duane A. Kasulka).

During the Battle of the Coral Sea SBD Dauntlesses sunk the small carrier *Shoho* and disabled the fleet carrier *Shokaku*. This SBD-3A (A-24 Banshee) was delivered to the US Army from the US Navy production line at El Segundo between June and October 1941. The 91st Bombardment Squadron A-24s fared badly in the Dutch East Indies and they met with equal misfortune in Australia, where only one of seven 8th Bombardment Group A-24s returned from a mission to Buna on 29 July 1942 after being intercepted by Zeros (McDonnell Douglas).

by Rear-Admiral Aubrey W. Fitch, was a former battle-cruiser which had been converted to a carrier by a provision of the Washington Naval Treaty of 1921.

When America entered the war on 8 December 1941, carrier squadrons normally operated three types of aircraft. Fighter squadrons flew the stubby Grumman F4F-3 Wildcat while scout and bomber units operated the Douglas SBD-2 Dauntless, and torpedo squadrons flew the Douglas TBD-1 Devastator. At the time of Pearl Harbor the Dauntless was considered obsolete, but the prolonged development of its intended successor, the Curtiss SB2C, which did not finally enter service until the end of 1943, saw the Douglas aircraft enjoy a long and successful career which was unsurpassed by any other dive-bomber in the world. The TBD-1, designed in 1934, was the first all-metal

of Rear-Admiral Frank J. Fletcher. The task force was made up of two carriers, seven cruisers and a screen of destroyers. The carrier *Yorktown*, sister of the *Enterprise*, was Fletcher's flagship and had been the fourth carrier to join the Pacific Fleet after being transferred from the Atlantic shortly after Pearl Harbor. The second carrier, *Lexington*, commanded

When America went to war in the Pacific in 1942 about 100 TBD-1 Devastators were available and just twenty-five took part in the Battle of the Coral Sea in May 1942. The poor torpedoes then available required that runs be made at altitudes of 80 feet at no more than 80 knots (92 mph) with release no further than 1,000 yards from the target. Even so, the torpedoes often failed to work properly (McDonnell Douglas).

monoplane carrier aircraft in the US Navy when it joined the Fleet in 1937, but by modern standards it was too slow, had a poor rate of climb and its range was limited. It also carried a very unreliable torpedo, the Mk 13, whose pre-war development had suffered badly because of lack of funding and limited testing. Each American squadron totalled eighteen aircraft of these respective types so a typical air group consisted of thirty-six Dauntlesses, eighteen Wildcats and eighteen Devastators, or seventy-two aircraft.

Ranged against them was Rear-Admiral Takagi's main strike force comprising the aircraft carriers *Zuikaku* and *Shokaku*, two cruisers and a screen of destroyers. The carriers between them had on board forty-two Mitsubishi A6M5 Zero fighters, forty-two Nakajima B5N Kate torpedo bombers and forty-one Aichi D3A Val dive-bombers. The US Navy outnumbered the Japanese in dive-bombers but more importantly, American carriers were equipped with radar and many of the *Yorktown*'s aircraft carried IFF (Identification, Friend or Foe) equipment, two innovations the Japanese carriers lacked.

The Port Moresby invasion force consisted of five Navy and six Army transports plus a number of other vessels and a destroyer escort. The Japanese strike force sailed from Truk on a course well to the east of the Solomons in order to avoid American reconnaissance aircraft for as long as possible. On 3 May Inouye ordered a small strategic strike force under Rear-Admiral Shima to attack and occupy Tulagi. By 1100 hours the island was under Japanese domination. Next day Fletcher despatched his aircraft from *Yorktown* to attack Tulagi.

At 0630 hours the first aerial strike force consisting of twelve Devastators of VT-5 (Torpedo) and twenty-eight Dauntless dive-bombers of VS-5 (Scout) and VB-5 (bomber) headed for Tulagi. Bad visibility shielded the aircraft until they were twenty-miles from the island, which was just as well because the crews could only rely on their own machine guns for protection; all eighteen Wildcat fighters of VF-42 (Fighting Squadron 42) were required for combat air patrol over the carrier. Starting at 0815 hours the two Dauntless squadrons and one Devastator squadron made their attacks on shipping and land targets on Tulagi. Each squadron attacked targets independently as was the practice of the time. Altogether, two air strikes succeeded in sinking three minesweepers, while the destroyer

Kikuzuki and a patrol craft were badly damaged for the loss of one Devastator. A third attack by twenty-one Dauntlesses dive-bombed landing barges but they succeeded in sinking only four. The most successful action was the destruction of five Kawanishi H6K Mavis flying-boats. By 1632 hours the last of the returning bombers was safely back on the carrier deck of the *Yorktown*. Two Grumman F4F-3 Wildcat fighters, which had strayed off course on the return to the carrier, had crash-landed on Guadalcanal but their pilots were picked up later and returned to the ship.

Generally, bombing results had been poor and the Devastator had proved most unsatisfactory. The Dauntless strikes had fared little better considering the high number of bombs dropped but crews were jubilant, believing they had sunk two destroyers, one freighter and four gunboats among others. Admiral Takagi's force carried on, and on 5 May passed Cristobal, turned west and passed north of Rennell Island. Allied reconnaissance aircraft failed to find the strike force in the prevailing bad weather, but the first H6K to sight the American flat-tops was shot down by Wildcats of VF-42.

At 0930 hours on 6 May Takagi turned south. Meanwhile, the Port Moresby invasion force, commanded by Rear-Admiral Kajioka, was underway from Rabaul. Kajioka in his flagship, *Yubari*, rendezvoused with Rear-Admiral Marushige's support group off Buin, Bougainville and headed for the Jomard Passage. As the American and Japanese fleets played cat and mouse, at noon at H6 flying-boat sighted and reported the position of the *Lexington* and the *Yorktown* but the report was not passed on to the Japanese carrier commander for eighteen hours. The *Shoho*, operating in support of the invasion force, was spotted by USAAF B-17Es during the day but no immediate action could be taken. During the evening of 6 May, in squally weather, the two opposing US and Japanese task forces were only seventy miles apart but neither force was aware of the other. During the night both forces change course and the gap between them widened again.

Before dawn on 7 May Fletcher instructed Rear-Admiral Crace's force (Crace was an admiral in the Royal Navy and he commanded an Allied force of two Australian cruisers, a US cruiser and a destroyer escort) to close the southern exit of Jomard Passage. Meanwhile, Fletcher's Task Force

17 held a steady westward course 225 miles south of Rennell Island. At first light he sent off two reconnaissance aircraft to try and locate the Japanese carriers.

At this time the Port Morseby invasion force was just off the Louisiade Archipelago. At 0815 hours one of the American reconnaissance aircraft reported seeing 'two carriers and four heavy cruisers'. Their position was radioed to the *Yorktown*. Although the ships were part of Rear-Admiral Goto's covering force, Fletcher, believing it to be the main force, ordered a strike. Between 0926 and 1030 hours ninety-three aircraft were flown off, leaving forty-seven for combat patrol. The Dauntless scouts soon returned, however, and it soon became apparent that the ships were in fact two heavy cruisers and two destroyers, the error having been made during encoding. Nevertheless, Fletcher allowed the strike to continue in the hope that a more profitable target would present itself.

Indeed it did. Shortly after 1100 hours, Lt-Commander Hamilton, who was leading one of *Lexington*'s Dauntless squadrons, spotted the aircraft carrier *Shoho* with some cruisers and destroyers near Misima Island in the Louisiades. The *Shoho* was only thirty-five miles south-east of the original target location so it was an easy matter to re-direct the air groups to the new target. The two air groups overwhelmed the Japanese defences even though the *Shoho* was protected by four cruisers and a destroyer. Commander W. B. Ault led the first attack and succeeded in knocking five aircraft over the carrier's side. His attack was followed at intervals shortly after by successive waves of Hamilton's ten Dauntlesses, the *Lexington*'s Devastator torpedo squadron and the *Yorktown*'s Dauntless attack group, all of which scored thirteen bomb and seven torpedo strikes on the carrier, leaving it on fire and listing. The *Shoho* sank shortly after 1135 hours. Some 600 of the 800 complement went down with the carrier. Six American aircraft were shot down. Lt-Commander Robert Dixon, leading *Lexington*'s other Dauntless squadron, radioed his ship and said 'Scratch one flat-top!'

The loss of the *Shoho* deprived Inouye's invasion force of air cover and he was forced to delay north of the Louisiades until the Jomard Passage has been cleared. Early in the afternoon Rear-Admiral Crace's force was attacked in strength by successive waves of shore-based torpedo bombers, but the Japanese crews failed to sink any of the Allied ships. *Shokaku* and *Zuikaku*, meanwhile, had been kept unnecessarily busy launching some sixty sorties which resulted in the sinking of the oil tanker USS *Neosho* and the destroyer *Sims* after the ships had been mistaken in earlier reports for a carrier and a cruiser. Realising the error, some twelve D3A Val dive-bombers and fifteen B5N Kate torpedo bombers were launched just before 1630 hours from *Shokaku* and *Zuikaku* with orders to attack Fletcher's carriers if they managed to locate them. The weather worsened during the afternoon and prevented any patrols from taking off from the American carriers. Fletcher had to rely on reports from shore-based aircraft such as the B-17Es. The Japanese were even further hampered in their search mission. They had no radar so the attacking aircraft could only search the area where they estimated the American carriers to be. It proved fruitless although they were closer to the American task force than they realised. The Japanese attack force was picked up on American radar and a combat patrol of F3F Wildcats of VF-3 from the *Lexington* was vectored to engage them. The Wildcats shot down nine bombers while the Vals accounted for the loss of two fighters which tried to dog-fight with the dive-bombers.

Nearing nightfall the Japanese crews finally gave up their search. They dropped their torpedoes into the sea and began the flight back to their carriers. At 1900 hours three Japanese planes were spotted blinking in Morse code on Aldis lamps on *Yorktown*'s starboard beam. They managed to get clean away, but twenty minutes later three more attempted to join the *Yorktown*'s landing circuit and one was shot down. A further eleven bombers failed to land back on their carriers and crashed into the sea in darkness. Only six of the original twenty-seven managed to return safely to their carriers.

Inouye's invasion plans were now in tatters. With the *Shoho* sunk and his path through the Jomard Passage into the Coral Sea blocked by Crace's cruisers, the Port Moresby invasion force remained north of the Louisiades until it was ordered to withdraw. Fletcher's and Takagi's carrier forces remained to fight it out alone like two colossi until one emerged victorious. During the night of 7 May the two task forces sailed further away from one another, neither admiral daring to risk a night attack.

Next morning brilliant sunshine replaced the previous day's murk over Fletcher's task force but the

Japanese task force was covered by a low overcast. At 0600 hours the Japanese carrier planes mounted a search mission and a short while later eighteen reconnaissance planes from the *Lexington* set out to find the elusive Japanese fleet. At 0815 hours and almost out of fuel, one of the Dauntless dived through thick cloud and squalls and the excited radio-navigator exclaimed, 'Ships at two o'clock!' The pilot dived for a closer look and the aircraft was rocked immediately by an explosion as a shell from one of the ships exploded near the port wing-tip. The pilot pulled up on the stick and headed for the safety of the clouds while his radio-navigator sent a Morse code message back to the US task force pinpointing the Japanese task force's position, 175 miles to the north-east of Fletcher's position. Fighters and bombers aboard the *Lexington* and *Yorktown* were prepared for take-off from the rolling carrier decks. At around 0850 hours the *Yorktown* group of twenty-four Dauntless dive-bombers with two Wildcats and nine Devastators with four Wildcats were flown off her deck and they turned on course to their target. Aboard the 'Lady Lex' Fitch ordered off his aircraft starting at 0900 hours. Some twenty-two Dauntlesses, eleven Devastators and nine Wildcats got airborne and they proceeded independently of the *Yorktown* strike force to their target. By 0925 hours all the American aircraft had left the decks of the two American carriers. Meanwhile, in the same period, the Japanese had launched a strike force of fifty-one bombers and eighteen fighters for a concerted attack on the American carriers.

The opposing Japanese and American pilots passed each other en route to their targets, oblivious of one another, high in the sky above the Coral Sea. At 1030 hours the Dauntless pilots spotted the Japanese ships first. Down below the Americans could make out the *Shokaku* and *Zuikaku* eight miles apart heading for their own carriers protected by two cruisers and several destroyers. The Dauntless crews hid in low cloud and rain while they waited for the slower Devastators to arrive. The *Shokaku* emerged from the squally overcast and at 1057 hours the American bombers attacked. The Dauntless crews from the *Yorktown* made their attacks but only two bombs hit the *Shokaku*. Torpedoes launched from the Devastators either missed or failed to explode, probably because they had been released too soon. The Japanese carrier

took violent evasive action to miss them. Japanese fighters rose up to attack as the Dauntlesses went in with their bombs, and they shot down three American aircraft. The bombs which had hit the *Shokaku* exploded with one setting the engine repair shop on fire and the other damaging the flight-deck preventing the launch of any further aircraft. The twenty-two Dauntless dive-bombers from the *Lexington* air group failed to find the enemy in the expected location and, low on fuel, they were forced to break off, leaving only four Dauntless scouts, eleven Devastators and six F4F Wildcats to continue the search. They soon sighted the enemy carriers, but patrolling Zeros intercepted the strike while it was still fifteen miles out. They succeeded in driving off the Wildcat escorts but the low flying Devastators managed to launch their torpedoes.

Despite claims to the contrary, none of the torpedoes found their mark, but a bomb dropped by a Dauntless hit the *Shokaku* and caused more damage. The attack cost the Americans five bombers and one fighter and had almost been in vain. The small carrier was burning but none of the bombs had hit below the waterline. Most of her aircraft were transferred to the *Zuikaku*, which had briefly emerged from the murk only to slip back into it again before the American aircraft could draw a bead. At 1300 hours the *Shokaku* left the battle zone with 108 dead strewn on her decks, and limped home to Truk.

Meanwhile, the American battle fleet had been discovered at 1055 hours bathed in bright sunlight and with little fighter cover. The incoming raid by thirty-five Val dive-bombers, eighteen B5N Kate torpedo bombers and eighteen A6M5 Zero fighters was detected on the radar screens some sixty-eight miles from the *Lexington*, which was charged with overall fighter direction, but the fighter defences had been badly positioned to meet the attack. Low on fuel, a dozen Wildcats on combat air patrol at 10,000 feet were forced to circle the ships, unable to climb at full power or zoom off into the distance and intercept the dive-bombers flying at 18,000 feet. Only three fighter pilots spotted the Japanese strike force before the attack began. Twelve Dauntless SBDs, their pilots schooled to expect the Japanese attack at low level (which was the tactic adopted by the US Navy torpedo squadrons), had been positioned three miles outside the destroyer screen at 2,000 feet. The Kates and their Zero escorts flew over the SBDs at 6,000 feet and only dropped down to

F4F-3 Wildcats are spotted on the smouldering flight-deck of the USS *Lexington*, hit during a Japanese air strike in the Battle of the Coral Sea (US Navy).

low level after clearing the destroyer screen. Even so, the SBDs defended magnificently, shooting down two Kates before torpedo release and destroying two more B5Ns, a Val and two Zeros for the loss of four SBDs.

The *Yorktown* twisted and turned as bombs rained down from the bellies of the Vals while the Kates launched eight torpedoes against her port quarter. Only violent evasive action ensured that all of them

missed the huge carrier. Five minutes later, at 1123 hours, the carrier came under attack from the Vals. An 800lb bomb went right through the flight-deck and exploded three decks below killing sixty-six sailors. A fire broke out and thick black smoke poured through a hole in the deck, but the *Yorktown* remained afloat.

The Japanese bombers fanned out and made a low-level torpedo attack on the *Lexington*, attacking

Sailors are evacuated off the USS *Lexington* before being abandoned on 8 May 1942 during the Battle of the Coral Sea (US Navy).

USS *Lexington* afire and sinking after being abandoned on 8 May 1942 during the Battle of the Coral Sea (US Navy).

both bows at once from barely a thousand yards out and at heights ranging between 50 and 200 feet. The carriers sustained two hits and water flooded the three boiler rooms. At the same time Aichi Vals dive-bombed the carrier from 17,000 feet, scoring two hits. Listing heavily, the *Lexington* limped away. The jubilant Japanese pilots broke off the attack and returned to their carriers, having hit both the American carriers. However, the carriers remained operational, and returning air crews were still able to land on the 'Lady Lex'. Fletcher still had thirty-seven attack aircraft and twelve fighters left. Most of the Japanese returned to the crippled *Shokaku* and had to ditch. Only nine aircraft were left operational.

In total the Japanese had lost eighty aircraft and approximately 900 men while the Americans had lost sixty-six aircraft and 543 men. The greatest loss occurred later in the day. Escaping fuel vapour built up inside the *Lexington*, and at 1247 hours, ignited by a still running motor generator, a great internal explosion rocked the ship. A second major explosion occurred at 1445 hours and the fires soon got out of control. At 1710 hours her crew were taken aboard the *Yorktown*. At 1956 hours the destroyer *Phelps* put five torpedoes into her and the 'Lady Lex' sank beneath the waves.

The Battle of the Coral Sea was unique in that it was the first sea battle in which the opposing ships neither engaged nor even saw each other. America is generally adjudged to have emerged victorious

A Japanese Zero fighter beached on a reef after being shot down during the Battle of the Coral Sea (US Navy).

not only because Japan was forced to cancel the amphibious invasion of Port Moresby in favour of a much more difficult overland campaign but also because of significant losses to the Japanese fleet which she could ill afford for campaigns to come. Apart from the loss of the small carrier *Shoho* and the destroyer *Kikuzuki*, the damage to the *Shokaku* and the *Zuikaku* and their air groups meant that both were unable to take part in the Battle of Midway a month later.

The American post-mortem, meanwhile, revealed that not enough Wildcats were embarked; when the *Yorktown* sailed to Pearl Harbor and, incredibly, was ready for sea again after just three days undergoing repairs in port, its fighter complement was increased from eighteen to twenty-seven. The aircraft were new type F4F-4s which were among the first of the newer types to reach the US Navy. The F4F-4, which had arrived in Hawaii just too late for service aboard *Lexington* and *Yorktown* in the Battle of the Coral Sea, was produced with folding wings for greater accommodation aboard the carriers, and fitted with six machine-guns instead of four. The Devastators, which had proved totally unsuitable for modern combat operations, remained aboard only because there was no time to embark the new Grumman TBF-1 Avengers. The *Yorktown* was needed for immediate action to the north because, even as the Battle of the Coral Sea was being fought, Fleet Admiral Isoroku Yamamoto, the architect of the attack on Pearl Harbor, and his staff officers in Japan were planning an even bigger operation, the seizure of Midway Island and the occupation of Kiska and Attu in the Aleutians. Yamamoto would then use Midway as a base for further raids on the Hawaiian Islands, and for the destruction of what remained of the US Pacific Fleet.

CHAPTER 2
The Battle of Midway

Yamamoto hoped to surprise the Americans and take Midway Island, 1,300 miles north-west of Oahu, with little difficulty. Its capture would give Japan a wider defence perimeter and prevent further American air raids on the Home Islands. Lt-Col Jimmy Doolittle's strike on Tokyo with sixteen B-25 Mitchells operating from the carrier *Hornet* on 18 April 1942 had been a small beginning but had proved most embarrassing for the Japanese military. However, American intelligence services had broken the Japanese code and Admiral Chester Nimitz and his staff were well aware of the Japanese strength and intent long before their plan was put into effect. This information was absolutely invaluable to the Americans because it allowed Nimitz to make best use of his meagre resources in the Pacific, and he could plan his defence of Midway safe in the knowledge that he need not spread his limited resources too thinly.

Yamamoto's battle strategy was complex. The Japanese architect of the raid on Pearl Harbor decided on a strong diversionary strike on the westernmost Aleutian chain lying off Alaska, which would be occupied to deter the Americans from

VF-6's F4F Wildcats and VT-6's SBD Dauntless aboard the USS *Enterprise* on 15 May 1942. During the Battle of Midway 110 SBDs from three carriers destroyed all four Japanese carriers and turned the tide of the Pacific war (Grumman).

sending reinforcements south into the Pacific. Although it was only a diversionary force, Yamamoto knew he had to include enough important vessels such as the fleet carrier *Junyo* and the light carrier *Ryujo* – which would have been invaluable at Midway – to persuade the Americans to split their defensive forces. Vice-Admiral Chuichi Nagumo's I Carrier Striking Force aimed at Midway was composed of four carriers – the *Akagi*, *Kaga*, *Hiryu* and *Soryu* – as well as the light carrier *Hosho*. The Japanese could also call upon an impressive number of battleships, destroyers and other craft. The light carrier *Zuiho* was part of a central covering force which could be diverted to help in the Aleutians or Midway depending on how the battles developed.

The Americans could immediately call upon only two carriers, the *Hornet* and the *Enterprise*, which had taken part in the Tokyo raid. Fortunately, the repair crews at Pearl Harbor managed to perform miracles and got the badly damaged *Yorktown* ready for sea again after her heavy involvement in the Battle of the Coral Sea. Her Air Group was a combination of her own and the survivors from the

Vought SB2U Vindicator, the type flown by US Marine Corps Squadron VMS-B231 from Midway Island (Vought).

late lamented *Lexington*. The battle-hardened pilots and crews provided the US task force with the experience that fliers on the *Hornet* and *Enterprise* generally lacked. On 30 May Admiral Fletcher took *Yorktown* north-westwards to join the two cruisers and five destroyers which formed the remainder of Task Force 17. The *Yorktown* rendezvoused with Task Force 16, whose flag ship was the *Enterprise*, commanded by Admiral Raymond Spruance. While Nimitz was thus able to call upon a third, highly valuable flat-top, Nagumo could only ponder the loss of the *Zuikaku* during the Coral Sea battle and the badly damaged *Shokaku*, which could not be repaired in time to join the battle fleet heading for Midway. Even so, the Japanese naval forces closing in on Midway from two directions were formidable.

Nimitz's defence plan was announced to his senior officers on 27 May, two days after the first of two Japanese task forces sailed for the Aleutians. On Midway itself ground forces worked tirelessly and without sleep to turn the island into a fortress while the airborne elements were brought up to strength. The defence of the island was entrusted mainly to the US Marine Corps' MAG 22 (Marine Aircraft Group 22), whose seven F4F-3 Wildcats and twenty-one obsolete Brewster F2A-3 Buffaloes were led by Major Floyd B. Parks. Major Lofton R. Henderson commanded MAG 22's seventeen Vought SB2U-3

Vindicators – or 'Wind Indicators' as the US Marines sardonically referred to them – and nineteen Douglas SBD-2 Dauntless dive-bombers. In addition, USAAF B-17E Flying Fortresses of the 26th, 31st, 72nd and 431st Bomb Squadrons in the 11th Bomb Group and a few B-26 Marauders and USMC Avengers helped swell the defences.

Meanwhile, Nagumo's I Carrier Striking Force and the main body, led by Yamamoto in the massive battleship *Yamato*, approached the island from the north-west while the Occupation Force commanded by Vice-Admiral Kondo and consisting of the Second Fleet Covering Group and an additional three groups comprising Transport (under Tanaka) Support (commanded by Vice-Admiral Kurita) and Mine-sweeping headed for Midway further to the south.

For three days (31 May to 3 June) two Aichi E13A Jake reconnaissance floatplanes searched in vain for the American task forces, but on 3 June a PBY Catalina about 700 miles west of Midway sighted ships of the Japanese fleet. It was assumed the force was the main Japanese task force and a bombing strike was ordered. At 1230 hours nine B-17Es of the 11th Bomb Group led by Lt-Col Walter C. Sweeney, which had arrived at Midway from Hawaii on 29 May, took off in search of the Japanese invasion fleet. At 1623 hours the Japanese invasion force was sighted some 570 miles from Midway.

The nine B-17Es attacked in three flights of three. Sweeney and his two other B-17s in the first flight picked out a large ship and bombed it. Sweeney wrote, 'At the bomb-release line we encountered very heavy anti-aircraft fire. It continued throughout the attack and, as in the attacks that followed, was plenty heavy. My flight didn't claim any hits on this run. We hit all around the enemy but we didn't see any evidence of damage.' Capt. Clement P. Tokarz led the second element in *The Spider*. Sgt Horst Handrow, his tail gunner, wrote, 'There below was a task force that spread all over the Pacific. We didn't have enough gas to look any farther so we picked out the biggest battlewagon we could find and started to make a run on it with the bomb bay doors open. The anti-aircraft was coming up now and the sky was black with it. Bang! We had a hit in no. 4 engine. On we went on our run. Bombs away! The third element, led by Capt. Cecil Faulkner, went after another vessel. Capt. Paul Payne, in *Yankee Doodle*, had two bombs hang up on

the first attack so he made an additional individual run through the ack-ack, scoring a near miss on a large transport.

Despite claims that they had hit two battleships or heavy cruisers and two transports it was later confirmed that the enemy force was in fact the Midway Occupational Force and the 'battleships' and 'cruisers' were in reality tankers and transports. No hits were scored on the ships until four Catalinas from Midway discovered them in bright moonlight in the early dawn of 4 June and torpedoed a tanker. Meanwhile, at 0415 hours, fifteen B-17Es cleared Midway Island and assembled in the vicinity of Kure Island to attack the same fleet they had bombed the previous afternoon, but word was received that another enemy task force, complete with carriers, was approaching Midway and was now only about 145 miles away.

At 0430 hours Lt Joichi Tomonaga's strike force of thirty-six Nakajima B5N Kate torpedo-bombers carrying 1,770lb bombs, thirty-six Aichi D3A Val dive-bombers and thirty-six A6M5 Zero fighters took off from Nagumo's carriers and headed for Midway Island. The softening-up operation of the American bastion, if successful, was to be followed two days later by an amphibious invasion force. At the same time ten Dauntless scout dive-bombers were flown off the *Yorktown* and they began a search mission in a wide arc to the north of the island. Six Japanese reconnaissance aircraft were also launched, although the second of two Jake floatplanes launched from the cruiser *Tone* was delayed until 0500 hours when a troublesome catapult was finally repaired. As luck would have it his search sector corresponded with the American task force's location. The breathing space afforded the American ships would prove significant. With the decks of the Japanese carriers *Akagi* and *Kaga* clear, the second wave of Kates, armed with torpedoes this time, were hoisted up on deck ready for a follow-up raid on any American shipping which might be uncovered by the first wave.

At 0534 hours a Navy Catalina reconnaissance flying-boat flown by Lieutenants Howard Ady and William Chase radioed Midway with the news that the Japanese carrier fleet had been sighted. *Yorktown*, only 250 miles to the east, was tuned to Midway's radio frequency and intercepted the message. Fletcher recalled the Dauntless scouts and despatched Rear-Admiral Spruance on the

Grumman TBF-1 Avengers making a torpedo run on their target. Six TBF-1s took off from Midway island on 4 June 1942 to attack the Japanese fleet but only one returned (Grumman).

Enterprise, with *Hornet* and the rest of Task Force 16, to attack the Japanese carriers.

At 0553 hours the radar operators on Midway picked up Tomonaga's strike force of some 108 aircraft and the island's defence forces quickly got airborne. Midway was mainly defended by the obsolete Brewster F2A-3 Buffaloes of VMF-221 which had arrived on the island on Christmas Day 1941. The B-17s and flying-boats which were already in the air were told to stay away as the twenty-one Buffaloes and seven Wildcat fighters set off in two groups to attack the incoming Japanese forces. Major Parks's group of seven Buffaloes and five Wildcats intercepted the enemy while Major Kirk Armistead's group was further westward where another strike was expected.

The American fighters intercepted the bombers, shot down four and damaged a few others before Tomonaga's escort of thirty-six Zeros intervened. Although two Zeros were shot down in successive dog-fights, the superior Japanese force soon completely overwhelmed Parks's outnumbered group. Vicious dog-fights continued until almost all over the island Armistead's fighters joined in the one-sided battle. It was too late. Although they fought valiantly, the Marine corps fighters were hopelessly outclassed by the nimble Zeros. Altogether, thirteen Buffaloes and three Wildcats were lost in the engagements and seven others were damaged beyond repair. Of the twenty-seven fighters that had engaged the Japanese (one F2A developed engine trouble and had to abort), only three survived intact. Major Parks was among the sixteen pilots killed. Three Japanese aircraft shot down by anti-aircraft fire over the island was small consolation.

Six new Grumman TBF-1 Avenger torpedo bombers of VT-8 commanded by Lt Langdon K. Feiberling and four Army Air Corps B-26 Marauders in the 22nd and 38th Bomb Groups, led by Capt. James F. Collins, which had also taken off from Midway fared almost as badly. The Marauders and Avengers located the Japanese carriers and bored in at low level for their attacks. Seventeen Zeros already on patrol dived on the torpedo bombers from upwards of 3,000 feet but failed to prevent the torpedoes from being launched. The unprotected bombers turned away after launching and were easy prey for the Japanese fighters. Machine-gun fire from the Zeros and intense ack-ack fire from the ships destroyed seven aircraft and badly damaged three others. Only one Avenger, flown by Ensign Bert Earnest, with a dead gunner and wounded radio operator aboard, and two B-26s, survived to crash-land back on Midway. All the torpedoes missed their targets.

Lt Tomonaga realised that a second strike by Japanese bombers was needed to destroy the defences on Midway. Nagumo agreed with him, his decision influenced by the succession of enemy torpedo attacks on his carriers. At 0715 hours he ordered the Kates to be re-armed with bombs, a procedure which involved bringing the torpedo bombers back below decks and re-arming them. The time taken would have severe consequences for the Japanese, particularly in view of the signal he received some thirteen minutes later from the *Tone*'s Jake floatplane which had spotted 'what appears to be ten enemy surface ships' some 240 miles from Midway. Nagumo agonised, wasting a precious fifteen minutes weighing up the information before finally ordering the re-arming of the Kates to stop and that all aircraft be prepared to attack the US task force. He was only stopped when the Jake floatplane confirmed at 0809 hours that there were no carriers in the US formation, only cruisers and destroyers. Nagumo knew these posed no immediate threat to his carriers because they were well out of range. However, he had more immediate problems to think about when sixteen SBD dive-bombers of Marine scout Bombing Squadron VMSB-241 and fifteen Flying Fortresses of the 11th Bomb Group appeared overhead at heights ranging to 20,000 feet, followed by eleven Marine Corps Vindicator scout bombers led by Major Benjamin W. Norris.

The carriers circled under broken cloud and the Marine Corps and Fortress crews had to search for them. In the Fortress formation Capt. Payne spotted the first carrier which was seen to break cloud cover. Payne directed the formation over his radio and the B-17s went into the attack. Col Sweeney wrote, 'The enemy started firing as soon as we opened our bomb bays. The fire wasn't effective but was a bit disturbing. The fighters came up to attack, manoeuvring beautifully, but they failed to follow through. It appeared that their heart was not in their work and in no case was their attack pressed home. We

divided our ships into three groups. Each group was instructed to take a carrier and we bombed away. We are fairly certain we hit the first carrier but we didn't claim it. The second group, under the command of Captain Faulkner, hit its carrier amidships. Lt-Col Brooke Allen, commanding the last flight, secured hits on the third carrier. We didn't have time to wait and see them sink but we left knowing they were badly crippled.' Sgt Handrow in Capt Tokarz's plane wrote, 'We started our run but couldn't get in. The clouds covered up the target and the anti-aircraft was thick. No. 4 engine went out again and we played around at 22,000 feet with the clouds and the anti-aircraft. Then we saw the big *Kaga* carrier come out from under the clouds. The rising sun on it looked like a big bullseye and we used it as such. Down went the bombs from three planes; the deck got three hits, the waterline four; she was sinking and burning at the same time. Zero fighters attacked us on the way home but wouldn't come in close enough so we could get a good shot at them.

'We got a radio report that Midway was being bombed. What a funny feeling we got; what if we couldn't get in there, what the heck were we going to do? We didn't have enough gas to go back to Hawaii. As we drew closer we could see a cloud of black smoke hang over the island. Something was really burning there and our hopes sunk with that sight. In we came and to give us a cheer we saw that the marine ack-ack batteries had kept the runways open even if everything else seemed to be hit.

'We landed and started to gas up and load bombs again for another run on the Japs, who were only ninety miles away now. Up again and this time we picked out a big cruiser but just as we started on the run, six Navy dive-bombers dove down on him; at last we were getting help from the Navy. So we picked out a nice transport loaded with Japs. Two hits and the Japs were swimming back to Japan. Home we went again, still fooling around with No. 4 out, then No. 2 started giving us trouble.

'It looked like our little fun picnic was over because we were ordered to go back to Hawaii. Take-off from Midway was made at 0200 hours. It was a tired-out crew that landed at Hickam that night. All the men in the crew got the Silver Star for this battle.'

Despite the number of American attacks, they were too unco-ordinated and widespread to be effective and no bombs or torpedoes hit the Japanese fleet. Eight Dauntlesses were shot down by intense ack-ack fire from the ships and by the defending Zeros. Major Henderson, the Marine Corps squadron commander, was among the dead. The Vindicators, which were last in, were forced off their targets by the Zeros, which by now had expended almost all their ammunition. Even so, they managed to shoot down two of the Marine Corps SB2Us.

Meanwhile, Nagumo's repeated insistence that the pilot of the *Tone* floatplane should positively identify the enemy ships he was shadowing finally had some effect. At 0820 hours the pilot of the *Tone* floatplane chillingly reported to Nagumo that one of the American ships 'appeared' to be a carrier. Nagumo did not want to risk his air task force and instead of proceeding to attack Midway with the second wave, he abandoned it. He could not attack the American task force either because his remaining torpedo-carrying aircraft would have to be brought up from below deck. Ten minutes later the same floatplane reported the sighting of two more cruisers. Nagumo wanted to attack the American ships immediately but most of his bombers were improperly armed for such a strike and his Zero fighters were low on fuel and ammunition after engaging the Marine Corps attacks and would be unable to escort the bombers. Before he could order the fighters to be re-armed and refuelled, Tomonaga's strike force returned to the carriers and Nagumo ordered that all aircraft which would have made up the second wave were to be kept below deck so that Tomonaga's air group could be recovered. The first wave survivors, which amounted to thirty-six Vals and fifty-four Kates, were re-armed with torpedoes and refuelled aboard the four Japanese carriers. It was at this moment that Nagumo was informed by his vessels to the south that a very large formation of American aircraft was approaching the task force. Spruance had taken advantage of Nagumo's problems in recovering the first wave and had despatched his air groups.

Lt-Cmdr Clarence W. McClusky, the Air Group Commander aboard the *Enterprise* who would lead the attack, had assembled thirty-three Dauntless dive-bombers from VB-6 and VS-6 for the strike. There was no time for them to form up because of the need to bomb the Japanese carriers before they got their own aircraft away. The SBDs took off and flew on alone in two groups led by Lt Richard H. Best and Lt Wilmer E. Gallaher. The rest of the air groups abroad the *Enterprise* and *Hornet* followed at intervals, but even using double launching methods, getting the large formations airborne took about an hour to complete. The time-lag between take-offs and a build up of layers of broken cloud en route scattered the formation and ruled out effective fighter protection for the slow-flying Devastators. The *Enterprise*'s fourteen TBDs in VT-6, led by Lt-Cmdr Eugene E. Lindsey, flew on to their targets alone while the ten Wildcats in VF-6, commanded by Lt James S. Gray, followed, thirty-six F4F-3s remaining behind to take it in turns to patrol over the task force.

The *Hornet*'s ten Wildcats in VF-8, led by Lt-Cmdr Samuel G. Mitchell, failed to make contact with Lt Cmdr John C. Waldron's fifteen Devastators in VT-8 and tacked on to the thirty-five Dauntlesses divided into Bombing Squadron 8, led by Lt-Cmdr Robert R. Johnson, and Scouting Squadron 8, commanded by Lt-Cmdr Walter F. Rodee, leaving Waldron's torpedo bombers to fly on alone. The Devastators took up station alone, flying along at wavetop height while the protective screen of F3F-3 Wildcat fighters and trailing Dauntless dive-bombers were stacked up to 19,000 feet. In the lead was Cmdr Stanhope C. Ring, *Hornet*'s Air Group Commander

In the time since take-off from the American carriers, Nagumo's task force had changed course to the north-east. The four air groups therefore arrived at the anticipated position and found no carriers. The *Hornet*'s dive-bombers decided to search south, but finding nothing and getting low on fuel, many of the Dauntlesses were forced to land back on *Hornet* or refuel at Midway. Unfortunately, the Wildcats burned up fuel far quicker and all ten were forced to ditch in the sea.

At 0910 hours Gray's fighters spotted the enemy ships but they did not wish to break radio silence and failed to inform the other squadrons. The much lower-flying torpedo bombers sighted smoke on the horizon, turned north and found the Japanese carriers just after 0930 hours. Waldron could not afford to waste precious fuel waiting for the fighter support and he must have known it was now a suicidal mission as he turned the formation into their attack positions and prepared to launch torpedoes from a height of just 300 feet. Meanwhile, Gray's

F4F Wildcat of VF-6 below deck on the USS *Enterprise* is prepared for combat (Grumman).

Wildcats remained on station 6,000 feet above them waiting for the pre-arranged call for assistance from Lindsey, not realising that the Devastators below belonged to Waldron's torpedo squadron. Upwards of fifty Zeros attacked the fifteen Devastators and wreaked havoc. One after the other of Waldron's torpedo bombers were blasted out of the sky by the Japanese fighters and supporting fire from the ships in the Japanese task force. Only one of the pilots, Ensign George H. Gay, who piloted the last plane in the formation, remained. He heeded the words of his commander, John Waldron, who before the raid had urged, 'I want each of us to do his utmost to destroy our enemies. If there is only one plane left to make a final run in, I want that man to go in and get a hit.' Despite the loss of his gunner and receiving wounds to his arm and leg, Gay managed to get his torpedo away before he skimmed over the bow of

the carrier and crashed into the sea. Gay miraculously emerged as his aircraft began to sink with his dead gunner aboard. He swam away from the wreckage as Zeros circled overhead. Luckily, his rubber seat cushion floated clear and Gay grabbed it. He bobbed in the sea clutching it until dusk when he finally inflated his dinghy without fear of being strafed by the Zeros. Gay was picked up by a PBY Catalina the following day.

Twenty minutes later Lindsey's fourteen Devastators arrived. Without fighter support now that VF-6 had left the target area, they singled out the *Kaga* and began their attack on the starboard side. Quite by chance the *Yorktown*'s air group appeared on the scene and flew in on the port side

TBD-1 Devastators of VT-6 on board the USS *Enterprise* prior to take-off in the Battle of Midway on 4 June 1942. Only five of forty-one Devastators launched returned (McDonnell Douglas).

at the same instant, proposing to attack the *Soryu*. The air group consisted of twelve TBD Devastators, commanded by Lt-Cmdr Lance E. Massey, six Wildcats of fighting Squadron Three, led by Lt-Cmdr John S. Thach, and seventeen Dauntlesses split into two groups led by the CO, Lt-Cmdr Maxwell F. Leslie and Lt Wallace C. Short. Their arrival drew some of the Zeros away from the *Enterprise*'s Devastators but even so eleven of the torpedo bombers, including Lindsey's, were shot down in a hail of gunfire.

Equally bravely, Massey's Devastators closed in on the Japanese carriers, protected only by Thach's six fighters. The small strike force penetrated to within only three miles of the Japanese carriers before shell fire from one of them alerted the Zeros, which were still busy dealing with the remnants of VT-6. The Wildcats were outnumbered and out-manoeuvred as about forty defending Zero fighters soon overwhelmed them. Nine A6Ms from *Hiryu* fought with the F4Fs, shooting one down and badly

damaging two others which were forced to break off. Thach and his two remaining wingmen, greatly outnumbered, were unable to help the TBD crews directly but they drew some of the Zeros away before they too were forced to break off and return to the *Yorktown*. The cumbersome Devastators, meanwhile, came under a fusillade of fire from the ships and were cut to pieces as they split into two sections. Massey's TBD was hit, burst into flames and careered into the sea. In the confusion, five Devastator crews who managed to get their torpe-does away, aimed them at any target which pre-sented itself before they were blasted out of the sky. Altogether, ten of Massey's Devastators were shot down and once again none of the torpedoes had found its mark, although two torpedoes passed within only fifty yards of *Kaga*

The Devastators' suicidal attacks had not been in vain however. Their action kept the defending Zeros occupied at low level so that when McClusky's and Leslie's Dauntlesses appeared high overhead, seven-teen Zeros that still had enough fuel were unable to gain enough altitude in time to intercept the SBDs before they began their dive-bombing. Three of McClusky's SBDs peeled off and aimed their 1,000lb bombs at the *Akagi* crowded with aircraft far below.

One bomb hit Nagumo's mighty flagship amidships, opposite the bridge and just behind the aircraft lift. It ripped through to the hangar below where it exploded among stored torpedoes. A second bomb exploded among the Kates and the deck erupted into a blazing inferno. Other explosions went on for some time as petrol tanks, bombs and torpedoes were enveloped in the conflagration.

McClusky's remaining Dauntlesses concentrated their attacks on the *Kaga* which received four direct hits, including one which exploded a petrol tanker near the bridge. The petrol ignited and a searing burst of flames burned everyone on the bridge, including the captain, to death. The other three bombs hit the aircraft ranged for take-off on the carrier deck and they were quickly enveloped in an inferno. Not to be outdone, Leslie's dive-bombers screamed down in a near vertical dive over the *Soryu* in three waves, aiming their 1,000lb bombs at the massed aircraft on the carrier deck. Three bombs

TBF Avengers and F4F-4 Wildcats on board a carrier deck prepare for take-off. The Grumman F4F-4 had arrived in Hawaii just too late to see service aboard the *Lexington* and *Yorktown* in the Battle of the Coral Sea, but by the end of May VF-3, VF-6 and VF-8 had each been equipped with twenty-seven F4Fs and took part in the Battle of Midway, 4–7 June 1942 (Grumman).

found their mark, including one which penetrated to the hangar deck and exploded. The other two bombs exploded among the aircraft ranged on deck and caused mayhem among the crews. Although the *Soryu* continued to remain afloat, as did the *Akagi* and the *Kaga*, the raging fires could not be extinguished and all three carriers were finally abandoned and sunk by Japanese or American torpedoes. Seven Dauntlesses were shot down in dogfights while eight Zeros were shot down. Eleven SBDs from the *Enterprise* were forced to ditch after running out of fuel on the return flight to the carrier.

The *Hiryu*, meanwhile, had become separated

Japanese cruiser of the Mogame class on fire after attack by US Navy aircraft during the Battle of Midway (US Navy).

from the main Japanese force and it became a haven for twenty-three Zeros which were diverted from the damaged carriers. Its total complement of about forty Zeros, eighteen Vals and ten Kates now posed a threat to American carriers like the *Yorktown*. A Yokosuka D4Y-1C Judy reconnaissance aircraft from *Soryu* located the American task force and, alone with Jake floatplanes, shadowed the carrier's every move. Admiral Fletcher, meanwhile, had

F4F Wildcat taking off from the deck of a carrier (Grumman).

ordered ten SBDs aloft to search for the Japanese carrier while twelve Wildcats took off and flew a defensive patrol. At around 1100 hours *Hiryu* launched eighteen Aichi Vals with mixed bomb loads and six Zeros led by the wily veteran, Lt Michio Kobayashi. Shortly before noon the radar operators on the *Yorktown* picked up the specks of the Japanese air striking force forty-six miles west of them and heading their way behind the returning Dauntlesses.

The Wildcats intercepted the Japanese formation about fifteen miles out at 10,000 feet and shot down seven Vals and four Zeros. The surviving D3As broke away from the engagement and dived on the *Yorktown*. Six Vals were shot down, including two by ack-ack fire from the American cruisers. The thirteenth victim, which fell to the anti-aircraft guns, succeeded in lobbing a bomb onto the flight-deck before it broke up and the explosion started a fire in the hangar below. A second bomb caused extensive damage to the ship's insides and knocked out most of the boilers so that the carrier's speed was severely reduced and then finally halted. A third bomb, which penetrated to the fourth deck, caused a serious fire which threatened to engulf the forward petrol tanks and ammunition stores. Despite severe losses and damage to her decks the crew of the *Yorktown* managed to dampen down the raging fires and soon the ship was underway again. The Wildcats were refuelled and re-armed aboard *Enterprise* and were almost ready when a second wave of ten Nakajima Kate torpedo bombers and six Zeros, led by Lt Joichi Tomonaga, who had led the first attack on Midway, appeared on radar forty miles distant. Only four Wildcats got airborne to join with six already in the air when the Japanese arrived in the area. The F4F pilots screamed into the attack, trying to get at the Kates but they were fended off by the Zero pilots who lost three of their number. Four Wildcats fell to the Zero guns. The Kates flew ruggedly on, despite the curtain of withering fire put up by the cruisers and the gunners aboard the *Yorktown*, and attacked the cruiser from four angles. Five of the torpedo bombers were shot down but the survivors, who launched four of their deadly torpedoes from only 500 yards, scored two hits below the waterline. The ship's fuel tanks were sliced open and the lower decks flooded. *Yorktown* began listing badly and the order was given to abandon ship.

F4F Wildcats taxi out on deck for take-off on another mission against Japanese fighters (Grumman).

The remaining five battered but jubilant Kate crews zoomed off back to the *Hiryu*, unaware that the same fate was about to befall their carrier. Now, only five Kates, four Vals and about twenty-five Zeros remained of the carrier's original sixty-three aircraft. Soon after they had been recovered, the *Hiryu* came under a surprise attack by fourteen Dauntlesses of VS-6 from the *Enterprise* led by Lt Wilmer E. Gallaher, together with ten more which had been transferred from the *Yorktown* after that carrier had been damaged in the Japanese attack. Close behind were sixteen Dauntlesses from the *Hornet*. Thirteen Zeros on patrol intercepted the SBDs and one of the leading dive-bombers was shot down during its dive with two more falling after bomb release. Despite the attacks, Gallaher's dive-bombers succeeded in getting four hits on the *Hiryu* which caused uncontrollable fires and destruction. *Hornet*'s SBDs, which arrived to find the *Hiryu* burning fiercely, turned their attentions to a battleship and cruiser instead but made no hits. Some USAAF B-17Es en route to Midway from Oahu also joined in the attack on the *Hiryu*, but their bombs

The USS *Yorktown* (CV-5) burns after being bombed in the first Japanese attack on 4 June (US Navy).

missed. The surviving Zero pilots made a few passes at the Fortresses before ditching in the sea to be picked up by ships of the task force. That evening thirteen bombers from VMSB-241, now led by Major Benjamin Norris, took off from Midway but failed to find the *Hiryu* and returned guided by the fires still raging on the island. Major Norris failed to return after crashing into the sea. The *Hiryu* was finally abandoned the next morning and finished off by Japanese torpedoes.

To all intents and purposes the Battle of Midway was over. However, Yamamoto, believing the Americans to have only one carrier in the vicinity of Midway, proposed to move his main body up to replace the now almost non-existent Striking Force and recall the Aleutian task force to join him in a joint attack on the island. It was only after pilots returning to the *Hiryu* late on 4 June reported the existence of the other American carriers that Yamamoto ordered his invasion force, in the early hours of 5 June, to withdraw.

The Americans, unaware of the true situation aboard the Japanese flagship, and knowing the lack of experience their pilots had in flying at night, waited until dawn of 5 June before getting their aircraft into the air. By then the Japanese main body had retreated well to the west and the fifty-eight Dauntlesses which were sent to look for the enemy force returned empty-handed. Later, however, a dozen dive-bombers succeeded in crippling the heavy cruisers *Mogami* and *Mikuma* after they had collided while taking avoiding action after sighting an American submarine. No bombs hit the *Mikuma*, but a Dauntless flown by Capt. Richard E. Fleming; crashed onto the cruiser's after-turret and petrol fumes sucked into the engine-room ignited and exploded, killing the entire engine-room crew. A further attack by dive-bombers sunk the *Mikuma*, but the *Mogami* managed to limp home to Truk. The crippled but still floating *Yorktown* was not as fortunate, finally being sunk by two torpedoes from a Japanese submarine on 7 June after she had been taken in tow.

The Battle of Midway proved to be the decisive turning-point in the Pacific War. Although Japanese fighters had scored an impressive victory over the American aviation units, which lost eighty-five out of 195 aircraft, a large part of the élite in Japanese naval aviation had also perished. The loss of her carriers meant Japan would never again dictate events in the Pacific. Her shipyards could not hope to replace the carriers lost in action at Coral Sea and Midway, while in America US shipyards were already building fleet carriers in large numbers and factories were turning out more powerful aircraft to put aboard them. Midway marked the beginning of the way back for the Americans which would see the liberation of the central Pacific and the final destruction of the Japanese home islands. It would, however, take a long and bloody island-hopping campaign fought over by ground troops supported by US Navy, army, air force and marine corps pilots.

CHAPTER 3

Wildcats and Corsairs versus Zeros

J. Hunter Reinburg

''Where the hell are those bombers?' I yelled to myself while strapped in the cockpit of my airborne Wildcat fighter aircraft. My voice was barely audible to me above the roar of the single Pratt & Whitney radial engine up front. Frequent glances back to the east towards Guadalcanal did not reveal a view of our bomb-carrying friends.

We had been circling the rendezvous point, Savo Island, for about five minutes. I led the twelve-plane fighter formation in a slow climbing spiral to stay over the volcanic atoll which was thirty miles west of our base on Guadalcanal. The additional altitude gained while waiting could be used to glide into position over the dive-bombers we were assigned to escort, when and if they arrived. Thus, a little of our precious fuel could be saved.

We had been instructed to escort fifteen Douglas Dauntless SBD dive-bombers for an attack on a newly-built Japanese airfield. The target was located at Munda Point on New Georgia Island, about one hundred and seventy nautical miles west of Savo. This mission appeared especially attractive since it seemed reasonable that the Japs would

surely send up some fighters after such easy targets as the SBDs. We looked upon the bombers as 'Zero-bait'. My flight had yet to see a Jap plane in the air, much to our consternation.

I was part of Marine Fighter Squadron (VMF) 121 based at Henderson Field on Guadalcanal. We were working to keep the Jap forces from obtaining a permanent toehold in and around the Solomon Islands. Henderson Field had been named in honour of Major Lofton R. Henderson, a Marine flyer killed in the Battle of Midway back on 4 June 1942. Now it was the day after Christmas 1942.

It seemed wise to make another check of our fighter formation. My division, counting myself, consisted of four Grumman Wildcat (F4F-4) fighters; my three companions were in loose position on each flank. Another division of four more identical airplanes was considerably behind us where it was difficult to keep track of them. Four army P-39 Airacobra fighter aircraft rounded out the escort. For clarification, a division consisted of four planes and a flight usually contained eight planes. My eyes

Grumman F4F-4 Wildcat in flight (Grumman).

strained to the east, and then a glance at my watch caused me to swear.

Damn! Ten minutes after scheduled rendezvous time. What in hell's detaining those guys? No sign of them. Wish I could use the radio; might find out something if the lousy thing worked.

Our aircraft radios were weak and frequently temperamental, which made it very discouraging even to try to use them. If we broke radio silence, the Japanese were always listening and then would know a raid was imminent. Consequently, they would be ready with their heavy anti-aircraft guns and have their Zeros positioned up-sun, waiting for us with the altitude advantage. Of course, we were most anxious to have a dog-fight, and since they hadn't accepted our challenges lately we were in the mood to take them on under any circumstances.

At the end of twenty minutes, it was doubtful that we could complete the escort mission and have sufficient fuel to get home if the Japs chose to tangle. It was obvious that we all were tired of waiting, but it seemed a shame not to complete some sort of a useful mission since we were airborne and already part of the way towards the enemy airbase. A thought flashed through my mind: I'd invent an alternate mission! 'This is Red One. We're heading for the alternate mission. Out!'

Well, guess we could make a fighter sweep of Munda. Maybe the breaking of radio silence will be a good thing. Maybe the Jap Zeros will be waiting for us and we'll finally have a good fight . . . Yeah, that's it! We'll sweep the area and knock down anything and everything that we can catch. That's a legitimate alternate assignment. We should be there in about an hour . . . I glanced at my watch. It was about 2 p.m. the day after Christmas, 1942. I knew it was the normal time of day in the tropical area for rain squalls. Many were already visible near the centre of the land. When about thirty miles from Munda, cruising at 11,000 feet, I noticed a cloud layer up ahead and about 2,000 feet below us.

Those clouds could help us approach undetected. However, they could also make it difficult for us to find the target.

My 'alternate mission' was now pretty firm in my mind, and it seemed time to talk to the formation. If the Japs had not already figured out we were coming, a radio broadcast at this time wouldn't hurt much since we would be on them in a few minutes. 'This is Red One. We'll check over the field for

bogies. If we don't find any airborne, I'll strafe with my division and then you follow us, Red Five. Red Nine, cover and strafe if you see anything worth shooting at. Everyone stay in the area so we can protect each other, and in the meantime clean house on anything we can find.' Red Nine was the division of four Airacobras.

The clouds were not thick enough to prevent our finding the airfield. I put on more engine power while going into a shallow dive to pick up speed and I strained my eyes for enemy aircraft. My companions began falling back in a wide staggered column. Another perusal of the clouds below us revealed no holes.

That looks like a hole coming up . . . Yeah, and there's the field down there . . . It looks so quiet and peaceful from up here.

Several swishes of my airplane's tail indicated I wanted the squadron in column. Quickly I rocked my wings indicating it was time to attack, and then dove through the hole. Munda was already in my sights as I descended in a near fifty-degree dive.

I had intended to level off under the clouds and search thoroughly for airborne airplanes. However, my gaze was transfixed by a Zero rolling rapidly down the taxiway very near the western end of the runway. It never occurred to me to be a sport and let him get airborne. Out of the corner of my eye, I saw another Jap fighter taxying along not far behind the first one. The urge to kill overtook me completely. The two tempting targets made me forget to look further for airborne aircraft. *Oh Boy! What a setup – I'll get both of these on the first pass!*

With fiendish exhilaration, I manoeuvred to take the two earth-bound Zeros in quick succession and squeezed the trigger on my control stick while passing through at 1,000 feet. The chatter of my six 50-calibre machine-guns made encouraging conversation. I watched my tracers converging on the helpless enemy plane. A moment later, it was rewarding to see my bullets tear off pieces of the target. I released the trigger after about a four-second burst, figuring that was his share and his friend should be given an equal portion. Still in a dive, I suddenly became fearfully aware that my speed was excessive, so I initiated a change of course toward the second Zero. The change of direction caused G-forces to strain my body but by flexing my stomach muscles, a blackout was retarded. In spite of the body strain, I managed to get my reflector gunsight locked on my intended victim and a generous squirt of lead quickly followed. Tracers bounced on and around him, kicking up flecks of dust and debris. Following this enervating moment, I was suddenly seized with fear that there was insufficient altitude left to make a safe pull-out.

Fortunately, my plane cleared the treetops with less than an inch to spare. I continued to guide it in a flat left turn towards the northern side of the airdrome. Fear was quickly overshadowed by a desire to observe my recent victims. I turned my head as far to the left as my strained neck muscles would allow and saw people scurrying in all directions on that side behind me.

Looks like we really caught them by surprise. Look at 'em run like so many crazy jackrabbits. Ha, ha, some fun! Both Zeros are burning.

I quickly returned my vision to what was ahead of me and saw several heavy rain squalls. They were just north of the enemy airdrome and obscured the rising ground covered with dense jungle.

Above the roar of my engine I heard what sounded like the chattering of machine-guns. I preferred to assume they were from unfriendly sources and consequently zigzagged while staying as low as the trees would permit. We had figured that the 'jinking' manoeuvre was the best way to upset ground gun aim. Finally, it seemed safe to gain some altitude beyond the hill near the edge of the rain curtain.

Having reached sanctuary, I reversed my fighter's course to a right climbing turn and headed back towards the airdrome. While looking for a new target I noticed only two, instead of three, Wildcats in staggered column behind me. I wondered what had become of my fourth man. No other aircraft were in sight, friendly or otherwise. Black smoke from these spots on the taxiways gave accurate evidence that the fuel tanks of three Zeros were burning. But then I began to wonder if one of the spots could be from my missing fourth fighter. I had faintly hoped to see the second division make a run across the field but they were nowhere in sight. I jealously wondered if they might have tangled with airborne Zeros. There seemed to be too many planes on the field; few could have gotten airborne. However, we could only stay alert and hope that we were being covered from above because the grounded airplanes were very inviting targets.

Seeing more Zeros in the revetments, I concentrated only on them as my next victims. I was really congratulating myself that we had caught the enemy in such a state of unpreparedness. Just before aligning my gunsight on another parked airplane, I heard the chatter of machine-guns again. Suddenly, tracer bullets were flashing by from what appeared to be several directions. A ground anti-aircraft gun emplacement was just short of my new target, requiring me to push harder on the controls to give the gunners a good blast in self-defence. A moment later, I jerked the stick back and converged my cone of fire on an earth-bound Zero. The distance must have been just right. None of the load seemed to miss the airplane, which obligingly burst into flames several seconds later. This time a safer pull-out was made above the trees.

The rainstorms to the north discouraged me from going in their direction again. They offered cover from the anti-aircraft guns but I had a fear of hidden rocks ('cumulo-granites' as we called them). Consequently, I retired south of the field and proceeded over the water. Upon gaining some altitude over the straits of Rendova, I made a climbing turn for a new look at our victims. My two faithful comrades were whizzing across the cut-up coconut grove behind me. They were wrecking more aircraft in revetments. I continued to wonder where my fourth fighter was.

While climbing and searching for more targets, another Zero was moving down the runway, presumably planning to join us in the air. This sort of insolence could not be tolerated, so I tightened my turn and dove straight at him. We were attacking each other head-on, which gave me fiendish delight since I was the one who was airborne and therefore had the upper hand. Just before pulling the trigger, I saw the pilot jump out of the moving airplane. He was a moment too late. My bullets cut him down as he hit the ground. An instant later his abandoned airplane ground-looped into a tree and caught fire. My plan was to switch aim to another plane before having to pull out. Luckily, another parked Zero was not too far to the left. A hard turn allowed my guns to give him a destructive blast and I had to pull up rather sharply to miss the north-side hills. Then I was forced to fly into one of the rain squalls. This momentarily frightened me more than the Jap gunners! Fortunately, a continued hard left turn brought me quickly back into the clear.

Looking down on the ridge, I was alarmed to see several more machine-gun emplacements. This new danger caused me to zigzag violently with erratic up-and-down manoeuvres. Tracers surrounded me and it seemed an eternity before out-distancing them. Those gun emplacements were my next victims.

It was easy to see my buddies jinking behind me. At this moment, a voice came over my radio: 'This is Red Five. My engine is running rough again and I'm low on gas. Let's go home.' I noted the transmission but was more concerned with the action at hand, and decided to say nothing. Not hearing from Red Nine (the Airacobras' leader), I presumed he was still somewhere above. I sprayed another gun nest and exploded a nearby parked plane. *Christ! What a sport . . . like shooting fish in a barrel.'*

Hunter Reinburg and his division returned safely to Guadalcanal after they bluffed two low-flying Zeros by diving on them, their guns either jammed or ammunition exhausted. One Zero splashed into the water in panic. Red Four was back at base after experiencing engine trouble over Munda.

More missions followed, and then on the morning of 15 January 1943 eleven Wildcats in VMF 121 escorted twelve SBD Dauntless 'Speedy Ds' up the 'slot' (the channel between the New Georgia and Santa Isabel Islands, north-west of Guadalcanal) to attack the Tokyo Express. The Tokyo Express was the Japanese transport and combat ship task force that raced down the slot almost nightly to reinforce the hard-pressed troops on Guadalcanal. It was soon apparent that the Tokyo Express was under the command of Rear-Admiral Raizo Tanaka, a seasoned fighter. The American formation spotted enemy destroyers in the slot and attacked. Hunter Reinburg scanned the sky for enemy fighters. 'Suddenly, my heart skipped a beat as I opened up on my radio: 'Bogies, ten o'clock, slightly lower than we are.' Automatically, my legs tapped out a tattoo on the rudder pedals in nervous anticipation. Every plane in my fighter formation simultaneously dipped its left wing and took in the sight.

Hot damn! I'm going to get one of those bastards today! I waggled my wings, put on full throttle and said over my radio, 'Let's go get 'em!'

As we got closer, it was easy to tell that they were Zeros by their silhouettes. They were in close formation and I counted nine.

They're not well deployed for combat. I wonder if they see us yet? We have a slight altitude advantage and the sun is at our back, to the east. Guess they can't see us in the bright morning light. Gotta get that first shot in before they wise up. Gotta shoot them from any angle just to get as many as possible before they know what hit them. If we give them a chance to manoeuvre, they might get the best of us. They can out-turn and out-climb us. Our only advantage is that we are flying a more rugged airplane with better fire power. Oh, oh, the leader must see us now. He's about a half-mile away and climbing directly towards us.

We were closing on the Zero formation, head-on. A moment later their red ball insignia or 'meatballs' were easy to see. Our rate of closure must have been well over 400 knots, fast for that era. Before they were within the range of my machine-guns, I already had my gunsight on the leader. It was a wonderful no-lead shot. I never gave any thought to the fact that he was probably coaching himself the same as I was and that he had an equal and reciprocal no-lead shot at me. He probably figured, as I did, that if he first picked off the Wildcat leader our formation would scatter and be easy pickings for their superior dog-fighting Zeros. A 'no-lead' shot meant I was head-on or coming up directly behind the enemy fighter. Consequently, there was no need to aim ahead of him. A 'deflection' or 'full-deflection' shot meant I was approaching the other aircraft somewhere between zero and ninety degrees (in the latter case, his flight-path would be perpendicular to mine). In a deflection shot, I had to lead my target (like in duck hunting), so my shot and the enemy aircraft arrived at the same place simultaneously.

The excitement of impending battle did not allow me to think of any personal danger. All I could think of was shooting down Zeros. When about 1,200 feet away, I squeezed my trigger and heard the welcome chatter of the Wildcat's pounding guns. An instant later, tracers leapt from the Zero's leading edges but I was only concerned with seeing where my bullets went. I was elated to see my gun fire converge on the Zero's engine and kick off sparks like a grinding wheel does. The fear of crashing into the Jap never occurred to me. It was a distinct possibility, and could be caused either by miscalculating a high-speed closure rate or just by plain carelessness. An instant later, when it seemed as though I might collide with my opponent, he passed harmlessly beneath me. I had hoped to see him explode right in front of me but our head-on speed made that impossible. Also, since my bullets were hitting his metal engine, it would more than likely stop them from getting to the Zero's gas tank. However, they would surely wreck his power plant and at least turn his fighter into a glider.

Desiring to see if my adversary had been destroyed, I threw the Wildcat into a hard left turn and craned my neck to the left rear. It was easy to see the rapidly scattering formation. But, much to my consternation, I could not be sure which airplane was my recent target.

Then my attention was diverted by a Zero diving down in front of me and I had to assume that another enemy fighter formation was pouncing on us from above. There was no time to worry if this were really true or not. If it was, we were now outnumbered. The fight was on, to the finish. It was obvious that I must kill or be killed. I manoeuvred for an easy tail shot at another Zero. Out of the corner of my eye I could see we were a great big ball of milling Wildcats and Zeros, diving, fighting and zooming in all three dimensions. Many collisions seemed imminent between friend and foe alike. There was no time to worry about slamming into one another, normally an extreme point of fear for every fighter pilot. I just wanted to pump my bullets into another Jap and to hell with the details.

Just as my guns began to bark at the Zero dead ahead of me, he made a violent pull-up. This made my bullets pass harmlessly below him, so I also pulled back on my control stick in an attempt to re-establish proper aim. High G-loads bore down on my body and prevented me from getting my airplane's nose at the correct angle. I needed to get the gunsight 'pip' slightly above the Zero for the proper lead. Suddenly, the G-loads relaxed and I squeezed my trigger. Simultaneously it dawned on me that I was looking at the horizon upside down! The damn

Jap had led me into a tight inside loop! His acrobatic abilities did him little good though, as my concentrated lead converged on him: the Zero exploded with surprising suddenness.

The sight elated me, and I rolled over to an upright position (thereby completing an acrobatic manoeuvre known as an Immelmann). I was surprised to see one of my Wildcat fighters flying fairly close formation on my right, slightly aft. I immediately returned to searching for more Zeros and did not have long to wait. Another Jap blasted by in front of me, right to left. My Wildcat fell in behind. As I opened fire on the meatball, he rapid-rolled to the left. I had to quit firing as my aim slipped off. *Christ, this must be the Jap Air Force's acrobatic team. The last Zero was a looper and now I've got a roller!*

I was about to open fire again when I was rudely disturbed by tracers whizzing past me. My personal safety suddenly became paramount. I forgot the guy in front and instantly jammed the stick forward. This manoeuvre might help me get out of his gunsight if I performed it fast enough. A quick glance in my rear-view mirror verified my suspicions. Damn! The Zero was sitting on my tail and I could see his muzzles flashing. He intended to murder me! Fortunately, my manoeuvre was the correct one and I was below his line of fire a split-second before his bullets could reach me. I knew my immunity would not last unless some new gyration was executed. I made a quick and hard left turn. For some reason the Jap did not choose to follow me; maybe one of my buddies got him. At any rate, the Zero bothered me no more.

Situations change incredibly fast in a dog-fight. Halfway through my left turn I spotted another

Mitsubishi A6M2 Zero-sen 'Zeke' in flight. This one was restored but was destroyed in a fire in June 1994 (Author).

Zero. He was slightly below and coming directly towards me. I stopped my turn and began pumping bullets his way. My tracers indicated hits. He did not exchange 'arrows' with me. I figured he did not see me or was too confused to know what to do. Unfortunately, like his leader, he passed rapidly and awfully close under me. I bounced on his slip-stream. I resumed my hard left turn hoping to see him disintegrate while getting my guns on yet another enemy airplane. I flexed my stomach muscles to retard blackout while in the hard turn; we had learned that this prevented too much blood from leaving the head and upper torso during high-G manoeuvres. Upon reversing course, I eased off on the stick and scanned the air. There was no sign of any Zero which could have been my recent target. *Did he blow up as he passed under me, and is he already falling earthwards in little pieces?*

I scanned the entire sky. There were still several planes in sight diving and zooming but none were very near me. I looked down and saw three black smoke plumes extending vertically. I hopefully assumed they were all enemy and that one was my last victim. Two parachutes were visible a few thousand feet below me and I wondered if they were friend or foe. If they were friends, they were in for a rough time as they were deep in Jap territory (better than 200 miles up the slot from Guadalcanal). Up to that time, we could not do much for our pilots downed in the slot since, for all practical purposes, it was considered a Jap lake. We had never dared to send our surface ships that far. We had some big PBY seaplanes at a seadrome on the Florida Islands near Guadalcanal. They had picked up pilots much nearer Guadalcanal, but to the best of my knowledge they had not dared venture this far up the slot in the daytime.

Upon seeing the parachutes, I was reminded that there were probably more Zeros in the sky nearby and if they were not annihilated, they might turn me into another smoke trail or a flowery parachute. I swivelled my head again and soon came to the realization that all of the planes around me were Wildcats. I checked my altimeter.

Christ! We started this dog-fight at 16,000 feet and here we are already down to 6,000. In the heat of the battle it was never evident that we were descending all the time. Man! We finished off those Zeros in a hurry. Eleven of us originally attacked nine Zeros and I could swear more jumped us from above. How many Wildcats do we have

left? Let's see . . . one, two, three, four, five . . . that's all! Christ, only six of us left! That means we've lost five? Maybe I'll find several on the way home. This fight only took a couple of minutes, now that I think about it. Wow! What a show. Guess we used the best tactics. Shoot them from any angle you can get your sights on them. The Zeros are crapped out fast. Maybe some of them got chicken and ran for home. Maybe I did get those two that I took head-on. Since I couldn't see them upon reversing course, perhaps they did just blow up and float down in little pieces. I hope one of the other guys can confirm them for me. Intelligence reports indicate that the Zero is cheaply built and has no armour or neoprene-lined gas tanks to keep them from blowing up.

Recounting the Wildcats raised the total to nine.

Hey, that's good, three more located! Now we're only missing two: my wingman [Sandy Hearn] and who else? No wonder we made short order of those Japs. If each of us got one on the first pass, that would have been eleven gone immediately. Maybe we did tangle with a second formation of Zeros.

Natives brought in Sandy Hearn some days later, wounded in the leg. Two SBDs were lost but the Wildcats claimed ten Zeros destroyed and six probables. Reinburg concludes, 'This certainly confirmed that we had been jumped by another enemy formation soon after contact with the original nine Zeros. We deplored losing one pilot and three Wildcat aircraft, but we supposed it was a fair exchange for at least ten Japs.'

On 27 January Hunter Reinburg and his fellow pilots tangled with Zeros again, about ten miles west of Henderson Field. 'The sight of enemy planes exposed my killer instinct. Intending to retake the lead and attack, I waggled my wings, tapped my head and dove away to the right. As soon as my plane was diving vertically, I sighted on an enemy Zero who did not seem very far below me. I was not concerned with the fact that my steep angle of dive would cause me rapidly to go below him since he was flying level. My approach was designed exactly as we had attacked tow sleeves many times in practice. My gunsight pipper was sufficiently in front of the Zero for a full deflection shot. I tripped the machine-gun trigger when about 1,200 feet above him and began pulling out of the dive in order to keep sight on the Jap. At this instant he apparently saw me because he executed a sharp climbing left turn. Since his manoeuvre was the smartest thing that could be done under the circumstances, it appeared my opponent was an experienced flyer. Fortunately for me, I had become quite proficient at this overhead type of attack during gunnery training. In order to keep my guns on him, I was forced to roll left, which in turn further steepened my dive. I quit firing at him when passing behind his tail.

My plane was still moving vertically down towards the earth and my excess speed carried me 2,000 feet below the Zero before I regained level flight. Excessive G-loads strained me and the airplane in the pull-out in an attempt to retain sight of my enemy. However, the pull of gravity was so great on my body that my eyesight went dim as blood was forced down and out of my head, and I could not keep track of my adversary. I was sure my bullets had hit the Zero, but I went below him so quickly it was impossible to ascertain what damage I had inflicted. However, as full sight returned to me following a near blackout, I was happy to see his plane burning and plunging towards the Guadalcanal jungle. *That'll fix that bastard!*

Knowing there were many more enemy planes in the area, I let my victim fall and used my excess speed to zoom back to the higher altitudes. Upon levelling off at about 20,000 feet on a westerly course, I spotted another Zero about 3,000 feet below, coming towards me. It was immediately apparent that I would have to execute another overhead pass to bear my guns on him quickly. There was no time to manoeuvre for an easier tail shot and he did not appear to see me. I rolled over and dove straight for him. Just as I pressed the trigger, he performed the same evasive action as his buddy. I screwed into the same left diving turn, which again increased my dive angle and gave me less time to shoot at him. I passed quite close to him in the opposite direction. With the Jap climbing and me diving, we separated rapidly. By the time the 'Cat was out of the dive and climbing again in the direction I had last seen the Jap, there was no trace of him.

Moments later, I saw another Zero, or perhaps the same one, 2,000 feet below me, a half-mile distant and going away from me at right angles. Since my plane was already running at full throttle I took up the chase. He apparently saw me and turned to meet the challenge. Having the altitude advantage, I wanted to keep it. He was climbing almost towards me and I was trying to climb up over him, hoping to execute another of those overhead passes. When the time seemed right, I rolled over and dove at him.

Realizing he might make my shot harder by continuing a left turn like his two buddies, I opened fire at 1,500 feet. I was upside down, pulling into a vertical dive. At this point, I was about 900 feet from him which is the distance where my six 50-calibre machine-guns converged to a point. It was the ideal distance, and I was exhilarated to see his plane explode from the concentrated bullets. An instant later, I was executing another straining pull-out below the confettied enemy fighter plane.

Man, this is fun! I wonder if Shorty [Mueller, who replaced Hearn as Reinburg's wingman] *followed me and is getting a few. Come to think of it, I don't remember seeing him since I tried to get him to follow me after these Japs. Well, might as well head west again and try to find some more Japs. There's Savo Island up ahead so I'm still over the western end of Guadalcanal.*

A little later, while climbing through 17,000 feet, I began seeing airplanes above and ahead of me. I quickly counted six Zeros in a spread-out formation, heading west. The rearmost one was just 2,000 feet ahead and above me. My plan was to creep up under him and blow his plane out of the sky with an easy stern shoot. If the others still did not see me, I would go after the next nearest Jap. If they saw and took after me, I'd dive straight down and run for the field, which was only fifteen miles behind me. A glance at my gas gauge indicated my fuel situation was pretty low and I'd better get home soon. This excessive use of fuel was understandable since I had been running at full throttle.

In about thirty seconds, I had carefully sneaked up under the Zero and was about to pull the trigger. My airplane was straining in the steep climb, barely maintaining 120 knots flying speed and hanging on the prop, which was turning at full power. I pulled the trigger and, damn! Only the outboard right-wing gun fired! This offset recoil action coupled with slow airspeed caused my 'Cat to snaproll into a diving right turn. An instant before pulling the trigger, I noticed out of the corner of my eye that several of the other Zeros were turning around, probably to attack me. Since I had been forced into a dive anyway, it seemed best to remain vertical and run for home while I was still a winner. Holding the plane in the steep dive, I left the throttle wide open. I cringed behind my armour-plated seatback, expecting Jap bullets to bounce off it and the airplane any second. En route home, I reassessed my fortunes.

USMC F4U-1 Corsair in flight with 1,000lb bomb on Brewster centre lines (Vought).

The first and third Zeros were definitely destroyed. There was no trace of the second one after I pulled out from my straining dive. A few tracers entered that fourth Zero before I was flipped into the dive. They could have been enough to kill the pilot but I'll never know.'

Next day VMF-121 was sent to the rear area for a well-deserved rest on Espiritu Santo Island and eight pilots, including Reinburg, were transferred to VMF-122 to begin operations with the new Chance Vought Corsair. VMF-122 was commanded, temporarily as it turned out, by the colourful Major Gregory 'Pappy' Boyington. 'Pappy' had fought in China in P-40 Warhawks with the Flying Tigers and he was to become even more famous in the months ahead for his exploits with VMF-214, the 'Black Sheep Squadron'. The squadron was fourth in line to be equipped with the new fighter but there was no time to work up on Corsairs because on 10 April 1943 VMF-122, with twenty-four Wildcats, was ordered to Guadalcanal to help defend it against a new Japanese offensive to retake the island. The offensive failed however, and after flying CAP (Combat Air Patrol) the squadron returned to the rear and resumed training on the Corsair.

Early in June 1943 the squadron returned to Guadalcanal to begin operations. Hunter Reinburg

was now a major and acting Squadron Commander on Boyington's recommendation.

The Corsairs of VMF-122 were soon in action and on 30 June Major Reinburg took off from Fighter Strip Number One at Guadalcanal to fly a CAP over assault landings on Rendova Island, 200 miles to the west. 'As we approached the Jap-held Munda airfield and were passing through 23,000 feet, my engine quit completely with frightful suddenness. The Corsair was our newest type fighter airplane, just completing its fourth month of combat. It soon endeared itself to all of us because it was a match for the Zero. The engine was new, the most powerful yet built, but in the last few months we had had a number of mysterious high-altitude engine failures. We felt sure these were caused by unwarranted spark-arcing within the unpressurised magnetos while flying in the rarefied upper air. The obvious cure was pressurised magnetos. These had been ordered from the States, but in the meantime, the war had to go on.'

Reinburg glided down through 9,000 feet and began to get very concerned about having to make a water landing. 'I jerked off my uncomfortable oxygen mask. By then I had made three tries to revive the dead engine (by moving the mixture control to the auto-rich position), but with no success. While the mixture was off, and before my fourth try, I saw a formation of airplanes ahead and slightly below, coming towards us. I counted eight aircraft and was then sure, by their silhouettes that they were Zeroes. *Christ! What a spot! Japs about to attack and my engine's dead!* I was more concerned with starting my engine than warning Sims. Besides, he also had eyes, he was trained and he was presumably ready for combat. *He damn well better cover me or . . .?*

The Jap pilots did not appear to see us as I automatically turned my powerless machine towards them. My actions were purely based on the best means of survival, rather than heroic intentions. I knew my guns would work so my plan was to get a couple of Japs head-on since I had the altitude advantage, for the moment anyway. Then there would be fewer to bother me in my continued glide towards the water. Moreover, experience had taught me that the enemy would usually scatter in confusion if attacked first. While moving my control stick to commence the attack I moved the mixture control up to the auto-rich position. I was surprised and elated when my engine roared to life, at full power. Those 2,000 horses made sweet music to my ears and the fight was on.

The Jap Zero leader had now seen me and was manoeuvring directly towards me. We were coming at each other, almost head-on, at a terrific closing rate. I was ready for him. I placed my gunsight pipper just in front of him to allow for the proper lead and squeezed the trigger at about 500 yards. An instant later, his leading-edge machine-guns were spitting flame as he exchanged lead with me. My tracers struck his airplane in the engine, and since every third bullet fired was a tracer, I knew he was getting hit thrice per tracer flash. My finger released the trigger as he flashed by, close under me.

I never felt my Corsair being struck by his bullets and I had no time or cause to give the matter more thought. Before completing a hard left turn, I was in firing position to kill another Zero. I felt this was more important than trying to confirm the leader's destruction. It was almost a no-lead shot and my cone of fire blew him up with a two-second burst.

There was no time to relax and shout joyous words of victory. Another Zero was looming up in the distance, slightly below and coming head-on, emulating his leader's recent manoeuvre. A forward push on the control stick instantly established the proper lead and my trigger finger flexed. Again I observed my tracers drill into him as he passed beneath me. He did not return my fire and I

again turned hard left hoping to observe him disintegrate. Halfway through the turn, a Corsair passed in front of me, presumably Sims. He was on my level and about 1,000 yards away, passing left to right. Tracers were chasing him and a glance down their path led me to a very unfriendly fellow. The red 'meatball' was very easy to see from the sideview. *You can't do that to my wingman!* I reversed my turn to bring my guns to bear on the enemy. The Zero was slightly out of range and both he and Sims were flying a nearly straight and level course. It was imperative that I shoot the Jap quickly because he had already had ample chance to hurt Sims. My rate of closure was slow so I decided to try some long-range shooting. If he could not be fatally hit, my bullets would at least scare him into leaving my wingman alone.

Surprise and exhilaration surged through me as the Jap exploded from a three-second burst of my machine-guns. I must have hit him at about 1,200 feet, as my tracers crossed before reaching him; they were set to converge at 900 feet. While concentrating on Sims's tormentor, I neglected to notice a Jap fighter closing on my tail in much the same manner as I had stalked my now defunct victim. The sudden silence of my own guns revealed that bullets were dancing on and about my machine. My attacker had apparently been shooting at me almost as long as I had been doing the same to his friend. A glance in my rear-view mirror confirmed his presence. I instinctively rammed my stick forward to get below his line of fire, a technique that had served me well in past flights. This caused the subsequent hail to miss me but it was too late. My right wing's internal gas tank was on fire and several large holes were easily discernible. It was obvious he had scored with his cannons because they had an explosive charge when they hit; Zeros had two 20mm cannon, as well as machine-guns.

I thought (and hoped) the fire would go out before it melted the wing off or the whole works exploded. A cloud was very close by so I ducked into it for greater safety while considering the fire situation. While enshrouded in the mist, I noticed fog beginning to fill the cockpit. The smell of smoke told me I had erred, and that the fog was actually smoke. It became difficult to breathe and to see the instruments. A glance to the left indicated I was suddenly out of the cloud. Flames were now intermingled with the smoke coming from the top of my

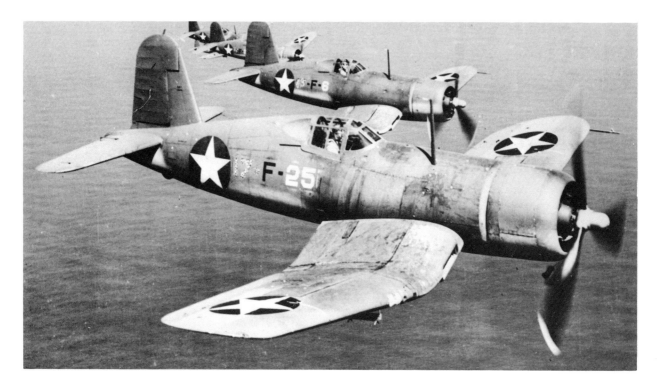

Vought F4U-1 Corsairs in flight. These F4Us belong to VF-17 (US Navy).

engine. *Christ, now I've got a fire in the engine!* This was it. I was a mass of flames and had to get out – in a hurry! The plane was expendable but I sure as hell was not. I was determined to bale out as fast as possible and avoid being cooked.'

Reinburg baled out successfully and landed by parachute in the sea. The Corsair pilot spent several very uncomfortable hours adrift in a one-man 'pararaft' before being picked up by an American destroyer.

Seven Corsairs in VMF-122 attacked fifteen 'Betty' bombers escorted by about twenty Zeros about 120 miles south-east of Kahili, a large enemy airbase on Bougainville Island, on 15 July. Hunter Reinburg dived on the formation and in one pass shot down the leader and damaged his left wingman. He turned and climbed and singled out a straggler. 'The Betty was not too near any other planes in the formation, so I would not be able to shoot at two in the same attack. His speed caused me nearly to flatten out behind him before getting close enough to shoot. The tailgunner was already shooting at me. All six of my guns needed only to bark at the bomber for less than a second before he disintegrated.

As near as I could tell, the gunner never hit my plane. In the next instant, I had to pull back the stick to avoid flying through the debris of the exploding bomber. It was a gruesome and yet rewarding sight. For an instant, several human bodies could be seen among the falling mess. The rest of the bombers were now four hundred yards ahead and it took me long excruciating minutes to gain any attack position again, high on their right side. I realized that it would be impossible to destroy all of the bombers alone. I decided to get on the radio and broadcast the location, course, altitude and speed of the enemy formation. Many flights of friendly fighters were supposed to be in the area and perhaps some of them might be close enough to join and finish what I had started. After transmitting the blanket broadcast twice, I was almost ready for another attack.

My plane started to roll left for the attack when I realized that tracer bullets were whizzing by me. My first thought was that the tailgunners were responsible. A glance into my rear-view mirror cleared up the mystery. A Zero was there pumping 'arrows' at me. That distant speck I had noticed a short while ago had now grown to a full-sized and very unfriendly airplane. I chopped my throttle while putting the Corsair in a left skid. This decelerating manoeuvre was designed to catch my attacker by surprise, confuse his aim and cause him to scoot by before he could recognize my actions and his mistake. Then, when my potential nemesis appeared in front of me; I would have him at my mercy. This caper had worked well in practice so I automatically used it.

My trigger finger itched while I strained my eyes for the first glimpse of the Jap in my gunsight. It was then that I began to suspect that my attacker was no amateur, because he never flew in front of me. My head swivelled on my shoulders as I fearfully tried to relocate my opponent. There was no sign of him anywhere. I then threw the airplane into a right skid but still could not see him. In my frantic search, I did happen to notice that the bombers were now a half-mile ahead of me because I had reduced my speed, hoping to trick the Zero. Seeing them again dispelled my fear as I returned my thoughts and efforts towards destroying more of those easy targets.

It took several minutes to attain a good attacking position again. But tracers once more began to whizz by and strike my wings. The reappearance of the Zero was confirmed by a glance in the mirror. Without thinking, I executed the same evasive skidding caper. This eliminated the 'arrows' like before, but again no Zero appeared in front. An alternate

skid to the right still did not reveal the phantom. By now I was getting more angry than frightened. Another search of the sky revealed the Betty bombers but nothing more. Where was that bastard? But seeing those juicy 'sitting-duck' bombers crowded the fears from my mind as I resumed the chase.

The enemy pilot apparently was an acrobat. He was diving on my tail from higher altitudes and using his excess speed to loop over me when my skidding manoeuvre caused him to overrun my plane before he could aim properly. This would explain his quick disappearing and reappearing. I should have suspected his manoeuvre at the time, as I had already fought with some acrobatic enemy pilots. Amazingly, the whole situation was repeated identically for a third time. However, this time the Zero, having more than his fair share of practice, sent a very hostile bullet into the cockpit. He must have been shooting from slightly on my left side, because the bullet entered just outboard of the armour plate (behind me on the left) and shattered the altimeter on the instrument panel. The bullet just

Vought F4U Corsairs of Fourth Marine Air Wing over the Marshalls later in the war, in 1944 (US Navy)

missed my arm as it passed through the crook of my elbow. The real danger from the rear now rudely awakened me. I lost my hero complex and devoted my full thoughts towards getting away from the Jap and giving him no further opportunity to kill me. I recalled that a few seconds before it was hit, the altimeter had registered 17,000 feet. I put the Corsair into a left skid and did a sloppy half-roll. I left the throttle wide open and, when inverted, pointed the airplane straight down. I continued jinking to spoil his aim as he kept the aircraft on its nose. I headed for the earth in a full-power, vertical plunge in the hope that the Zero's wings would break off.

Damn! Will my plane hold together? His bullets have struck and could have weakened its structure. Too late now; I'm already in my dive. Gosh! He's still after me and still shooting. He must be their highest ace. I'll have to

---

On 15 July 1943 fifteen G4MO1 Mitsubishi 'Betty' medium bombers of the Japanese Navy escorted by about twenty Zeros approximately 120 miles south-east of Kahili, a large enemy airbase on Bougainville Island, were attacked by seven VMF-122 Corsairs. Hunter Reinburg shot down two of the 'Betty' bombers and damaged a third (Marine Corps).

make this pull-out a tough one to finish him . . . or maybe me.

The volcanic peak of Kolombangara was helpful in gauging my altitude. At what I guessed to be 2,000 feet, I commenced easing back on the control stick with both hands. When my eyes began to see more grey than light, I refrained from pulling back on the stick further. I froze it in that position while hoping the recovery would continue. When halfway out of the steep dive, I commenced a right rolling turn and could barely see the island shoreline and the sea beyond. *Am I going to make it? The island seems to be coming up at me awfully fast!* Perspiration stung my eyes. The strain of gravity prevented me from watching the Jap in the Corsair's mirror. *Made it!*

I levelled off just above the treetops of the jungle and continued my hard right turn away from the mountain peak and towards the shoreline. As the loads of gravity lessened on my body, I tried to see behind me, hoping to observe the Jap fighter crash. But, if he survived, I wanted to get on his tail and give him some more 'arrows' in return, and show him how he should have hit me. After making a complete turn, there was no sign of the Jap. I started worrying that he might be close under my tail, in my

blind spot, and would soon be drilling me again. Several swishes of my tail calmed my fear.

Another circle of the area revealed no Zero. *Hey, what's that?* Black smoke began to rise out of the jungle at about the place where I would have crashed, if unsuccessful with my pull-out. The smoke volume rapidly increased and the blackness was indicative of a petroleum fire.

Hot damn! That just has to be that Zero, but I'll never know for sure, I guess. I just barely made the recovery so it seemed impossible that he could have. I guess I can't even claim him as a probable even though the evidence is pretty conclusive that he crashed. Anyway, he's not around to bother me. Boy, that fire's really burning fiercely now, and only gasoline could make such a blaze.

One more circle of the area for good measure still did not produce an airborne Zero. I flew low and slow over the fire, but could not see through the thick smoke and foliage. The jungle had swallowed another mystery.

A weak thought prodded me to take up the bomber chase again. The Bettys, however, were now out of sight. A glance back into my cockpit revealed a frightening fact; only sixty gallons of gas registered on my fuel gauge.

Golly! I'd better scoot for 'Canal. It's well over 200 nautical miles away, and it's going to be close on that little gas. I'd better lean out the mixture and pull the rpms back.' (Reinburg made Henderson Field with only ten gallons of fuel to spare and managed to put down safely despite a complete loss of hydraulic fluid.)

In August 1943 Reinburg was among the first Marine Corps fighter pilots to complete three combat tours fighting the Japanese. While assigned to VMF-121 and VMF-122, Reinburg had scored seven confirmed aerial victories and nine unconfirmed. In April 1945, at the end of World War Two, Reinburg had been awarded twelve Air Medals and six Distinguished Flying Crosses.

CHAPTER 4

To Hell and Back

Ploesti – 1 August 1943

Ploesti lies on the Romanian plains fifty miles north of Bucharest. In World War Two it was the greatest single source of fuel for the German war machine in all Europe. In 1941 Ploesti refined a large portion of the 2.1 million tons of Romanian oil supplied to the Third Reich. To bomb it and destroy it would be a great morale boost for the Allies.

One strike had already gone ahead in 1942. A tiny force of twenty-three B-24Ds under the command of Col Harry H. Halverson, code-named 'HALPRO', originally en route to China to bomb Tokyo from the Chinese mainland, attacked at dawn on the morning of 12 June. Ten bombed through solid cloud cover and hit the Astra Romana Refinery while one B-24D blasted the port of Constanta. Another two released their bombs on unidentified targets. There was no serious fighter opposition and all thirteen Liberators landed in neutral countries. Results, though poor, were a boost to morale. Though it was a small beginning, American heavy bombers had bombed a European target for the first time. The HALPRO detachment remained in the Middle East and in July 1942 they were absorbed into the 376th Bomb Group, better known as the 'Liberandos'. Late that month they were joined by the 98th Bomb Group, commanded by Col Hugo Rush, which was established at Ramat David, thirty-five miles east of Haifa in Palestine. The group's B-24Ds had been painted in 'Desert Pink', more popularly known to crews as 'Titty Pink'.

On 1 August 1942 the 98th Bomb Group, later more popularly known as the 'Pyramiders', attacked an enemy convoy ninety miles off Benghazi and sank one of the five tankers supplying fuel to Rommel's Afrika Korps. Further raids were made by the 98th and 376th Bomb Groups in support of the Eighth Army, and as the British moved to the offensive the Liberators were used to disrupt communications at El Alamein. In November Lt-General Lewis H. Brereton was authorised to activate Ninth Bomber Command. On 22 November the 98th and 376th Bomb Groups attacked Tripoli and in 1943 they moved further afield, bombing targets in Sicily and southern Italy. On 6 March Field Marshal Erwin Rommel launched what proved to be his last offensive; it failed and he was recalled to Berlin. The path was now clear for another strike on the oilfields at Ploesti. The refineries had become even more crucial to the German war machine after the failure of their Soviet

Capt. (later Colonel) William R. Cameron, pictured late in 1943 when he was a Major (Bill Cameron).

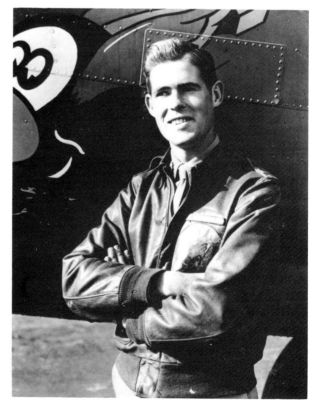

adventure and the loss of the anticipated Soviet oil supplies from the Baku area on the Caspian Sea.

In April 1943 bomber chiefs in London pressed Brereton for another attack but he was anxious to contain his bombing force for the Tunisian and Sicilian battles that lay ahead. On 6 May 1943 Operation 'Husky', the invasion of Sicily, began. Early in June Brereton was informed that three Eighth Air Force B-24D Liberator groups from England would join the 98th and 376th Bomb Groups for a second attack on Ploesti. This time the planners had opted for a low-level strike. B-17 Flying Fortresses were ruled out because they did not possess the required low-level range. The B-24D could make the trip to the target, some 1,350 miles, and back again. Eighth Air Force crews should have been alarmed at the prospect but many, like Col William R. Cameron of the 44th Bomb Group, based at Shipdham, Norfolk, felt differently. 'The whole Ploesti episode began on a high note as far as I was concerned. After six months of combat operations in very cold and hostile winter skies over Europe, we were shifted, without explanation, to low-level formation practice over the green fields of England. We were told, for the time being, at least, there would be no combat – and it was springtime. There were new crews and new B-24s to replace those that had been lost, and losses had been severe for our group. We didn't understand then that this relatively pleasant interval was designed to prepare us for an exceptional mission – one that would put it on the line for all of us.'

The three groups – the 44th 'Flying Eightballs', 93rd 'Flying Circus' and the 389th 'Sky Scorpions' – began at once flying low-level practice missions over East Anglia at less than 150 feet en route to their target range over the Wash after a five day orientation course. Rumour and speculation increased as ground crews sweated to remove the Norden bombsights and replace them with low-level sights. Heavier nose armament and additional fuel tanks in the bomb bays gave the men clues as to their new role. By increasing the Liberators' fuel capacity to 3,100 gallons they could just make it to Ploesti from the North African desert. At Hardwick, Norfolk, Col Addison Baker, CO of the 93rd, led his Liberators flying wing-tip to wing-tip at 150 feet over the hangar line on the base which was used as a target. On some days the 93rd were joined by the 44th and the 389th from Hethel in flights over the

base in waves of three aircraft. Col Leon Johnson's 44th were old hands, but Col Jack Wood's 389th had only arrived in Norfolk in mid-June. The group was under extra pressure to be ready for the flight to North Africa and it says something for its organisational ability that the 'Sky Scorpions' were ready on time. The 44th, 93rd and 389th crews had been trained in the art of high-altitude precision bombing and were quite unused to low-level flying. It led, on 25 June, to a mid-air collision involving two 389th Liberators. One B-24 made it back to Hethel but the other crash-landed and one man was killed. The 389th were the youngest and most inexperienced of the three 101st (Provisional) Wing Groups.

Bill Cameron recalls: 'After those few weeks of preparation, we took off singly on 30 June. It was a dark morning and we flew, at very low altitude, to Portreath airfield in Cornwall. The next day we crossed the Bay of Biscay, again low enough to escape German radar, and passed through the Straits of Gibraltar to Oran in Algeria. After a brief but interesting stay, we proceeded to Benina Main, near the coastal city of Benghazi in Libya. It was nearly dark when we climbed down from the *Buzzin' Bear* and waited to be directed to our billet. As we waited – and waited – Sgt Gerald Sparks, our radio operator, entertained us with his guitar. Eventually, someone came by in a truck and threw off a large canvas bundle, which we were informed was our billet. We knew then that we were not destined to feel at home in this strange new environment – and we never did.' Altogether, 124 Liberators flew in from England for Operation 'Statesman', as the Ploesti operation was codenamed. Forty-one Liberators of the 44th Bomb Group were joined by forty-two B-24s of the 93rd Bomb Group and thirty 389th Bomb Group Liberators, based near Benghazi. The 'Sky Scorpions' had only completed two weeks' training in Norfolk. For the 93rd the long overseas flight meant a return to the African desert they had forsaken in February 1943. 'Ted's Flying Circus' (named after the CO, Col Ted Timberlake), had provided a temporary detachment in support of 9th Air Force operations.

The 93rd and 389th resided at bases near Benghazi while the 'Eightballs' were based at Benina Main, one of Mussolini's former airfields, fifteen miles from Benghazi. It was an opportunity to meet the 345th Bomb Squadron of the 98th Bomb

Colonel (later General) Leon W. Johnson, CO, 44th Bomb Group, a thirty-nine-year-old West Pointer who led his group on the Ploesti low-level mission to 'White V' – Columbia Aquila. The refinery was put out of production for eleven months. On 17 August Johnson was awarded the Medal of Honor, America's highest military award, which was presented to him at a ceremony at Shipdham on 22 November, by which time he commanded the 14th Combat Wing (Bill Cameron).

Group which had been formed from the 44th in March 1942. However, there was very little *esprit de corps* prevailing when it was discovered that the 98th were withholding the best rations. By using up the less desirable items and withholding the best footstuffs, only the choicest rations would remain for the 98th when the 44th returned to England. Col Leon Johnson took the matter up with Col John 'Killer' Kane, now the 98th CO, but things did not improve during the 'Eightballs' stay in Benina Main.

On 5 July the Liberators took off on the first of ten missions in support of the Italian campaign. Most of these missions were flown without escort and soon losses began to assume the proportions sustained at the height of the raids on the U-Boat pens in France. The rush of missions meant that some crewmen quickly racked up enough to complete their tour. Bill Cameron recalls: 'After missions over such targets as Messina, Catania, Foggia and Naples, I completed my required twenty-five in a borrowed ship, the *Suzy-Q*, over Rome on 19 July.'

After the Rome mission, the Liberator groups concentrated on training for Ploesti, as Bill Cameron recalls. 'We plunged into low-level formation practice once again, but this time it was over the dry Libyan desert. It occurred to me at the same time that I was not really expected to fly this low-level mission, whatever the target was, but I was swept up in the preparation for it primarily out of loyalty to my crew, and perhaps some curiosity that caused me to want to see it through. For almost two weeks, B-24s in small groups were crisscrossing the desert in all directions, practising low-level formation flying. Eventually, the groups became larger as the training progressed towards a full dress rehearsal

B-24D Liberators pictured making a low-level practice run over the desert prior to the mission on 1 August 1943 (USAF).

involving the total force of 175 B-24 Liberator bombers.'

On 6 July Brereton told his five group commanders that a low-level, daylight attack would be made on Ploesti to achieve maximum surprise and ensure the heaviest possible damage in the first attack. Brereton had studied target folders for two weeks before making his decision. The attack would be made at noon to minimize losses among the slave labour work force. On 20 July the five groups began twelve days' training for 'Tidal Wave' (the codename for Ploesti), with practice flights against a mock-up target in the desert. Bill Cameron recalls: 'Target models had been set up in the desert. When we were considered ready, the entire force of 175 bombers took off, assembled in group formation, and lined up one group behind the other. Proceeding just as we would against the actual targets in Romania, we arrived at the practice IP [Initial Point] and each unit then swung approximately ninety degrees to the right. This manoeuvre put five units of aircraft flying side by side at a very low level and racing towards our simulated target. In this manner, all our aircraft were streaking over their small targets at nearly the same moment. The units were then to turn to the right, which meant

that once again the five groups would be lined up one behind the other as they left the target area.

'A day or two before the mission, we were brought into the briefing room and the great secret was unveiled. The presentation was quite elaborate and included movies of models of each of the several refineries we were to attack. The movies simulated the view of the target as a pilot would see it approaching at very low altitude. Everything would depend on surprise and exact timing. It was explained that the defences were relatively light and we would not have to concern ourselves too much about Rumanian anti-aircraft because Sunday was a day of rest for Romanians – even in time of war. Some of the edge was removed from this optimism by Lt-General Lewis H. Brereton, who addressed us all at an open-air meeting in the African sunshine. 'This job' he told them 'is a dangerous mission, but we feel that if the refineries are demolished, and the entire force wiped out, it will still be worth the price.' T/Sgt Donald V. Chase, radio operator in the crew of *Heaven Can Wait* flown by Charles Whitlock, in the 44th BG, recalls: 'Brereton warned that aircraft

General Lewis H. Brereton addresses Liberator crews prior to the low-level raid on 1 August 1943 (USAF).

losses might reach fifty per cent or more. That Russian roulette figure aroused our apprehension. Nevertheless, all ten crewmen willingly readied for the assault. But orders called for a crew of only nine, not the usual ten, the tunnel gun position to be unmanned because of weight restrictions for the 2,500 mile flight and because our low attack altitude and 200 mph ground speed would cancel the effectiveness of a single, belly-fired, hand-held .50.'

'The four mid- and rear-section gunners drew straws to determine which one would remain on the desert on P-Day. Young waist gunner Ralph Knox drew the 'unlucky' straw. He complained and cursed and, feeling abandoned, withdrew from the rest of the crew, not to speak until just before take-off, when, woefully, he wished us luck. Ralph was dejected by this fracture in the brotherhood of battle. There wasn't much reason to stash aboard beer or extra water for the Ploesti run; we wouldn't fly high enough to chill it. But one of the ground men fastened a canteen in the already crammed bomb bay. 'Just for luck, okay?' He punctuated his words with the universal, jabbing thumbs-up salute.'

It was barely daylight, 1 August, when the Liberators took off. Brereton had decided on seven forces from the five groups. First away at 0700 hours was 1/Lt Brian W. Flavelle's *Wongo Wongo!* of the

B-24D Liberator *Forky II*, 42-40182 of the 66th Bomb Squadron, 44th Bomb Group, was flown by Capt. Rowland M. Gentry who led the last wave of five aircraft in vee formation to 'White V', the Columbia Aquila refinery complex, which they were to bomb from just 400 feet. Explosions in the target area killed William L. Leisinger, the tail gunner, and Stanley Wilson, the left waist gunner, and set two engines on fire. Three fighters finished off the B-24, killing Gentry and others in the crew before *Forky II* crashed in a cornfield and buried its nose in the ground. Only S/Sgt Charles T. Bridges, the right waist gunner and a veteran of fifty-three operational missions with the RAF, staggered out, his back broken, before the B-24 exploded (via Steve Adams).

Low-flying Liberators photographed by a B-24D Liberator of the 389th Bomb Group make their way to the oil refineries at Ploesti (USAF).

376th and the lead plane of 'Tidal Wave', which lifted off from Berka Two. On board was the mission navigator Lt R. Wilson. The other twenty-eight B-24s of the 376th BG 'Liberandos', led by the Group CO, Col Keith Compton, and Brigadier-General Uzal G. Ent (CO, 9th Bomber Command) in the command ship, *Teggie Ann*, followed. (Brereton had intended to go in the command aircraft but an order from General Hap Arnold in Washington forbade it.) Compton's target was 'White I', the Romana American Refinery. Behind them came thirty-six B-24s of the 93rd Bomb Group, led by Col Addison Baker and Major John 'The Jerk' Jerstad in *Hell's Wench*. Baker was assigned 'White II', Concordia Vega while Major Ramsey D. Potts led the balance

TO HELL AND BACK

of the 93rd (fifteen aircraft) to 'White III', the Standard Petrol Block and Unirea – Spiranza. They were followed by forty-seven B-24s in the 98th BG formation, led by Col John 'Killer' Kane in *Hail Columbia*. Some 389th crewmen flew with the 98th as fill-ins. Kane's target was 'White IV', the Unirea-Orion and Astra Romana refineries. Next came thirty-seven B-24s of the 44th Bomb Group, led by Col Leon Johnson and Bill Brandon in the venerable *Suzy Q*. Johnson's intention to lead in *Suzy Q* had been placed in jeopardy the night before when a broken spark-plug was diagnosed in engine number two. After an anxious night of maintenance and repair the sick patient was pronounced well enough to fly. Seventeen B-24s were headed for 'White V' – Columbia Aquila. Bill Cameron recalls: 'Our formation consisted of, first, a three-plane element led by Col Leon Johnson with Bill Brandon as his pilot. Next would come six bombers trailing to the right, which we were leading in the *Buzzin' Bear*. Off to our left would be the remaining six air-craft, led by Dexter Hodge. Trailing behind would be a spare aircraft, piloted by Bob Felber. It was arranged that we would move into the lead should *Suzy Q* falter for mechanical reasons en route to Ploesti. As it turned out, only one of the thirty-seven aircraft of our 44th failed to reach the target area, a tribute to our maintenance men. I think it was also due in some measure to our dedication to Leon Johnson.' Johnson's deputy, Major Posey, led his force of nineteen B-24s to 'Blue' target – Creditul Minier Brazi.

Last to take-off were twenty-six B-24s of the 389th Bomb Group, led by Col Jack Wood in Major Kenneth 'Fearless' Caldwell's Liberator. The 'Sky Scorpions' had been allocated the longest route in the target ('Red I', Steaua Romana at Campina) because their Liberators were the only ones fitted with fuselage tanks containing an additional 400 gallons of fuel. However, this additional weight made them very vulnerable and meant that each B-24 could only carry four 500lb bombs. The 389th carried bombs with only 10-second delay fuses while the other groups carried twenty-minute acid core fused bombs which would not explode until the bombs dropped by the 389th created a concus-sion wave in the target area. Any that did not explode in the concussion wave would eventually explode by means of the acid core fuse. The fuel and bomb load preyed on the minds of the 389th crews

Major James T. Posey, a West Pointer from Henderson, Kentucky who succeeded Leon Johnson as Group CO at Shipdham on 3 September 1943, led twenty-one B-24s on 1 August 1943 in a very accurate strike on 'Blue I', Creditul Minier Brazi, five miles south of Ploesti. Only two of Posey's twenty-one Liberators were lost and Creditul Minier was put out of commission for the rest of the war (Bill Cameron).

at take-off. Earl Zimmerman, the radio operator in Lt Harold L. James's crew, recalls: 'We were made to drain the gas gauges on the flight-deck prior to taking off because they figured that if we got hit by ground fire it would be less likely to catch fire.'

One B-24 from the 389th, *Kickapoo*, which was flying with the 98th, had an engine failure on take-off and crashed on landing. Only two men, badly burned, scrambled out of the wreckage. As Bill Cameron circled to take his place in the 44th forma-tion he saw a large column of black smoke and orange flame blossom up. 'We knew someone had not made the take-off. It was a tragic end for one crew and it did nothing to relieve our tension. Shortly afterwards, we settled down and began the long, silent ride across the Mediterranean, barely visible in the hazy skies below and around us. Ahead of us were the 376th, 93rd and 98th Bomb Groups, in that order. The intercom cut into my concentration. Capt. Jim DeVinney, our bombardier, called attention to a column of smoke rising from the sparkling sea below us.' Nearing landfall at the German occupied island of Corfu, *Wongo Wongo!*, the 376th lead ship, had gone down out of control. It veered up, fell over on its back and plunged into the sea.

The realisation that the lead navigator had gone down with it began to sink in for those, like Bill Cameron, who crossed over. 'Had I known at the time that the alternate leader had followed the leader down to look for survivors, I would have been even more concerned. At the time, however, I did not realize that we had lost the two crews that had been specially briefed and trained to lead the entire formation to Ploesti.' *Brewery Wagon*, piloted by Lt John Palm, took its place at the head of the 376th. 'What a moment that must have been for Brig.-Gen. Uzal G. Ent and Col Keith Compton – flying in the third and remaining aircraft of that lead element – to suddenly find that command of this vital mission had been so unexpectedly thrust on them.

'We were still puzzling over the smoke rising from the sea below when a bomber well in front of us swung out of formation and turned back towards us with two port engines out.' Bill Dabney added: 'We saw his bomb bay doors open and his bombs drop into the sea as he lightened the load on his two good engines for the long headlong dash home. The engine-eating sand of the desert had claimed another victim and I guess we all gave a little prayer for the boys in that ship. It was almost too much to take. The gods just didn't seem to be with us. So many bad breaks so early in the game was pretty disheartening.'

As the five-mile-long formation headed for Corfu, inevitable malfunctions reduced the numbers and seven of Kane's 'Pyramiders' were forced to abort. Three more B-24s from other groups also returned early. After Corfu, crews veered right, to the east, and headed overland to Ploesti. At the Greek border commanders were confronted with the Pindus Range rising to a height of, at most, 11,000 feet. The

horizon was blotted out with cumulus clouds towering to 17,000 feet and a decision had to be made whether to continue as briefed and risk collision or climb above them. Bill Cameron observed, 'I felt a foreboding of trouble for the first time.' Compton elected to climb above the cloud tops to save fuel and time and the 93rd followed him. 'Killer' Kane, whose group was following the 376th, had his mind made up for him. Many of the 'Pyramiders' aircraft were not equipped with oxygen for this low-level mission so the 98th circled and entered the cloud in threes, and after the range repeated the manoeuvre before setting course again. Bill Cameron continues: 'The skies were clearer now, less hazy and we could see the aircraft of the 98th group very clearly and, beyond, numerous specks that would be the B-24s of the 93rd and perhaps the 376th as well. At any rate, the latter two groups were some distance ahead, not quite the way we have flown it in practice.'

Bill Dabney called the crew in the rear to tell them they were going up so that they could get a little oxygen in the event any of them needed it. Cameron continues: 'As we approached the clouds, they grew more menacing. It was vital that one group follow the other into the target area. Our success and our salvation depended not only on surprise but also on a simultaneous sweep across our various targets. We must arrive together, attack together and depart together. How would this be possible, we began to ask ourselves, if we were now to be separated penetrating the clouds? Would the mission now be abandoned? Would radio silence be broken to announce our recall? Then one of the leading groups disappeared in the clouds and we had our answer. The only question now was could we find that same hole and follow straight through it? 'As the 98th, leading us, came closer to that solid wall, we searched for the opening until it became obvious we couldn't find it. The formation veered off to look for another opening and at that moment, I knew that it was to be a new ball game.'

Bill Dabney adds: 'Bill and I watched our engine instruments with hopeful eyes. The climbs had always meant trouble for our engines and we were really sweating this one out, every foot of the way. An abortive, or turn back, would mean an ignominious end to all our plans, so we nursed the *Buzzin' Bear* along with careful hands. Slowly we got our altitude and I called Frank Maruszewski, our tail gunner, to check on the boys in our formation. 'Right on the old agate sir', he called. 'The number three man is a little wide but he'll be okay.' 'The mountains weren't getting any smaller by this time. They reminded me of the towering Rockies of Colorado. Away off to our left, dodging in and out of the clouds, we could see the other group but they were drawing farther and farther away as we flew on.' Bill Cameron continues: 'The lead groups continued on course to Ploesti, while we lost time searching for a route through the clouds. It would not be a co-ordinated attack and from that time on we would be alone with the pink-coloured airplanes of the 98th. Adding to our concern was flight engineer Sergeant Gibby's announcement, 'Fighter at ten o'clock, two thousand above!' A fighter? Had we been spotted so soon? We were miles from the target. 'Hey look!' someone yelled. 'It's a biplane.' 'Strangely enough, that's what it was and I agreed with co-pilot Bill Dabney's opinion that the pilot was a lot more startled to see us than we had been to see him! Nevertheless, we had been spotted.

'Some minutes later we were clearing the clouds with only the aircraft of the 98th in sight ahead of us. Our own 44th was coming along in good shape. Even with this combined force of some seventy bombers, it felt very lonely. Maruszewski looked in vain for the 389th behind us. Nothing. I think we must have all felt threatened now and the formation began to tighten up. We began our slow descent that would eventually take us below the treetops in the vicinity of Ploesti. We had now descended the Balkan east slope. It was almost peaceful as we droned on a straight course, mile after mile. Because of the relatively few bombers we could see, the skies seemed strangely empty and nothing appeared to be moving on the green hills below.' Dabney adds: 'Tom Clifford called to say we were a little off course and he hoped like hell we'd come out at the right place. Down we went, so I pulled back the rpms to help keep us in position, but even so we slid on by the *Suzy-Q*. For an awful moment we had terrible visions of ruining the whole deal by messing up the formation, but finally *Suzy* pulled ahead and Cameron called for more power as we swung back into position.'

Cameron continues: 'I didn't know how our timing was and it couldn't matter much now since we were obviously separated from the two groups in the lead. The 98th formation was still stretched out in front of us and the 389th now appeared behind us and very high. We were down to about 3,000 feet as we crossed the Danube and had a very clear view of the Romanian countryside.' Bill Dabney adds: 'Every few minutes we'd pass over a country town with its dusty streets and avenues of trees. It was hard to believe we were deep inside Europe in a strange country. They might have been Indians and those little Indiana country towns. The little groups of people watching us as we roared over would have gaped just like that back home.' Cameron continues: 'Ploesti was still more than 160 miles away. Pitesti, the first of three checkpoints before we began the turn on our bomb run, was now less than 100 miles ahead. We didn't know it then but the two lead groups were some sixty miles ahead of us. They had reached the first checkpoint on time but turned on the second checkpoint and streaked on a correct course, but for the wrong target!' Due to a navigational error, the 'Liberandos' had turned south too soon, at Targoviste, instead of at the correct IP at Floresti, and the 93rd followed. Nearing Ploesti, Compton and Ent prepared to take the 376th over the refineries alone. He overtook *Brewery Wagon* and nosed *Teggie Ann* into the lead slot. *Brewery Wagon*, which was on course, took the route as briefed and was shot down soon after. The 376th's error led to the 93rd's subsequent tactical mistake in bombing the 98th's and 44th's targets and caused approximately twenty ineffective 376th sorties.

When the mistake was realised, Compton and Ent decided to make the best of the situation and head for the Astro Romana, Phoenix Orion and Columbia Aquila refineries, which were the intended targets of the 98th and 44th Bomb Groups. The 'Liberandos' saw the 93rd already desperately fighting its way through to the target area, and split to attack targets of opportunity instead. As the 'Liberandos' passed Ploesti and began climbing up the foothills east of the city they saw the 'Pyramiders' coming towards them. The plan was in ruins with groups coming in from the wrong directions and bombing any target which presented itself. The 93rd had followed Compton's force and trailed over Ploesti. Some Romanian fighters attacked the 93rd formation and the tail gunner of *Joisey Bounce* became the first casualty of the Ploesti battle.

Baker and Jerstad turned *Hell's Wench* 90 degrees left and headed for the smokestacks of Ploesti.

A B-24D Liberator of Col John R. 'Killer' Kane's 98th Bomb Group roars low over 'White IV', or the Astra Romana refinery, the largest in Europe, amid smoke and flame. The 'Pyramiders' destroyed half the refinery's productive capacity at a cost of twenty-two Liberators and their crews (USAF).

Ramsey Potts in *The Duchess* and the second formation of 93rd B-24s followed. The flak batteries enveloped the 'Flying Circus' with their fire and at only twenty feet they were sitting targets. During the five-minute bomb run the group was torn to shreds. *Hell's Wench* was hit and caught fire. Baker jettisoned his bombs but he and Jerstad decided to continue to the target. At Ploesti *Hell's Wench* was enveloped in flames and surged up to 300 feet before falling back and crashing to the ground. Both pilots were awarded posthumous Medals of Honor for their sacrifice. Capt. Walter Stewart, the deputy leader in *Utah Man*, took over the 93rd lead and despite severe damage to the bomber, managed to land again in Libya fourteen hours later. K. D. McFarland, flying *Liberty Lad* on two engines, was the last home by another two hours. Nine other 93rd B-24s, including two which collided in cloud, did not return. Among the survivors were *Joisey Bounce*, which made it home with a shattered tail, *Thar She Blows*, *Ball of Fire Jr*, *Bomerang* and *The Duchess*. Meanwhile, the 98th, led by 'Killer' Kane in *Hail Columbia*, and the 44th, crossed Ploesti from the north-west. The 'Pyramiders' suffered the highest casualties of all five groups, losing twenty-one of the thirty-eight B-24s that started out from North Africa. At least nine were destroyed by the blasts from delayed action bombs dropped by the 376th.

The 'Eightballs' had arrived at Ploesti at 1515 hours, immediately plunging into a hail of flak, ripping tracers, smoke, fire and explosives. Bill Dabney observed: 'The IP was just as we'd memorised it – a ridge of green mountains sprinkled with oil derricks which dotted a trail down on to the plain and to Ploesti itself. The only thing we hadn't seen before were the guns, which appeared in every field and patch of woods; even the houses fell apart, revealing heavy flak guns and way up ahead we could see men hastily setting up positions between the derricks. 'Get ready boys, this is it!' Bill called and those were the last words we heard before the run. We turned ninety degrees to the right, dropping in directly behind Brandon to begin the dive to the target.'

Bill Cameron continues: 'We were keenly aware of the smoke and the flame that was now becoming visible in the target area. We could begin to guess what was happening but we did not know that those huge fires came from the very targets we had been assigned to attack at near ground-level! 'With the aircraft of the 98th stretched out before us we had passed Pitesti and Targoviste and were nearing the turning-point at Floresti. As Floresti came into view, with our altitude approximately 1,500 feet, things began to get very busy. By now it was clear that our target had already been bombed and was in flames. What followed was probably the most action-packed thirty minutes of my life.'

'The long gaggle of pink-coloured 98th B-24s began a wide descending turn to the right and there we were, turning on the bomb run to the target labelled 'White V', the Columbia Aquila refinery. Col Leon Johnson and Bill Brandon in the *Suzy-Q* turned their three-ship element inside the 98th and all together some fifty bombers began to drop rapidly to their assigned bombing altitudes, flying parallel to a railroad on our right, which led directly towards our target. As we made the turn, we pulled our six-ship flight into position directly behind *Suzy-Q* and the remaining seven bombers fell in line behind us – sixteen 44th bombers in all. The last element numbered four Liberators instead of three because Bob Felber, in the spare B-24, refused to go home and stayed with us all the way [subsequently going into 'Blue' target with Posey's formation,

which split off at this point to attack the Brazi refinery, five miles to the south of Ploesti].

'As we approached the target area, several B-24s were coming in straight for us from our left but there was no time then to try to figure that one out! It was just one of several unexpected happenings that had to be accepted. Later, we learned that these were Liberators from the 93rd and 376th. Some of these aircraft had unfortunately dropped their bombs a few minutes earlier on the very target we were now rapidly approaching. As we raced towards Columbia Aquila, levelling off at our bombing altitude of 250 feet, my eyes were glued on the *Suzy-Q*. Her target would be almost exactly in line with the spot where our own bombs were programmed to go. We were expected to place our load into a low-profile building some 210 feet wide and 600 feet long. We were edging towards a train rolling side by side with us along the tracks on our right. It appeared to be exceptionally well equipped with anti-aircraft weapons of all calibres. By this time it seemed that almost all our own .50 calibre machine-guns were in action and, judging by the excited chatter on our intercom, they were directed towards the train. Bill Dabney adds: 'Our top turret snarled and I smelled cordite from the nose guns as the boys raked the cars up and down. A second later and their shots had taken effect. The whole damned train seemed to disintegrate in one fierce explosion. Undismayed by the flames that seemed to lick our very wingtips, Brandon still was bearing down on the target and we had short glimpses of smoke stacks and the cracking plant silhouetted against a sheet of raging fire.'

Cameron continues: 'The sky was becoming unusually crowded with pink aircraft sliding in on us from our left. Perhaps no moment of the entire episode worried me more than did the chilling knowledge that we were suddenly sandwiched between two bombers, one directly above us and one below! I could not have lifted either wing during those few seconds without bringing sure destruction to the three of us. Even now, I can visualise the rivets of the bomber above us, which I could see all too clearly. I could occasionally glimpse the bomber below but could only concern myself with the one above. Miraculously, both of our large neighbours slid away from us. We were now heading towards a point where the railroad disappeared into a great mass of smoke and flame –

the Columbia Aquila refinery. By this time, I am quite sure that green and pink B-24s were mixed together as we neared our targets. I will always believe that a few pink bombers crossed through our formation at just about the time we penetrated the smoke over the target area. I also became increasingly aware of the flames and huge columns of smoke just ahead of us. There were two raging areas of destruction. These were close together with a narrow tunnel of light in between. The wind was from our left and the smoke from the towering flame on the left stretched high and over towards the fires on the right side, forming a top to the tunnel I have described.

'It seemed to me that bombers were converging towards that one small area that was free of flame and explosions. And then *Suzy-Q* disappeared in that smoke and we were right behind. Below me in the nose section I could hear DeVinney and Clifford frantically trying to pinpoint our target. Then we were in the smoke – and then out of it. If you have ever flown an airplane through a lone, fleecy white cloud, you will remember how suddenly you pop out on the far side. To this day Bill Dabney maintains that our outside air temperature gauge reached its most extreme temperature reading as we sailed through the awful heat of those great fires that seemed to surround us!' Bill Dabney confirms this: 'Our own *Buzzin' Bear* was hot as an oven and I glanced at the air temperature gauge – it had passed the last mark! But the flak suit felt pretty wonderful and the 'chute reassuring. I started to call Jim to see if the bombs had gone but just then Brandon pulled up abruptly and we saw three tall smoke stacks pass under our wing as the target appeared for a brief second. Now we were in a diving turn to the right and there was blue sky ahead as the wind cleared the smoke. It didn't clear for long. The green fields below were suddenly alive again with belching guns and I could see the sweat-stained German gunners furiously following us with their barrels. We had no defence, I thought, but I didn't reckon with fast-thinking Johnson and Brandon. They dived so low that the gunners abandoned their triggers and ducked as we roared over where their heads had been a second before.'

Cameron continues: 'Just as abruptly, I pushed hard on the control column and headed for the ground, all in a split-second, and I am sure this near spontaneous action saved our lives. Staring up at us

were numerous shirtless anti-aircraft gunners in gun emplacements with long, black barrels pointing directly at us. We levelled and began a flat turn to the right. By 'flat' I mean that I pushed hard on the right rudder but kept our wings from banking with opposite aileron control. It may be that the skidding turn threw the gunners off, but whatever the reason we escaped destruction.'

Dabney continues: 'Now there was blue sky ahead, the wind was against us and we had left the fires and were skimming the tops of the waving corn. Bill called for less throttle, so I pulled her back, glancing quickly at the engine instruments to see if we'd been hit – but they were perking like the old cabriolet back home and by some miracle we were still going strong. Unable to find our building in the smoke (augmented by smoke pots), flames, exploding tanks and the general confusion of that instant, our bombs were held too long. I can only hope that they fell in an area that contributed to the general destruction in the target complex. Few, if any, aircraft came off that target lower than we did – at least at that moment. Every Liberator I saw was above us. The abrupt pitchdown from 250 feet dislodged the gunners in the rear, Sergeants Jerry Grett and Ernie 'Mac' McCabe, but they were on their feet again in an instant.'

'Everything was happening awfully fast now. The *Suzy-Q* and her two wingmen, Reg Carpenter and Ed Mitchell, were in their turn just ahead. My own two wingmen, Charlie 'Punchy' Henderson and Jim Hill, had dropped down with us and were doggedly hanging on in formation as we skidded around that turn. A B-24 ahead pulled straight up and then fell out of the sky. Two doll-like figures popped out of the waist windows, barely 200 or 300 feet above the ground. I learned later that both men actually survived that fantastic jump. As this was going on and we were still in our turn, a V-formation of five to seven Me 109s swung headlong into us, going from our left to right. I didn't know it but both Charlie Henderson and Jim Hill had received damage by this time. I have always assumed that Henderson was hit by those oncoming Me-109s, because the damage was in his nose section where both his navigator and bombardier were wounded. However, more official records give credit to a Ju-88. Jim Hill hit a barrage balloon cable that put a rip in his wing but otherwise came through okay. We took a hit somewhere along the line, ripping out hydraulic lines and putting our tail turret out of operation. There was a pretty fair-sized hole in the *Bear*'s tail but no-one was hurt. The loss of the tail gun turned out to be a great disadvantage during the next few minutes. In the meantime, there was a rather wild mixture of bombers and fighters and then we were levelling out and heading on the long road home. But we were not out of it yet.'

'The way things were developing, it had become almost a matter of individual survival, with little time to account for our companions. In fact, because of the personal nature of our targets, the three-ship elements were separated to enable each aircraft to attack its own aiming point. The formation was further widened by the smoke, flame and the tremendous barrage of anti-aircraft fire we encountered in the target area. And because we were using high – though not maximum – power settings, ships to the rear could not readily close up, especially if they were damaged. Nevertheless, the formation was beginning to assemble when all the fighters in Romania seemed to descend on us. From all directions came Me-109s, 110s, and 210s. All this took place not more than three to five minutes after leaving the target area.'

Bill Dabney wrote later, 'I was just patting myself on the back when it all began again. Out of nowhere twenty fighters appeared, coming straight for us in a long dive. I prayed that we were too low for anything but a passing shot as they went over. But three of the bastards were heading right for us. The top turret roared and in a flash they had passed – not over but under! And we thought *we* were on the deck! The ship vibrated as the waist guns chattered and from the tail Frank cursed the Jerries' passing speed. Cameron continues: 'The chatter on the intercom was pretty frantic by now but in all the excitement I understood that a Liberator off to our right was fighting for its life against repeated fighter attacks. Then in a cloud of dust it was on the ground and skidding to a stop. The war was over, apparently safely, for that crew. Nearby, an Me-110 went down and exploded, joined almost immediately by an Me-109, which crashed, leaving a fiery trail through a field of wheat.'

'I was pulling about 32 inches of manifold pressure and indicating 220 to 225 mph as we closed in towards the lead element when I noticed a twin-engined Dornier 217 just above and to our right. I usually left such matters to my eagle-eyed crew,

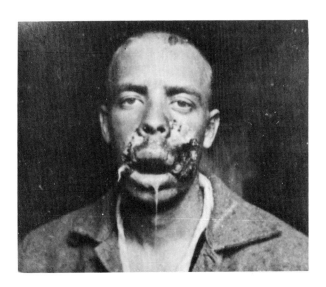

1/Lt Henry Lasco, pilot of *Sad Sack II*, in a Romanian PoW camp. A 20mm shell, fired from a Bf 109 after the target, passed through both cheeks and his palate. It was his seventh mission. Both he and his co-pilot, Lt Joe Kill, came from Chicago. Five of the crew, including Thomas M. Wood, the tail gunner, Sgt Leonard Raspotnik, who died on the way to hospital, and Sgt Joe Spivey, who was hit in the stomach, were killed (Elmer Reinhart via John Page).

who had scored five confirmed fighters over Naples not long before, but I yelled to Gibby on the intercom to bring this one to his attention. He called back that we could quit worrying about that one if we were to do anything about the several other fighters on our tail! With the tail turret out, both Gibby and the waist gunners were busy warding off a number of single- and twin-engined fighters that were to stay with us for the next fifteen to twenty minutes. In the meantime, we saw other fighters overshoot us in their pursuit of bombers ahead. It was what could accurately be described as a running fight! We were flying at about 100 ft now because I intended to pull into close formation directly behind and under Col Johnson and Brandon. To elude the fighters, if we could, we went back down below the level of the scattered treetops. We followed the terrain, once lifting slightly to rise up over a man ploughing a field directly in our path. He never left his plough and acted as though American bombers flew over those fields every day. I especially recall two well-spaced trees that I deliberately flew between, thinking to myself under circumstances that seemed very unreal that I might never have the chance to do that again – legally.'

'Now the fighters appeared to have turned off and we could begin to look around cautiously and take stock of our situation. As it turned out, the battle was over for us but we learned later that the fighting went on for many of the other crews. Some were still being attacked by fighters after they had reached the Mediterranean. By now we had lost track of Henderson and Hill, who had taken up a direct route for Malta. It was a long, lonely trip, but they made it. Ed Mitchell, who had been flying on *Suzy-Q*'s left wing, peeled off to land in Turkey. Worden Weaver, who was leading the flight behind [in *Lil' Abner*], was hit very badly over the target and crashed about forty miles away – about the same time as we passed over the man ploughing the field. Hit severely, with gaping holes in the fuselage and a missing vertical stabiliser, was the airplane flown by Bob Miller and Dexter Hodge, leading the fourth flight. Luckily, three of their engines were spared and miraculously they made it safely 1,100 miles back to Benghazi. Both of their wingmen were lost.'

'Some distance away, Col Jim Posey had led the other half of the 44th, twenty-one B-24s, on a very accurate strike against their separate target. Charles Whitlock was forced to abort forty minutes short of the target, near Craiova, as T/Sgt Don Chase recalls: 'Fuel transfer problems and . . ., as proved later, oiling difficulties caused us to shut down engine number one and feather the propeller. We were tail-end Charlie, eating everyone's prop wash. We kept lagging farther behind. Then engine number four lost power. We fell farther back. We had no choice. Navigator, Robert Ricks gave Whitlock a course heading to the nearest friendly landing field, in Cyprus, some five hours distant.' Posey's formation made it safely over the Creditul Minier refinery at Brazi but lost Elmer Reinhart a short distance from the target. Reinhart was able to gain some altitude, permitting his crew to bale out successfully. Bill Cameron recalls: 'Rowland Houston, an outstanding flyer, was shot down by a fighter moments later and was lost with his entire crew. Despite the two losses, the performance of Posey's bombers was one of the few success stories that can be told about the attack on Ploesti.'

General Leon W. Johnson talks with 2/Lt Gerald J. Totten, 2/Lt Richard H. Pendeleton and T/Sgt Frank D. Garrett (third from left) following their return to Shipdham in September 1944 after a year in a Romanian PoW camp. All three men were part of 1/Lt Elmer Reinhart's crew in *GI Gal*, the last B-24 away from Blue target. Part of the wing was shot off and Bf 109s shot away most of the tail turret but George Van Son emerged alive from the debris. Eighty miles from the target all the crew, except Flt Off. Charles L. Starr, the co-pilot, whose parachute failed to open properly, baled out safely (Elmer Reinhart via John Page).

Four dramatic photos of the Ploesti raid taken by a 389th Bomb Group photographer over the burning refinery at Steaua Romana, Campina. 'Red Target' was totally destroyed at a cost of six of the 'Sky Scorpions' twenty-nine Liberators, and put out of production for six years (via Earl Zimmerman).

The greatest success, however, went to the 389th BG bringing up the rear of 'Tidal Wave' and striking for the Steaua Romana refinery at Campina, eighteen miles north-west of Ploesti. The 389th, led by Col Jack Wood and Major Kenneth 'Fearless' Caldwell, had some anxious moments when the formation turned down the wrong valley, but they pulled up and flew on for perhaps three to four minutes before turning to the right.

Crews were also anxiously eyeing their fuel gauges, particularly those in the rear of the formation, as Earl Zimmerman recalls: 'Just before we hit the target Lt James got a little worried about the gas consumption because we were flying in the last element. Flying in the tail end of the formation you were constantly jockeying the controls. It takes a bit more manoeuvring to stay in formation and we were constantly being buffeted by prop wash. We were really burning up the gas. The engineer told me that if we had turned round then we could not have made Benghazi. We knew we were not going back no matter what happened over the target.'

The 389th started down towards the refinery, which was marked by a great pall of smoke, and split into three sections to hit the refinery from three different directions. 2/Lt James F Gerrits, the co-pilot of *Hitler's Hearse* flown by Capt. Robert Mooney of the 567th Squadron, recalls: 'As we started down and saw the target, Bob Mooney was all excited. He said to me, 'There it is, get those nose guns firing Hank!' (We had two .50 calibre guns specially mounted in the nose for shooting up the target a little and mostly to demoralise the ground gunners.) I had a toggle switch to fire them and I flipped it a couple of times and heard them roar.'

'We headed down on a long glide into the target. There were a lot of orange blips appearing all over from around the target area. We looked down the barrels of the guns as they were firing at us. Everything was fine and then suddenly there was a loud bang in the cockpit. It quickly filled with smoke. I flinched away and turned towards my side window. As the smoke cleared there was a horrible roar from a hole in the windscreen and I turned towards Mooney. He was leaning back, away from the control wheel. His hands were off the wheel and just held in front of him. Blood was running all down his face. It was evident right away that he wasn't conscious anymore. We were still going down on the target in a shallow dive and maybe 200 feet or so off the ground. I quickly grabbed the wheel and held the run for a few seconds. Then I pulled up and to the right and we went over the refinery structures a little to the right. I could feel something down the side of my face and my left arm hurt. I looked down and I had some blood on myself too. The air was roaring in through the hole in the windshield where the shell had entered to the left of Mooney's head. I was alone. Garret, the engineer, had disappeared too. I thought it was all over for us so I felt we should give them hell before we crashed. I pushed my intercom button and shouted 'OK, now give it to them, pour it at 'em. Let's go now. Keep those guns going!' I was talking to the tail gunner, who had good shots at the refinery as we were pulling away. Then we were low over the trees, past the target and still in the air.'

'Red' target was completely destroyed but the success was marred by the loss of four Liberators shot down. The bravery and determination of the men of the 389th was shown in the courage displayed by Lt Lloyd D. Hughes. He was posthumously awarded the Medal of Honor for refusing to turn back after shells had ruptured his fuel tanks. Despite fuel streaming over the fuselage, he and his co-pilot, Lt Horton, piloted the B-24 low over the blazing target. Heat engulfed the bomber and flames licked at its fuselage as the fuel ignited. Hughes struggled to complete the bomb run but after 'bombs away' his starboard wing dipped and ploughed into the ground. Only two gunners survived.

The 'Sky Scorpions' had been the last to arrive over the target area and had paid dearly for their lack of surprise. When *Hitler's Hearse* came off the target the only Liberator around was Lt James's B-24. Gerrits and his badly wounded engineer, Garret, with Mooney dead, nursed their shattered B-24 to Turkey, where, low on fuel, they managed to put down at Izmir without flaps and brakes. They were soon joined by Lt James's crew. Seven other 389th BG Liberators also landed in Turkey, and Cyprus. The seventeen survivors in the 389th formation headed for home in all directions. In the 44th formation Bill Cameron looked out across the Mediterranean for fellow survivors: 'Where was everybody? I had taken a position on *Suzy-Q*'s right wing and Reg Carpenter was trailing somewhat behind us.' Dabney adds: 'Up ahead Brandon was

Bill Dabney, Bill Cameron's co-pilot, aboard *Buzzin' Bear* on the Ploesti mission (Bill Cameron).

check our estimated time of arrival at base and he answered in his usual, matter-of-fact RAF manner (before coming to us he had been with the RAF, and was a veteran of the block-busting shows on Essen, Cologne and Berlin): 'If the petrol holds out Skipper our ETA is 2130.' This shook us pretty badly, since it would mean a total elapsed flying time of fourteen hours – right at the limit of our gas capacity – but we prayed some more and throttled back to conserve fuel.

'Brandon was our only company now. Henderson and Hill had dropped back to save their spluttering engines. Suddenly, a battered wreck that we recognised as the ship of Reg Carpenter crossed between us and fired a red 'Very' cartridge. 'He's in trouble', called Jim. That was a useless remark. We could see the hundreds of holes that dotted the rear of Carpenter's ship. 'P for Peter – R

The funeral of Capt. Robert C. Mooney at Izmir, Turkey on 2 August 1943. Personnel, left to right: Lt Harold L. James, pilot; S/Sgt John P. Morris, James's waist gunner; next, second row, Lt Rocky Triantafellu, Mooney's bombardier; unknown; next, second row, Lt James F. Gerrits, Mooney's co-pilot; S/Sgt Elvin H. Henderson, Mooney's tail gunner; S/Sgt Max C. Cavey, James's top turret gunner (behind); T/Sgt Harold M. Thompson, James's engineer; S Sgt Grover A. Edminston, James' bombardier (behind); S/Sgt Hugh R. McLaren, James's waist gunner/assistant radio operator; T/Sgt Earl L. Zimmerman (behind McLaren), James's radio operator; S/Sgt Robert L. Hamilton, James's tail gunner; Lt William R. Gilliat, James's navigator; unknown; Lt Robert W. Schwellinger, James's co-pilot (McLaren).

beginning to climb, so we eased up behind him and started the long haul back over the hills and across to the sea. The minutes crawled by and we prayed that the *Bear* would survive the climb and that our gas would hold out for a few more hours. We were really sweating it out by now. Bill called Tom to

B-24D Liberator *Suzy Q*, 44th Bomb Group lead ship on the Ploesti raid, flown by Major Bill Brandon and Col Leon Johnson, undergoing repairs in the North African desert (Cameron).

for Robert'', Reg called on the radio. 'Can you slow down a little. I'm having trouble.' We were almost stalling out as it was but Bill eased her back until we mushed along at 145 hoping Reg could hold out a few minutes longer. Then we saw the most welcome sight of my life – the grey shores of Africa under the darkening sky. We were home! The crew screamed and raved. We'd made it in one piece and ahead was safety and peace and quiet.'

Welcome home party for 44th Bomb Group survivors shot down on the Ploesti mission congregates on the lawn of the Paterson farm, Shipdham, after their return to Norfolk in 1944 (Elmer Reinhart via John Page).

Cameron continues: 'I could see wounds in *Suzy-Q*'s tail and wingtip but otherwise it was in good shape and so were we. However, Reg Carpenter and his crew failed to make it that night. They had slowly dropped back and below us. Eventually, they had to ditch. After twenty-nine very difficult and painful hours in a dinghy, they were picked up by an RAF launch in a rare night-rescue operation. It was dark now and at last we could see scattered points of light below, as trucks and jeeps and bombers manoeuvred into their parking positions on our home field. Col Johnson and Brandon wasted little time; we could see their wing lights peeling off into the traffic pattern. We were right behind, as we had been for the past thirteen hours and twenty minutes. As we pulled into our parking area and cut those four great engines, we were extravagantly greeted by Howard Moore and a number of our flight line people, Sgts Gilbert Hester, Ed Hanley, Marion Bagley and others. And so it ended up that only two of us were back out of the formation of sixteen assigned to attack 'White V'. It had been a long day.'

Dabney adds: 'When we landed, 'Pappy' Moore, our squadron commander who had already completed his tour of duty, gave Bill and me one hell of a bear-hug. 'I didn't think you'd make it', he cried and we all slapped each other again and roared happily off to interrogation in his jeep. There were some amazing stories that night and for many days to come! George Martin, who drove straight through a five-strand high-tension line but lived to tell the tale. Then there was the one about 'Killer'

Kane's boys who flew so low they bumped the ship on the ground and dented the nose. There were many more just as thrilling, just as frightening. Whatever praise, whatever glory is due goes to our pals who died. They took the brunt of the attack. They absorbed the hell we survived.'

Next morning results of the mission were pieced together. Of the 177 B-24s which had set out, 167 had actually attacked their targets and had dropped 311 tons of bombs on the refineries. Some fifty-four B-24Ds were lost over the targets and three more crashed at sea. Seven B-24D crews were interned in Turkey, while nineteen had landed in Cyprus (including Kane's *Hail Columbia*), Sicily or Malta. Of the ninety-two that returned to North Africa, fifty-five had varying degrees of battle damage. All five groups received Presidential Unit Citations, while five Medals of Honor (three posthumously) were awarded and every crew member received the DFC. The Liberators had only destroyed forty-two per cent of the plants' refining capacity and forty per cent of its cracking capacity. The refineries were repaired and operating at pre-mission capacity within a month. Repeated attempts were made to destroy the plants and the USAAF would lose in excess of 200 more bombers and over 2,000 further aircrew in raids on the Ploesti refineries before the end of the war in Europe.

CHAPTER 5

Double Strike

On 24 July 1943 the 8th Air Force mounted the long-awaited succession of attacks which would become known as 'Blitz Week'. Crews flew four missions in five days until, on 31 July, groups were told to stand down after a week of exhausting raids. Crews had flown themselves almost to a standstill and in a week of sustained combat operations VIII Bomber Command had lost about a hundred aircraft and ninety combat crews. This

General Ira C. Eaker, commanding general, 8th Air Force Bomber Command (USAF).

reduced its combat strength to under 200 heavies ready for combat. However, losses were made good and Major-General Ira C. Eaker, Chief of VIII Bomber Command, kept up the pressure on the enemy as he sent his bombers daily to targets in the Reich.

On 12 August 330 bombers hit targets in the Ruhr. Three days later VIII Bomber Command participated in the 'Starkey' deception plan which was created to make the enemy believe that an invasion of the French coast was imminent to help relieve some of the pressure on Russia and halt troop movements to Italy. Strikes against enemy airfields in France and the Low Countries continued on 16 August, then early that evening base operations staff throughout eastern England waited for their orders for the morrow; the anniversary mission of the 8th Air Force. Throughout the east of England staff waited in anticipation, none more so than at Grafton Underwood where Budd Peaslee's 384th had a special interest. Speculation had been rife on the base ever since late in July when the group had received an order from higher headquarters. Col Peaslee explains: 'It said 'Select one of the best of your lead crews, stand them down. Send them to headquarters, VIII Bomber Command for special briefing, thereafter they will not leave the base nor communicate with other crews. They will fly practice flights daily and practise high-altitude bombing on the Irish Sea bombing range whenever possible.''

Crews knew something special would be in the offing for the anniversary mission, but what? They had laid bets that the subterfuge was part of the preparations for the first ever American air raid on Berlin; for others, an attack on Hitler's mountain retreat at Berchtesgaden was thought likely. In fact Eaker and his planners had conceived a most ambitious and daring plan, to attack, simultaneously, aircraft plants at Schweinfurt and Regensburg. The selection of Regensburg and Schweinfurt as the targets for the anniversary mission of VIII Bomber Command came at a time when the Luftwaffe's operational fighter strength on the Western Front was showing a significant increase. Regensburg was the second largest aircraft plant of its kind in Europe – the largest was at Wiener Neustadt near Vienna – and it was estimated that the total destruction of the plant would entail a nine-month delay in production. Immediate results would be felt in operational strength, it was hoped, between one and a half to two months. Crews were told that production at Regensburg was estimated at 200 Me-109s a month, or approximately twenty-five to thirty per cent of Germany's single-engine aircraft production.

Few doubted the importance of mounting a mission against the plants, but hitherto, the campaign against the German aircraft industry had been waged within reasonable striking distance from the British mainland. The original plan to bomb all three plants on one day, 7 August, had been disrupted by bad weather, so the plan had been modified to bomb each target when the opportunity arose. On 13 August Wiener Neustadt was bombed by B-24s of VIII Bomber Command and on 14 August by B-24s of the 9th Air Force, both forces flying from North Africa. Not enough 1st Wing Fortresses were equipped with 'Tokyo tanks' and could not make the 725-mile trip, but now preparations were almost complete for the daring double strike. Such was the importance that the 'top brass' would lead the heavies deep into southern Germany. Even the loss of an eye in a bombing raid while he watched the Battle of Britain as an American observer was not enough to deter Brigadier-General Robert Williams, commander of the 1st Wing, and he would lead his force to Schweinfurt while Col Curtis E. LeMay led the 4th Wing to Regensburg.

To minimise attacks from enemy fighters it was decided that LeMay's B-17s would fly on to North Africa after the target. The 1st Wing, meanwhile, would fly a parallel course to Schweinfurt to confuse further the enemy defences and return to England after the raid. Despite this crews remained sceptical, as Howard E. Hernan, a gunner in the 303rd Bomb Group at Molesworth, explains: 'We had been briefed for this one three weeks before, so naturally the Germans knew we were coming. Since the previous mission had been scrubbed we were called in every day and told not to mention the target area. Intelligence seemed to think there were

Capt. Claude W. Campbell of McComb, Mississippi, pilot of *The Eightball* in the 303rd Bomb Group at Molesworth (Campbell).

a lot of spies in Great Britain.' Crews realised the risks better than anyone and were made aware how important the targets were. Claude Campbell, Hernan's pilot on the mission, wrote: 'Our target was the ball-bearing factory, or rather I should say the elimination of Schweinfurt and all its inhabitants. It is predicted that this is the strike that will break Hitler's back. We were told that within three months from this date Hitler will feel the blow so acutely that he will throw in the towel.' Despite the planning Eaker and his subordinates were under no illusions. They knew the B-17 crews would have a running fight on their hands but hoped that the P-47 fighter escort would keep losses down.

At Thorpe Abbotts, home of the 100th Bomb Group, part of the 4th Wing strike force, officers and men sat through the briefing. Among them was Lt Colonel Beirne Lay Jr., who as a captain had been one of Eaker's original 'seven' senior officers who had flown to England with the general in 1942. Lay had spent the early part of the war 'flying a desk' but had clamoured for action and had now got his wish. Lay would fly with the 100th as a special observer. His account, 'I Saw Regensburg Destroyed', first published in the *Saturday Evening Post,* is one of the classical passages in the history of air warfare. 'In the briefing room, the intelligence officer pulled a cloth screen away from a huge wall map. Each of the 240 sleepy-eyed combat crew members in the crowded room leaned forward. There were low whistles. I felt a sting of anticipation as I stared at the red string on the map that stretched from our base in England to a pinpoint deep in southern Germany, then south across the Alps, through the Brenner Pass to the coast of Italy, then past Corsica and Sardinia and south over the Mediterranean to a desert airdrome in North Africa. You could have heard an oxygen mask drop. 'Your primary', said the intelligence officer, 'is Regensburg. Your aiming point is the centre of the Messerschmitt 109 aircraft and assembly shops. This is the most vital target we've ever gone after. If you destroy it, you destroy thirty per cent of the Luftwaffe's single-engine fighter production. You fellows know what that means to you personally.' There were a few hollow laughs.

'After the briefing, I climbed aboard a jeep bound for the operations office to check up on my Fortress assignment. The stars were dimly visible through the chilly mist that covered our blacked-out bomber station, but the weather forecast for a deep penetration over the Continent was good. In the office I looked at the crew sheet, where the line-up of the lead, low and high squadrons of the group is plotted for each mission. I was listed for a co-pilot's seat. While I stood there, and on the chance suggestion of one of the squadron commanders who was looking over the list, the operations officer erased my name and shifted me to the high squadron as co-pilot in the crew of a steady Irishman named Lieutenant Murphy, with whom I had flown before. Neither of us knew it but that operations officer saved my life right there with a piece of rubber on the end of a pencil.

'At 0530 hours, fifteen minutes before taxi time, a jeep drove around the five-mile perimeter track in the semi-darkness, pausing at each dispersal point long enough to notify the waiting crews that poor local visibility would postpone the take-off for an hour and a half. I was sitting with Murphy and the rest of our crew near the *Piccadilly Lily.* She looked

sinister and complacent, squatting on her fat tyres with scarcely a hole in her skin to show for the twelve raids behind her. The postponement tightened, rather than relaxed, the tension. Once more I checked over my life vest, oxygen mask and parachute, not perfunctorily, but the way you check something you're going to have to use. I made sure my escape kit was pinned securely in the knee pocket of my flying suit, where it couldn't fall out in a scramble to abandon ship. I slid a hunting knife between my shoe and my flying boot as I looked again through my extra equipment for this mission; water canteen, mess kit, blankets and English pounds for use in the Algerian desert, where we would sleep on the ground and might be on our own from a forced landing. Murphy restlessly gave the *Piccadilly Lily* another once over, inspecting ammunition belts, bomb bay, tyres and oxygen pressure at each crew station. Especially the oxygen. It's human fuel, as important as gasoline up where we operate. Gunners field-stripped their .50 calibres again and oiled the bolts. Our top turret gunner lay in the grass with his head on his parachute, feigning sleep, sweating out this thirteenth start.

'We shared a common knowledge which grimly enhanced the normal excitement before a mission. Of approximately 150 Fortresses who were hitting Regensburg, our group was the last and lowest, at a base altitude of 17,000 feet. That's well within the range of accuracy for heavy flak. Our course would take us over plenty of it. It was a cinch also that our group would be the softest touch for the enemy fighters, being last man through the gauntlet. Furthermore, the *Piccadilly Lily* was leading the last three ships of the high squadron – the tip of the tail end of the whole shebang. We didn't relish it much. Who wants a Purple Heart?

'The minute hand of my wristwatch dragged. I caught myself thinking about the day, exactly one year ago, on 17 August 1942, when I watched a pitifully small force of twelve B-17s take-off on the first raid of the 8th Air Force to make a shallow penetration mission against Rouen. On that day it was our maximum effort. Today, on our first anniversary, we were putting thirty times that number of heavies in the air – half the force on Regensburg and half the force on Schweinfurt, both situated inside the interior of the German Reich. For a year and a half, as a staff officer, I had watched the 8th Air Force grow under Major-General Ira C. Eaker. That's a long time to watch from behind a desk. Only ten days ago I had asked for and received orders to combat duty. Those ten days had been full of the swift action of participating in four combat missions and checking out for the first time as a four-engine pilot. Now I knew that it was easier to be shot at than to be telephoned at. Staff officers at an Air Force headquarters are the unsung heroes of this war. And yet I found myself reminiscing just a little affectionately about that desk, wondering if there wasn't a touch of suicide in store for our group. One thing was sure; headquarters had dreamed up the biggest air operation to date to celebrate its birthday in the biggest league of aerial warfare.'

The 147 bombers of the 4th Wing could not be delayed for more than ninety minutes if they were to reach North Africa in daylight and for a time it looked as if their participation was at an end. Thankfully, the mist diminished slightly and the roar of over 500 Wright-Cyclones was heard throughout East Anglia as the Fortresses thundered into the overcast. That they got off at all was due entirely to the fact that Curtis LeMay's groups had been practising take-offs on instruments for the past few weeks. Col LeMay took off from Snetterton Heath at the head of the 96th Bomb Group formation which would lead the mission. Behind came the 388th and 390th Bomb Groups in the low and high positions, followed by the 94th and 385th making up the Second Combat Wing. Bringing up the rear of the formation were the 95th and 100th Bomb Groups, flying lead and low respectively, each carrying 250lb incendiaries to stoke up the fires created by the leading groups. Beirne Lay continues: 'At 0730 hours we broke out of the cloud tops into the glare of the rising sun. Beneath our B-17 lay English fields, still blanketed in the thick mist from which we had just emerged. We continued to climb slowly, our broad wings shouldering a heavy load of incendiary bombs in the belly and a burden of fuel in the main and wing-tip 'Tokyo tanks' that would keep the Fortress afloat in the thin upper altitudes for eleven hours.

'From my co-pilot's seat on the right-hand-side, I watched the white surface of the overcast, where B-17s in clusters of six to the squadron were puncturing the cloud deck all about us, rising clear of the mist with their glass noses slanted upwards for the long climb to base altitude. We tacked on to one of these clutches of six. Now the sky over England was heavy with the weight of thousands of tons of bombs, fuel and men being lifted four miles straight up on a giant aerial hoist to the western terminus of a 20,000 foot, elevated highway that led east to Regensburg. At intervals I saw the arc of a spluttering red, green or yellow flare being fired from the cabin roof of a group leader's airplane to identify the lead squadron to the high and low squadrons of each group. Assembly takes longer when you come up through an overcast. For nearly an hour, still over southern England, we climbed, nursing the straining Cyclone engines in a 300-foot-per-minute ascent, forming three squadrons gradually into compact group stagger formations, low squadron down to the left and high squadron up to the right of the lead squadron, groups assembling into looser combat wings of two to three groups each along the combat wing assembly line, homing over predetermined points with radio compass and finally cruising along the air division assembly line to allow the combat wings to fall into place in trail behind Col Curtis E. LeMay in the lead group of the air division.

'Formed at last, each flanking group in position 1,000 feet above or below its lead group, our fifteen-mile parade moved east towards Lowestoft – point of departure from the friendly coast – unwieldy but dangerous to fool with. From my perch in the high squadron in the last element of the whole procession, the air division looked like huge, anvil-shaped swarms of locusts – not on dress parade like the bombers of the Luftwaffe that died like flies over Britain in 1940 but deployed to uncover every gun and permit manoeuvrability. Our formation was basically that worked out for the Air Corps by Brigadier-General Hugh Knerr twenty years ago with 85 mph bombers, plus refinements devised by Col LeMay from experience in the European theatre of war. The English Channel and the North Sea glittered bright in the clear visibility as we left the bulge of East Anglia behind us. Up ahead we knew that we were already registering on the German RDF screen and that the sector controllers of the Luftwaffe's fighter belt in western Europe were busy alerting their Staffeln of Focke Wulfs and Messerschmitts. I stole a last look back at cloud-covered England, where I could see a dozen spare B-17s, who had accompanied us to fill in for any abortives from mechanical failure in the hard climb, gliding disappointedly home to base.'

Betty Boop, The Pistol Packin' Mama of the 390th Bomb Group pictured in August 1943 (Gus Mencow).

Four P-47 groups were scheduled to escort the Regensburg force but only one group rendezvoused with the bombers as scheduled. The overburdened Thunderbolts could not possibly hope to protect all seven groups in the 4th Wing. The long, straggling formation stretched for fifteen miles and presented the fighter pilots with an awesome responsibility. Fortresses in the rear of the formation were left without protection at all and the bomber crews' worst fears were about to be realised. Beirne Lay braced himself for the battle that lay ahead. 'I fastened my oxygen mask a little tighter and looked at the little ball in a glass tube on the instrument panel that indicates proper oxygen flow. It was moving up and down, like a visual heartbeat, as I breathed, registering normal.

'Already the gunners were searching. Occasionally the ship shivered as guns were tested in short bursts. I could see puffs of blue smoke from the group close ahead and 1,000 feet above us, as each gunner satisfied himself that he had lead poisoning at his trigger tips. The coast of Holland appeared in sharp black outline. I drew a deep breath of oxygen. A few miles in front of us were German boys in single-seaters who were probably going to react to us in the same way our boys would react, emotionally speaking, if German bombers were heading for the Pratt & Whitney engine factory at Hartford or the Liberator plant at Willow Run. In the making was a death struggle between the unstoppable object and the immovable defence, every possible defence at the disposal of the Reich, for this was a deadly penetration to a hitherto inaccessible and critically important arsenal of the 'Vaterland'.

'At 1008 hours we crossed the coast of Holland, south of the Hague, with our group of Fortresses tucked in tightly and within handy supporting distance of the group above us, at 18,000 feet. But our long, loose-linked column looked too long and the gaps between the combat wings too wide. As I squinted into the sun, gauging the distance to the barely visible specks of the lead group, I had a recurrence of that sinking feeling before the take-off – the lonesome foreboding that might come to the last man about to run a gauntlet line with spiked clubs. The premonition was well-founded.'

The Luftwaffe began its attacks as the formation entered enemy territory. Lt Richard H. Perry, co-pilot aboard *Betty Boop, the Pistol Packin' Mama*, flown by Lt Jim Geary in the 390th Bomb Group, recalls: 'Just after we reached the Dutch coast we were attacked by several FW 190s. A .30 mm calibre armour piercing shell entered the waist gun area and went right through the steel helmet of Sgt Leonard A. Baumgartner and struck him in the head. The shell also shattered a rudder control cable which made our landing in North Africa very difficult later. I went to the back of the airplane to administer to him. Baumgartner took his last breath in my arms.'

At 1017 hours near Woensdrecht, Lt-Col Lay saw 'the first flak blossom out in our vicinity, light and accurate. A few minutes later, at approximately 1025 hours, a gunner called 'Fighters at two o'clock low.' I saw them, climbing above the horizon ahead of us to the right – a pair of them. For a moment I hoped they were P-47 Thunderbolts from the fighter escort that was supposed to be in our vicinity but I didn't hope long. The two FW 190s turned and whizzed through the formation ahead of us in a frontal attack, nicking two B-17s in the wings and breaking away in half rolls right over our group. By craning my neck and back, I glimpsed one of them through the roof glass in the cabin, flashing past at a 600 mile-an-hour rate of closure, his yellow nose smoking and small pieces flying off near the wing root. The guns of our group were in action. The pungent smell of burnt cordite filled the cockpit and the B-17 trembled to the recoil of nose and ball turret guns. Smoke immediately trailed from the hit B-17s but they held their stations. Here was early fighter reaction. The members of the crew sensed trouble. There was something desperate about the way those two fighters came in fast right out of their climb,

without any preliminaries. Apparently, our own fighters were busy somewhere farther up the procession. The interphone was active for a few seconds with brief admonitions: 'Lead 'em more . . .'; 'Short bursts'; 'Don't throw rounds away'; 'Bombardier to left waist gunner, don't yell. Talk slow.'

'Three minutes later the gunners reported fighters climbing up from all around the clock, singly and in pairs, both FW 190s and Me 109Gs. The fighters I could see on my side looked too many for sound health. No friendly Thunderbolts were visible. From now on we were in mortal danger. My mouth dried up and my buttocks pulled together. A co-ordinated attack began, with the head-on fighters coming in from slightly above, the nine and three o'clock attackers approaching from about level and the rear attackers from slightly below. The guns from every B-17 in the group ahead were firing simultaneously, lashing the sky with ropes of orange tracers to match the chain-puff bursts squirting from the 20mm cannon muzzles in the wings of the Jerry single-seaters. I noted with alarm that a lot of our fire was falling astern of the target – particularly from our hand-held nose and waist guns. Nevertheless, both sides got hurt in this clash, with the entire second element of three B-17s from our low squadron and one B-17 from the 95th falling out of formation on fire, with crews baling out and several fighters heading for the deck in flames or with their pilots lingering behind under the dirty yellow canopies that distinguished some of their parachutes from ours. Major John Kidd, our twenty-four-year-old group leader, flying only his third combat mission, pulled us up even closer to the 95th Group for mutual support.

'As we swung slightly outside with our squadron, in mild evasive action, I got a good look at that gap in the low squadron where three B-17s had been. Suddenly, I bit my lip hard. The lead ship [*Alice From Dallas*], of that element had pulled out on fire and exploded before anyone baled out. It was the ship to which I had originally been assigned.' *Alice From Dallas*, piloted by Roy Claytor, who was leading the second element of the low squadron, was shot down by flak bursts at 1020 hours while over eastern Belgium. The B-17 erupted in flames and eight men managed to bale out safely. Edward Musante's – the right waist gunner – parachute fouled the horizontal stabiliser and he was killed when the aircraft exploded. The ball turret gunner

B-17F *Picklepuss*, 42-30063, piloted by Lt Robert Knox (front row, second left) in the lead squadron, was hit by fighters and knocked out of formation soon after crossing the River Moselle. A second attack inflicted more damage, and just south of Aachen the right wing was shot off in an attack by Me 110s. Three men, including Ernest Warsaw (front row, second from right), baled out safely and a fourth was blown out in the explosion before the bomber hit the ground (Thorpe Abbotts Memorial Museum).

---

was also killed after failing to get clear in time. For most of the crew it was only their tenth mission. Both Claytor's wingmen, Thomas Hummel and Ronald Braley's *Tweedle O' Twill* were shot down by a combination of flak and fighters. A B-17 in the 95th Bomb Group was also shot down. In addition, *Picklepuss*, piloted by Lt Robert Knox in the lead squadron, was hit by fighters and knocked out of formation soon after crossing the River Moselle. A second attack inflicted more damage and *Picklepuss* became separated from the rest of the group. The crew were faced with a decision: should they try to make Switzerland or fly back to England? Ernest Warsaw, the navigator, persuaded them that they

should try to get back to Thorpe Abbotts, so Knox headed for the German border. Just south of Aachen three Bf 110s from St Trond who had been detailed to pick off any returning cripples, attacked the ailing bomber. Two of the fighters, which attacked from the rear, were shot down but the third which attacked from head-on succeeded in shooting the B-17's right wing off with cannon fire. Warsaw, Walter Paulsen, the radio operator, and Clover Barney, the engineer, managed to bale out before the rapid descent pinned the crew to the inside of the spiralling bomber. A fourth man, Edwin Tobin, the bombardier, was saved when he was blown out in the explosion before the bomber hit the ground. Tobin knew nothing of his descent and only came round in a German hospital.

Lay continues: 'I glanced over at Murphy. It was cold in the cockpit but sweat was running from his forehead and over his oxygen mask from the exertion of holding his element in tight formation and the strain of the warnings that hummed over the interphone and what he could see out of the corners of his eyes. He caught my glance and turned the controls over to me for a while. It was an enormous relief to concentrate on flying instead of sitting there watching fighters aiming between your eyes. Somehow the attacks from the rear, although I could see them through my ears via the interphone, didn't bother me. I guess it was because there was a slab of armour plate behind my back and I couldn't watch them anyway. I knew that we were in a lively fight. Every alarm bell in my brain and heart was ringing a high-pitched warning. But my nerves were steady and my brain working. The fear was unpleasant but it was bearable. I knew that I was going to die and so were a lot of others. What I didn't know was that the real fight, the 'Anschluss' of Luftwaffe 20mm cannon shells, hadn't really begun. The largest and most savage fighter resistance of any war in history was rising to stop us at any cost and our group was the most vulnerable target.

'We absorbed the first wave of a hailstorm of individual fighter attacks that were to engulf us clear to the target in such a blizzard of bullets and shells that a chronological account is difficult. It was 1041 hours, over Eupen, that I looked out of the windows after a minute's lull and saw two whole squadrons, twelve Me 109s and eleven FW190s, climbing parallel to us as though they were on a steep escalator. The first squadron had reached our level and was pulling ahead to turn into us. The second was not far behind. Several thousand feet below us were many more fighters, their noses cocked up in maximum climb. Over the interphone came reports of an equal number of enemy aircraft deploying on the other side of the formation. For the first time I noticed an Me 110 sitting out of range on our level out to the right. He was to stay with us all the way to the target, apparently radioing our position and weak spots to fresh 'Staffeln' waiting farther down the road. At the sight of all these fighters, I had the distinct feeling of being trapped – that the Hun had been tipped off or at least had guessed our destination and was set for us. We were already through the German fighter belt. Obviously, they had moved a lot of squadrons back in a fluid defence in depth and they must have been saving up some outfits for the inner defence that we didn't know about. The life expectancy of our group seemed definitely limited, since it had already appeared that the fighters, instead of wasting fuel trying to overhaul the preceding groups, were glad to take a cut at us.

'Swinging their yellow noses around in a wide U-turn, the twelve-ship squadron of Me 109s came in from twelve to two o'clock in pairs. The main event was on. I fought an impulse to close my eyes and overcame it. A shining silver rectangle of metal sailed past over our right wing. I recognised it as a main exit door. Seconds later, a black lump came hurtling through the formation, barely missing several propellers. It was a man, clasping his knees to his head, revolving like a diver in a triple somersault, shooting by us so close that I saw a piece of paper blow out of his leather jacket. He was evidently making a delayed jump, for I didn't see his parachute open.

'A B-17 [*The WAAC Hunter*, piloted by Henry Shotland, whose crew were on their first mission] turned gradually out of the formation to the right, maintaining altitude. In a split-second it completely vanished in a brilliant explosion, from which the only remains were four balls of fire, the fuel tanks, which were quickly consumed as they fell earthwards. [Nine of the crew managed to bale out before the B-17 exploded and were made PoW.]

'I saw red-, yellow- and aluminium-coloured fighters. Their tactics were running fairly true to form, with frontal attacks hitting the low squadron and rear attackers going for the lead and high squadrons. Some of the Jerries shot at us with rockets and an attempt at air-to-air bombing was made with little black time-fuse sticks, dropped from above, which exploded in small grey puffs off to one side of the formation. Several of the FWs did some nice deflection shooting on side attacks from 500 yards at the high group, then raked the low group on the breakaway at closer range with their noses cocked in a side slip, to keep the formation in their sights longer in the turn. External tanks were visible under the bellies or wings of at least two squadrons, shedding uncomfortable light on the mystery of their ability to tail us so far from their bases. The manner of the assaults indicated the pilots knew where we were going and were inspired with a fanatical determination to stop us before we got there. Many pressed attacks home to 250 yards or less, or bolted right through the formation wide out, firing long, twenty-second bursts, often presenting point-blank targets on the breakaway. Some committed the fatal error of pulling up instead of going down and out. More experienced pilots came in on frontal attacks with a noticeably slower rate of closure, apparently throttled back, obtaining greater accuracy. But no tactics could halt the close-knit juggernauts of our Fortresses, or save the single-seaters from paying a terrible price.

'Our airplane was endangered by various debris. Emergency hatches, exit doors, prematurely opened parachutes, bodies and assorted fragments of B-17s and Hun fighters breezed past us in the slip stream. I watched two fighters explode not far beneath and disappear in sheets of orange flame; B-17s dropping out in every stage of distress, from engines on fire to controls shot away; friendly and enemy parachutes floating down and, on the green carpet far below us, funeral pyres of smoke from fallen fighters marking our trail.

'On we flew through the cluttered wake of a desperate air battle, where disintegrating aircraft were commonplace and the white dots of sixty parachutes in the air at one time were hardly worth a second look. The spectacle registering on my eyes became so fantastic that my brain turned numb to the actuality of death and destruction all around us. Had it not been for the squeezing in my stomach, which was trying to purge itself, I might easily have been watching an animated cartoon in a movie theatre.

'The minutes dragged on into an hour, and still the fighters came. Our gunners called coolly and briefly to one another, dividing up their targets, fighting for their lives and ours with every round of ammunition. The tail gunner called that he was out of ammunition. We sent another belt back to him. Here was a new hazard. We might run out of .50 calibre slugs before we reached the target. I looked to both sides of us. Our two wingmen were gone. So was the element in front of us – all three ships. We moved up into position behind the lead element of the high squadron. I looked out again on my side and saw a cripple, with one prop feathered, struggle up behind our right wing with his bad engine funnelling smoke into the slipstream. He dropped back. Now our tail gunner had a clear view. There were no more B-17s behind us. We were the last men.

'I took the controls for a while. The first thing I saw when Murphy resumed flying was a B-17 [*Escape Kit*, piloted by Lt. Curtis Biddick] turning slowly out to the right, its cockpit a mass of flames. Richard Snyder, the co-pilot, crawled out of his window, held on with one hand, reached back for his parachute, buckled it on, let go and was whisked

back into the horizontal stabiliser of the tail. I believe the impact killed him. His parachute didn't open.' Sgt Lawrence Godbey, the engineer, died from wounds sustained by a 20mm shell which hit him in the shoulder and hip. Dan Mackay, the bombardier, and John Dennis, the navigator, both badly burned, survived the bale-out and were treated in Frankfurt hospital for several weeks before being sent to a PoW camp. Biddick and Robert DeKay, the radio operator, were also killed. Snyder's remains were discovered months later hanging from his parachute in a tree. Lay continues: 'I looked forward and almost ducked as I watched the tail gunner of a B-17 ahead of us take a bead right on our windshield and cut loose with a stream of tracers that missed us by a few feet as he fired on a fighter attacking us from six o'clock low. I almost ducked again when our own top turret gunner's twin muzzles pounded away a foot above my head in the full forward position, giving a realistic imitation of cannon shells exploding in the cockpit, while I gave a better imitation of a man jumping six inches out of his seat.

'Still no let up. The fighters queued up like a bread line and let us have it. Each second of time had a cannon shell in it. The strain of being a clay duck in the wrong end of that aerial shooting gallery became almost intolerable. Our *Piccadilly Lily* shook steadily with the fire of its .50s and the air inside was wispy with smoke. I checked the engine instruments for the thousandth time. Normal. No injured crew members yet. Maybe we'd get to that target, even with our reduced firepower. Seven Fortresses from our group had already gone down and many of the rest of us were badly shot up and short-handed because of wounded crew members. Almost disinterestedly I observed a B-17 pull out from the preceding 95th Bomb Group and drop back to a position about 200 feet from our right wing tip. His right 'Tokyo tanks' were on fire, and had been for a half-hour. Now the smoke was thicker. Flames were licking through the blackened skin of the wing. While the pilot held her steady, I saw four crew members drop out the bomb bay and execute delayed jumps. Another baled out from the nose, opened his parachute prematurely and nearly fouled the tail. Another went out of the left waist gun opening, delaying his opening for a safe interval. The tail gunner dropped out of his hatch, apparently pulling the ripcord before he was clear of the ship. His parachute opened instantaneously, barely missing the tail and jerked him so hard that both his shoes came off. He hung limp in the harness whereas the others had shown immediate signs of life, shifting around in their harness. The Fortress then dropped back in a medium spiral and I did not see the pilots leave. I saw the ship though, just before it trailed from view, belly to the sky, its wing a solid sheet of yellow flame.

'Now that we had been under constant attack for more than an hour, it appeared certain that our group was faced with extinction. The sky was still mottled with rising fighters. Target time was thirty-five minutes away. I doubt if a man in the group visualised the possibility of our getting much farther without 100 per cent loss. I know that I had long since mentally accepted the fact of death, and that it was simply a question of the next second or next minute. I learned first-hand that a man can resign himself to the certainty of death without becoming panicky. Our group firepower was reduced to thirty-five per cent and ammunition was running low. Our tail guns had to be replenished from another gun station. Gunners were becoming exhausted and nerve-tortured from the nagging strain – the strain that sends gunners and pilots to the rest homes. There was an awareness on every-body's part that something must have gone wrong. We had been the aiming point for what looked like most of the Luftwaffe. It looked as though we might find the rest of it primed for us at the target.

'At this hopeless point, a young squadron commander [Major Gale Cleven, flying with Capt. Norman Scott in *Phartzac*] down in the low squadron, was living through his finest hour. The 350th squadron had lost its second element of three ships early in the fight, south of Antwerp, yet he had consistently maintained his vulnerable and exposed position in the formation rigidly, in order to keep the guns of his three remaining ships well uncovered to protect the belly of the formation. Now, nearing the target, battle damage was catching up with him fast. A 20mm cannon shell penetrated the right side of his airplane and exploded beneath him, damaging the electrical system and cutting James Parks, the top turret gunner, in the leg. A second 20mm shell entered the radio compartment, killing Norman Smith, the radio operator, who bled to death with his legs severed above the knees. A third 20mm shell entered the left side of the nose, tearing out a section about two feet square, and tore away

Major Gale 'Bucky' Cleven, CO, 350th Bomb Squadron, 100th Bomb Group, who led his squadron to Regensburg. He was shot down on the mission to Bremen on 8 October, captured and made a PoW (Thorpe Abbotts Memorial Museum).

the right-hand nose gun installations, injuring Norris Norman, the bombardier, in the head and shoulder. A fourth 20mm shell penetrated the right wing into the fuselage and shattered the hydraulic system, releasing fluid all over the cockpit. A fifth 20mm shell punctured the cabin roof and severed the rudder cables to one side of the rudder. A sixth 20mm shell exploded in the no.3 engine, destroying all controls to the engine. The engine caught fire and lost its power, but eventually I saw the fire go out. Confronted with structural damage, partial loss of control, fire in the air and serious injuries to personnel, and faced with fresh waves of fighters still rising to the attack, this commander was justified in abandoning ship. His crew, some of them

Corporal Jerome E. Ferroggiaro, tail gunner on the Regensburg mission in *Phartzac*, in the 350th Bomb Squadron, flown by 1/Lt Norman H. Scott, pictured in his normal office window manning two specially modified twin .50 calibre machine-guns. The towns listed are from a time spent fighting in the Spanish Civil War. After Regensburg, Scott was transferred out of the 100th Bomb Group and the gunners were sent to other crews. Ferroggiaro was shot down on 8 October 1943 on the mission to Bremen, captured and taken prisoner. RHEUDELL possibly refers to the Indian waist gunner 'Paddy' Blaizier who, sometime after Regensburg, went AWOL for twelve days in London and was put on the 'Victory Garden' detail at Thorpe Abbots (Thorpe Abbotts Memorial Museum).

comparatively inexperienced youngsters, were preparing to bale out. The co-pilot pleaded repeatedly with him to bale out. His reply at this critical juncture was blunt. His words were heard over the interphone and had a magical effect on the crew. They stuck to their guns. The B-17 kept on.

'Fighter tactics were running fairly true to form. Frontal attacks hit the low and lead squadrons, while rear attackers went for the high. The manner of their attacks showed that some pilots were old-timers, some amateurs, and that all knew pretty definitely where we were going and were inspired with a fanatical determination to stop us before we got there. The old-timers came in on frontal attacks with a noticeably slower rate of closure, apparently throttled back, obtaining greater accuracy than those that bolted through us wide open. They did some nice shooting at ranges of 500 or more yards and in many cases seemed able to time their thrusts to catch the top and ball turret gunners engaged with rear and side attacks. Less experienced pilots were pressing attacks home to 250 yards and less to get hits, offering point-blank targets on the break-away, firing long bursts of twenty seconds and in some cases actually pulling up instead of going down and out. Several Focke Wulf pilots pulled off some first-rate deflection shooting on side attacks against the high group, then raked the low group on the breakaway out of a sideslip, keeping the nose cocked up in the turn to prolong the period the formation was in their sights. I observed what I believe was an attempt at air-to-air bombing, although I didn't see the bombs dropped. A patch of seventy-five to a hundred grey-white bursts, smaller than flak bursts, appeared simultaneously at our level, off to one side.

'Near the Initial Point, at 1150 hours, one hour and a half after the first of at least 200 individual fighter attacks, the pressure eased off, although hostiles were still in the vicinity. A curious sensation came over me. I was still alive. It was possible to think of the target. Of North Africa. Of returning to England. Almost idly, I watched a crippled B-17 pull over to the kerb and drop its wheels and open its bomb bay, jettisoning its bombs. Three Me 109s circled it closely but held their fire while the crew baled out. I remembered now that a little while back I had seen other Hun fighters hold their fire, even when being shot at by a B-17 from which the crew was baling. But I doubt if sportsmanship had anything to do with it. They hoped to get a B-17 down fairly intact. We turned at the IP at 1154 hours with fourteen B-17s left, two of which were badly crippled. They dropped out after bombing and headed for Switzerland. The no.4 engine on one of them [042] was afire but the plane was not out of control. Major William Veal, leader of the high squadron [in *Torchy 2nd*], received a cannon shell in his no.3 engine just before the start of the bombing run but went into the target with the prop feathered.' Despite the fire and an oxygen failure, *Torchy 2nd* successfully bombed the target and the crew extinguished the fire and managed to reach North Africa safely.

In the one and a half hours preceding the bomb run, seventeen Fortresses altogether were shot down. The 385th Bomb Group lost three bombers while others, so badly shot up, would barely make it over the treacherous snow-covered Alps. Aubrey 'Bart' Bartholomew, a young Canadian-born ball turret gunner in *Raunchy Wolf*, was almost blown out of his turret at 19,000 feet after persistent attacks during the bomb run. Bart's turret door blew off as a result of an ill-fitting door hinge and only the toe of his left flying boot hooked under the range pedal of his guns saved him from being sucked out. Oxygen and interphone cables were severed and he lost contact with the rest of the crew. Somehow he managed to pull himself back into his turret and attract the attention of a crewman who cranked him back into the B-17.

The bombing was extremely accurate and might well have had something to do with the presence of Col LeMay, exponent of high-level bombing techniques, in the first wave. The 390th had placed fifty-eight per cent of its bombs within 1,000 feet of the MPI and ninety-four per cent within 2,000 feet. *Rick O'Shay* flown by Capt. Gerald F. Ritcher, circled

Regensburg after the bombing and the crew could see smoke towering up to almost 10,000 feet. It was a sight to cheer all the crews in the surviving 128 ships in the 4th Wing as LeMay led them off the target. The 2nd Combat Wing was forced to swing around in a 360 degree turn and make another bomb run after the target had been obscured by smoke from the leading wing's bombs. Then it was the turn of the last two groups over the target, the 95th and 100th, to add their incendiary clusters to the conflagration.

Beirne Lay wrote: 'And then our weary, battered column, short of twenty-four bombers but still holding the close formation that had brought the remainder through by sheer air discipline and gunnery, turned in to the target. I knew our bombardiers were grim as death while they synchronised their sights on the great Me 109 shops lying below us in a curve of the winding blue Danube, close to the outskirts of Regensburg. Our B-17 gave a slight lift and a red light went out on the instrument panel. Our bombs were away. We turned from the target towards the snow-capped Alps. I looked back and saw a beautiful sight – a rectangular pillar of smoke from the Me 109 plant. Only one burst was over and into the town. Even from this great height I could see that we had smeared the objective. The

Bombs away over Regensburg (via Ian McLachlan).

price? Cheap. 200 airmen.' Six main workshops were hit, five being severely damaged. A hangar was partially destroyed and storerooms and administrative buildings wrecked. Thirty-seven Me 109s at dispersal were at least damaged if not wrecked and all production at the plant came to an abrupt halt. Although unknown at the time, by way of a bonus, the bombing had destroyed the fuselage jigs for a secret jet fighter, the Me 262. Two of the 390th Group's Fortresses had been shot down in the target area and a third, out of fuel, headed for Spain. It crash-landed near Toulon in France and the crew were made prisoners of war. The surviving 128 B-17s, some flying on three engines and many trailing smoke, were attacked by a few fighters on the way to the Alps. LeMay circled his formation over Lake Garda near Verona to give the cripples a chance to rejoin the Wing but two smoking B-17s, one belonging to the 390th and the other, the 100th, *High Life* in the 100th Bomb Group, flown by Lt Donald Oakes, glided down towards the safety of Switzerland, about forty miles distant. Oakes landed wheels-up at Dübendorf, a military airfield near Zürich, to become the first B-17 to land in Switzerland. *Flak Happy* in the 100th Bomb Group piloted by Ronald Hollenbeck, which had been hit in the bomb bay shortly before the target and had jettisoned its bombs, tried to make for Switzerland with two engines out but the crew were forced to bale out over Italy.

Lt Donald Oakes's B-17F-85-BO *High Life*, 42-30080, at Dubendorf after the forced landing on 17 August 1943 (Thorpe Abbotts Memorial Museum).

Among the survivors in the 100th Bomb Group who headed for North Africa was Beirne Lay. 'We approached the Mediterranean in a gradual descent, conserving fuel. Out over the water we flew at low altitude, unmolested by fighters from Sardinia or Corsica, waiting for hours through the long hot afternoon for the first sight of the North African coastline. The prospect of ditching, out of gasoline, and the sight of other B-17s falling into the drink seemed trivial matters after the vicious nightmare of the long trail across southern Germany. We had walked through a high valley of the shadows of death, not expecting to see another sunset, and now I could fear no evil. Eventually, at dusk, with red lights showing on all of the fuel tanks in my ship, the seven B-17s of the group still in formation circled over Bertoux and landed in the dust after eleven hours in the air. Our crew was unscratched. Sole damage to the airplane – a bit of ventilation round the tail from flak and 20mm shells. We slept on the hard ground under the wings of our B-17 but the good earth felt softer than a silk pillow, and, waking occasionally, we stared up at the stars. My radio headset was back in the ship. And yet I could hear the deep chords of great music.'

Red lights were showing on all four fuel tanks in every ship and it was a ragged collection of survivors which landed at intervals up to fifty miles along the North African coast. Among the fourteen survivors in the 390th Bomb Group, which had set out from Framlingham with twenty B-17s, was *Rick O' Shay*, piloted by Capt. Gerald F. Ritcher and Winfred W. Alfred. After the target, *Rick O'Shay* fought a running battle with the fighters and a

Lt Robert Wolf's B-17F *Wolf Pack*, 42-30061, in the 418th Bomb Squadron (nearest) and three other 100th Bomb Group B-17s fly a ragged formation over the Alps after bombing Regensburg. Wolf's aircraft received 20mm cannon fire to the tail fin and a released life-raft hit the tailplane. The life-raft door can be seen opened above the port inner engine cowling. Top aircraft is *Laiden Maiden*, 42-5861, in the 349th Bomb Squadron (lost in action on 30 December 1943) flown by Lt Owen 'Cowboy' Roane (Thorpe Abbotts Memorial Museum).

20mm shell exploded in the tail position, severely wounding the gunner in the chest and arms. Ritcher nursed the ailing bomber over the Alps with his oxygen system shot out and headed for the Mediterranean. The crew were weary from lack of oxygen and from beating off fighter attacks. The Luftwaffe had attacked their B-17 in tens and twenties until they couldn't count them anymore. Apart from a six-minute respite over the target it seemed they had been under attack for the greater part of the eleven-hour flight. Now the calm, blue waters of the Mediterranean were in sight. No pilot in the group was certain he would make Africa and several aircraft commanders knew they would not. Ritcher wrote later: 'One by one they started slipping out of formation and headed down to the water. I saw three splash in before I realised that we'd have to go too. The crew threw everything overboard to lighten the aircraft. Guns, tools, ammunition,

helmets, camera and everything they could tear loose went over the side before we settled down to ditch.' Ritcher watched the waves, looking for a trough to set the B-17 in, when Alfred spotted the African coast straight ahead. Ritcher pulled up the

Closer view of the damage to the tail of Lt Wolf's B-17F *Wolf Pack*, 42-30061 (Thorpe Abbotts Memorial Museum).

Returning 100th Bomb Group crews gather for a press conference following the mission to Regensburg. Robert Wolf is far right, middle row, wearing a service forage cap (Thorpe Abbotts Memorial Museum).

Major John Egan, CO, 318th Bomb Squadron, who as second in command led the squadron to Regensburg on 17 August, points out the shuttle mission route on the map to members of 1/Lt Charles B. Cruickshank's crew (some wearing souvenir pith helmets and fezzes) of *Aw-R-Go*, 42-30725, in the 419th Bomb Squadron. Cruickshank's crew and Egan – flying with Lt John Brady's crew – were shot down on 10 October on the mission to Münster. Egan and Frank D. Murphy (far left, front row) were among those taken prisoner (Thorpe Abbotts Memorial Museum).

nose, prayed a little, and gunned the engines. *Rick O' Shay* made it, landing on a dry lake bottom. The pilots turned to taxi off to the side and the engines quit – out of fuel!

In the 100th Bomb Group *Oh Nausea*, flown by Lt Glen van Noy, was also forced to land on the sea. Van Noy put the B-17 down about ninety miles north of Sicily which crews had been briefed would be in Allied hands by the end of the day. The bomber floated for an hour and half and gave the crew ample time to get into their dinghies. The loss of *Oh Nausea* brought the 100th Bomb Group's total losses to nine; the highest loss in the 4th Wing, which had lost twenty-four bombers in total. Although they did not yet know it, the 4th Wing had encountered so many fighters en route because the 1st Wing had been delayed by thick inland mists for three-and-a-half hours after the 4th Wing had taken off, and this had effectively prevented a two-pronged assault which might have split the opposing fighter force. The delay gave the Luftwaffe time to refuel and re-arm, after dealing with the Regensburg force, and deal now with the Schweinfurt force.

The 91st Bomb Group from Bassingbourn led the 1st Wing to Schweinfurt with Lt-Col Clemens L. Wurzbach, the CO, and Col Cross of Wing head-quarters flying lead in *Oklahoma Oakie*. Brigadier-General Robert B. Williams, the task force commander, also flew in the 91st formation. The 381st Bomb Group from Ridgewell flew low group. Following close on their heels was the 103rd Provisional Combat Wing, led by Col Maurice 'Mo' Preston, CO of the 379th Bomb Group. 'I was positioned towards the front of the column and the 303rd from Molesworth flew the low box. The top box was a composite furnished by the 303rd and the 379th. The 379th provided the top element of six airplanes in this composite box.

'We began to encounter enemy fighters when we were about halfway to the target and had them almost constantly with us from there until we left the target area on the way out. There was every indication that the Germans were throwing at us just about everything they had in their inventory. We saw everything we had ever seen among those identification models we had hanging up back in our briefing room, and some we just couldn't identify. Certainly, there were FW 190s, Me 109s and 110s, Heinkels, Dorniers and at times I thought I saw even a Stuka or two. And the planes apparently came from many different branches of aviation. Probably they had interceptor units, tactical air (ground support) units and even training units. You name it; they were all there. Probably as a result of introducing units that were not combat-seasoned, the tactics employed were most unusual. The fighters queued up as usual out to the right front and up high but then instead of turn-diving down for attack on the lower elements, they turned in more sharply and delivered diving attacks on the topmost elements – woe be it to that 379th element in the composite box. That entire element of six aircraft was left in central Germany that day. This was the only time I ever saw the Germans employ such a technique and it may have been limited to the particular force that attacked my part of their formation. I don't know, but it was certainly unusual. Even so, it was effective, as our losses will attest. Here again I must say that although I had a box-seat for the whole show – riding up front where I was – I saw those bombers go down but I didn't witness the destruction of a single fighter.'

The 303rd Bomb Group flying in the low box also had its problems as Howard Hernan, in *The Old Squaw* piloted by Claude Campbell, recalls: 'On the way over we had two abortives from our squadron, leaving it under-strength. It looked bad. We had a P-47 escort part of the way in and they were to pick us up on the way back. By this time they were using belly tanks and pilots would tell crews over the intercom when the fighters were due to leave. Quite a long while before we reached the target there were a lot of Me 110s. The P-47s were supposed to leave us about ten minutes previously. Out on the right of us flying out about 2,000 yards were six Me 110s, flying in a stacked-up formation with the lead ship low. Occasionally, there would be a German fighter calling out our altitude to the ground for the flak gunners, but I'm sure these were not doing that. All the time I was watching these Me 110s, and then I suddenly saw the sun glint off four wings of planes above us. Right at that moment I couldn't identify them so I kept my eye on them. When they got above these Me 110s they dived down and I could see that they were four P-47s that were supposed to have been gone ten minutes before. Flying a finger-four to the right, they came down at a seventy or eighty degree angle, made one pass, and got all six Me 110s. They were just sitting-ducks. The rear gunner in the last Me 110 evidently spotted the P-47s commencing their dive and baled out!

'Immediately afterwards three enemy fighters came in at us from about one o'clock. A FW 190 was in the lead and right behind him came two P-47s on his tail. The FW 190 was making his turn to attack us and all six turrets were pointed at him. I'm sorry to say we got the FW 190 and the first P-47. The other Thunderbolt peeled off and headed for home. We felt bad about it and I doubt whether the P-47 pilot realised he was so close to the bomber formation. There was little flak from the target, which was battered from the bombs of other B-17s. We loosed our incendiaries into the middle of the town and, as we left, huge fires were burning. The trip out was a long one and fighters were many.'

The coast of England was a welcome sight for the survivors but not all the Fortresses were able to land back at their home bases. Lt David Williams, lead navigator aboard the 91st lead ship, *Oklahoma Oakie*, recalls: 'Our group had lost ten aircraft and we were one of only two aircraft which were able to make it back to Bassingbourn without an intermediate landing. At that, we had part of our left wing shot off from a 20mm frontal attack which resulted in our left wingman being completely shot out of the air. We discovered after landing that we also had an unexploded 20mm in our left main wing tank. A bullet of unknown calibre (I hope it was not a .50) came through the top of the nose, passed through my British right-hand glove, through my left pant leg and British flying boot without so much as breaking the skin, then out through the floor. It paid to be skinny at the time!'

At bases throughout eastern England anxious watchers counted in the returning Fortresses. Eighteen had taken off from Grafton Underwood but the watchers in the control tower had no need to count further than thirteen. At Molesworth things were a little different, as Claude Campbell explains: 'For some unknown reason there were no losses from the 303rd. The lead bombardier was hit in the stomach forty-five seconds from the target and the waist gunner was killed and the other wounded. It was the longest, most impressive, toughest and the

most important raid of the war. We got a bullet hole through our left aileron and one through the fuselage which went under Miller's [the co-pilot] seat and a fragment struck my hand. Following the raid the 8th got the biggest let-down of the war by the RAF. The British night bombers were to follow us and do most of the damage. Our job was merely to start fires so they could saturate the area with blockbusters. But they assumed the target was hit and enough damage done so they failed to follow. It was discovered later that Schweinfurt was not hit as terrifically as supposed. We sacrificed 600 men, sixty planes and many injured men to start those fires.'

Col 'Mo' Preston concludes: 'The first Schweinfurt was a matching of excessive efforts. We, for our part, put up a maximum all-out effort in an attempt to deal the Hun a telling blow and at the same time prove to one and all the decisive nature and the viability of the daylight programme. The Germans, on the other hand, felt themselves pricked at their sensitive heartland with their major industries threatened and the morale of their population in the balance. So they put up everything they had to stop the Yankee thrust and make it so costly it would not be repeated. The result was a mixed bag. Our effort fell far short of expectations but nonetheless achieved some of its purposes. But the losses suffered were certainly unbearable and could not be borne by us on a sustained basis.' VIII Bomber Command lost 36 Fortresses on the Schweinfurt raid

Col (later General) Maurice 'Mo' Preston (left), CO, 379th Bomb Group, who led the 103rd Provisional Combat Wing to Regensburg on 17 August, pictured with his bridge partner Major David Meyer (Preston).

with a further twenty-four being lost on the Regensburg strike, making sixty lost in combat (almost three times as high as the previous highest, on 13 June, when twenty-six bombers were lost). Worst hit were the 381st and 91st Bomb Groups which lost eleven and ten B-17s respectively. Twenty-seven B-17s in the 1st Wing were so badly damaged that they never flew again. Third highest loss of the day went to the 100th Bomb Group in the 4th Wing, which lost nine Fortresses. Sixty Fortresses had to be left in North Africa pending repairs, so in the final analysis, the 8th had actually lost 147 bombers to all causes on 17 August. The almost non-existent maintenance facilities in North Africa ruled out any further shuttle missions, but General LeMay and the 4th Wing earned the following accolade from General Frederick L. Anderson at Wing headquarters, Elveden Hall: 'Congratulations on the completion of an epoch in aerial warfare. I am sure the 4th Bombardment Wing has continued to make history. The Hun now has no place to hide.'

Colonel Curtis E. LeMay takes a salute from Louis Lonsway of the 385th Bomb Group at Deopham Green when group personnel were presented with DFCs for their part in the 17 August mission (via Ian McLachlan).

Young Arab boys salute the 100th Bomb Group at Bone, North Africa after the 17 August shuttle mission (Thorpe Abbotts Tower Museum).

CHAPTER 6
Black Thursday

On 1 October 1943 British Intelligence sources had estimated that despite round-the-clock bombing of aircraft factories and component plants, the Luftwaffe had a first-line strength of some 1,525 single- and twin-engined fighters for the defence of the western approaches to Germany. American sources put the figure at around 1,100 operational fighters. In reality, the Luftwaffe could call upon 1,646 single- and twin-engined fighters for the defence of the Reich; 400 more than before the issue of the 'Pointblank' directive. The Allies' figures confirmed their worst fears. The decision was therefore taken to attack the ball-bearing plant at Schweinfurt for the second time in three months, in the hope that VIII Bomber Command could deliver a single, decisive blow to the German aircraft industry and stem the flow of fighters to Luftwaffe units.

On the afternoon of 13 October, Brigadier-General Orvil Anderson, Commanding General of VIII Bomber Command, and his senior staff officers gathered at High Wycombe for the daily Operations Conference. They were told that good weather was expected for the morrow. At once a warning order was sent out to all three bomb division headquarters with details of a mission, no. 115, to Schweinfurt. The orders were then transmitted over teletype machines to the various Combat Wing headquarters. Anderson hoped to launch 420 Fortresses and Liberators in a three-pronged attack on the city of Schweinfurt. The plan called for the 1st and 3rd Bomb Divisions to cross Holland thirty miles apart while the third task force, composed of sixty Liberators of the 2nd Bomb Division, would fly to the south on a parallel course. The 923-mile trip would last just over seven hours and meant that the B-17s of the 1st Division which were not equipped with 'Tokyo tanks' would have to be fitted with an additional fuel tank in the bomb bay. However, this meant a reduction in the amount of bombs they

could carry. Each division would be escorted by a P-47 group while a third fighter group would provide withdrawal support from sixty miles inland to half way across the Channel. Two squadrons of RAF Spitfire Mk 9s were to provide cover for the stragglers five minutes after the main force had left the withdrawal area, and other RAF squadrons would be on standby for action if required. Despite these precautions, 370 miles of the route would be flown without fighter support. The plans then had been laid, but the success of the mission was in the lap of the gods. It needed fine weather and, above all, the fighters had to be on schedule.

During the early evening of 13 October and the early hours of 14 October, all the necessary information for the raid was teletyped to all Fortress and Liberator groups in eastern England. The 96th Bomb Group would lead the 3rd Division with Col Archie Old, CO, 45th Wing, in the lead ship while the 92nd Bomb Group, at the head of the 40th Combat Wing, would lead the 1st Division with twenty-one Fortresses. Its commander would be Col Budd J. Peaslee, deputy commander to Col Howard 'Slim' Turner of the 40th Combat Wing and formerly CO of the 384th Bomb Group. Budd Peaslee's pilot on the mission would be Capt. James K. McLaughlin of the 92nd Bomb Group. He recalls: 'I shall never forget the many target briefings that Ed O'Grady, my bombardier, Harry Hughes, my navigator, and I went through preparing for this famous raid. We had led our squadron [the 326th] on the first Schweinfurt raid on 17 August and, along with the others, did a pretty good job of missing the target too. We had all been apprehensive of the second raid because we'd been flying missions since we'd arrived in England in August 1942 and we had first-hand experience of how the Luftwaffe would punish us, particularly when we failed to knock out a target for the first time and attempted to go back.'

Capt. David Williams, lead navigator in the 91st Bomb Group at the time of the Schweinfurt mission, 14 October 1943 (David Williams).

Among the first of the 91st Bomb Group personnel to hear the news at Bassingbourn was David Williams, who in September had been promoted to captain and appointed group navigator. Like McLaughlin, Williams had also been on the first Schweinfurt raid. 'I vividly recall the operations order when it came over the teletype in Group Operations during the wee hours of the morning of 14 October, as I had to do the navigational mission planning while the rest of the combat crews were still asleep. Thus we had already overcome the initial shock which we were to see on the faces of the crews somewhat later when the curtains were dramatically pulled back to reveal the scheduled second deep penetration to Schweinfurt.' Col Peaslee recalls: 'From the beginning, mission no. 115 was in doubt. A persistent low overcast had hung over the English bases for three days. Over the Continent the target areas were also blanketed by varying degrees of cloud coverage that had led to the enforced rest period granted the combat crews. The weather had permitted the maintenance crews

to change many battle-damaged engines and patch up thousands of bullet- and flak-damaged bombers that had returned from the furious fights over north Germany and Poland. The night sky of 13 October showed no change, in fact there seemed to be some deterioration, as a damp mist fell silently from the dark windless sky. Nevertheless, those who might fly on the morrow must be prepared and at the bases the bars closed early.'

Crews slept in their beds piled high with blankets, uniforms and anything else they could lay their hands on to keep out the freezing east wind, dreading the knock at the door which told them the mission was on. Col Peaslee continues: 'The footsteps came in the early black hours of 14 October 1943, as inevitably as the approaching day. The footsteps came to hundreds of crewmen over the English countryside, and the doors rattled as they were yanked open and the darkness was ripped by the dazzling brightness of light-bulbs. The voices of the runners were harsh, with a barely discernible note of comparison, as they sung out, 'Crew thirty-seven hit the deck, briefing at 0500.' Black Thursday had begun.'

The same scene was being replayed at all the bases in the east of England. The sky was still dark and windless and a heavy mist clung to the buildings and surrounding countryside as thousands of men cycled or trudged their way to the mess halls for unappetising breakfasts of powdered eggs, toast and hot coffee. Soon they were on their way again to the briefing halls to hear about the part they would play in the forthcoming mission. Col Budd J. Peaslee describes the briefing at Podington: 'The briefing room filled rapidly as 210 crewmen and perhaps twenty-five briefing officers and key specialists, including flight surgeons, chaplains and unit commanders, completed the gathering. The senior officers, including the 92nd commander, Col William Reid of Augusta, Georgia, occupied the more comfortable seats near the stage in the front of the room. Ranged towards the rear on rows of hard chairs and benches were the crews . . . all these were present as the doors were closed and guarded against intrusion and prying eyes. The briefing was opened by a dignified middle-aged major. In civil life he had been a teacher in a small southern community. He had himself learned a thousand things never dreamed of when he volunteered to serve his country. Now he was an intelligence specialist, and a good one. He opened the briefing in a calm and scholarly voice: 'Gentlemen, may I have your attention? This morning we have quite a show.' So saying, he drew back the curtains that had covered a large-scale map of Europe and the British Isles. In the hushed room all leaned forward intently to study the map with its heavy black yarn marking the routes over Britain, the Channel and across the occupied countries to a point deep in Germany. 'It's Schweinfurt again', said the major. For a moment there was dead silence as the major's words struck home with full impact on the minds of the men. Then a buzz of intelligible comment filled the room, punctuated by whistles, curses, moans and just plain vocal explosions. Above all came one remembered phrase that stood out in the tumult of vocal sound: 'Son-of-a-bitch, and this is my twenty-fifth mission!' Eyes turned towards the speaker and there were expressions of sympathy and condolence until a baby-faced pilot spoke: 'What the hell are you crying about? This is my first!''

For the next half-hour the major and his aides spoke on the plan for the mission. Then it was the air commander's turn to say a few words to the crews he was to lead. Col Reid introduced Budd Peaslee to the expectant crews. Peaslee spared no punches. He told them straight out they were in for a fight. Their responsibility was to the group, not to the stragglers, and there was no room for useless heroics. He tried to think of something humorous to dispel the tension which had suddenly gripped the men but he could think of nothing funny about the situation. Finally, he said, 'If our bombing is good and we hit this ball-bearing city well, we are bound to scatter a lot of balls around on the streets of Schweinfurt. Tonight I expect the Germans will all feel like they are walking around on roller skates.' 'It was a weak effort', wrote Peaslee, 'but they all laughed loudly, too loudly, and the tension was reduced.'

The news that Schweinfurt was their target brought mixed reactions from men weary from days of bitter combat and fitful sleep. There were few men on the bases who doubted it was an excursion into Hell despite some officers' platitudes that it was going to be a 'milk-run'. Lt Edwin L. Smith, co-pilot in Lt Douglas L. Murdock's crew, sat through the 305th Bomb Group briefing at Chelveston. 'We had been briefed once before for Schweinfurt but because of the weather the mission was scrubbed. This particular morning when we

saw the tapes stretching that deep into Germany we all had misgivings. The gunners knew we were in for a fight and so they lugged extra ammo' boxes out to our aircraft.' Crews in the 3rd Division had not flown the first Schweinfurt raid and, in the words of Roy G. Davidson, a pilot in the 94th Bomb Group, 'didn't realise how bad Schweinfurt was. We knew we were in for a pretty rough time but we had no idea just how tough it was really going to be. Despite this I really looked forward to the mission because I thought the accomplishment would be great.'

At Thorpe Abbotts the 100th Bomb Group was still licking its wounds after the severe maulings of 8 October, when it lost seven crews, and 10 October, when it had lost twelve out of thirteen crews. Despite these extremely serious losses and an unsuccessful appeal by Col 'Chick' Harding, the Group CO, the 'Bloody Hundredth' was still expected to make some contribution to the tonnage of bombs to be dropped on Schweinfurt, as Lt Bob Hughes, pilot of *Nine Little Yanks and a Jerk*, explains: 'The call came for the Hundredth to mount a maximum effort but there were only eight crews available. Some of the key positions, therefore, had to be taken by personnel from other groups. The eight crews were broken down into flights. Four aircraft would be led by 'Cowboy' Roane, flying with the 390th Bomb Group, with four being led by myself flying with the 95th Bomb Group. [These two groups would fly in the 13th Wing, the last wing in the 3rd Division task force.] The mess hall seemed virtually empty as we had our usual breakfast of dried eggs, spam, coffee, toast and good old orange marmalade with vast amounts of good American butter to go on that wonderful dark English bread.' For many it was to be their last breakfast on English soil. There was little hope for any man holding low rank who wished to take leave that was owing to them either. It was a maximum effort and everyone was needed. At Framlingham, home of the 390th Bomb Group, Lt Richard H. Perry had hoped to receive a short period of leave in London after his crash four days before. 'The squadron CO, Joe Gemmill, felt differently. His view was that the best way to get the 'butterflies out of our stomachs' was to participate in another mission immediately. We did fly the Schweinfurt mission, which was no 'milk-run', and I think in our case his approach worked fine. Later, when I became operations officer, I used this approach on many other crews that had rough missions.'

As H-Hour approached the tension on the bases mounted. The weather in England was very bad but at 0900 hours an American-crewed Mosquito, in the 25th Bomb Group, 35,000 feet over the Continent, radioed back the news to 8th Air Force headquarters that all of central Germany was in the clear. An hour later Liberators and Fortresses began taking off. The weathermen had predicted overcast to only 2,000 feet, but the bombers were still flying around in cloud at heights of 6,000 feet and above forcing the lead aircraft to circle for two hours. Flares were fired in a vain attempt to pull the formations together. Sixty Liberators managed to take-off from their airfields in Norfolk and Suffolk but only twenty-four arrived at the rendezvous point. The remaining twenty-five managed to link up with fifty-three P-47s from the 352nd Fighter Group but such a small force would have been decimated by the Luftwaffe and the flak guns, so both fighters and bombers aborted after circling for half-an-hour. The B-24s and their P-47 escort were redirected on a diversionary sweep over the North Sea as far as the Frisian Islands to aid the Fortress formations.

Col Peaslee, the mission leader, and his pilot, Capt. McLaughlin, sat waiting in the lead Fortress of the 92nd Bomb Group on the runway at Podington. Green flares shot skywards from the control tower and the lead bomber moved to its take-off position. The time was 1012 hours. James McLaughlin released the brakes and throttled out towards the fading runway lights in the distance. Col Peaslee, sitting in the right-hand seat, listened intently as McLaughlin announced over intercom that he was taking-off on instruments. He directed Peaslee to watch the runway and if the B-17 should start to wander to one side or the other he was to overpower him on the rudder control and bring it back to safety on the runway. The lead bomber gathered speed and at 100 mph in the last hundred foot of runway it was airborne. Peaslee released the locks and pulled the 'gear up' lever. They were followed by a further twenty bombers, and crews peered into the overcast for recognition points on the ground. In the dimness of the approaching day there was only a brief glimpse of the dark shadows of the woodland on either side of the runway clear zone, but this was almost instantly blotted out as the bombers entered the overcast.

Peaslee and McLaughlin levelled out at 8,000 feet and they began craning their necks to spot other aircraft. McLaughlin recalls: 'After we were airborne and formed up, the first warning of what the day would be like came when we discovered that some of the groups and wings had not joined up in their proper sequences; the mission thus began in confusion because some group leaders could not find their wings.' The 92nd Bomb Group had cruised to the splasher beacon over Thurleigh and formed as a group, but at the second splasher, where the 40th Combat Wing was to assemble, the 305th Bomb Group failed to rendezvous. Peaslee therefore decided to continue with just the 306th Bomb Group to the third assembly area at Daventry in the Midlands and fly on at 20,000 feet to the English coast. Standing orders dictated that no air commander could send out a two-group combat wing; the risk of total annihilation of such a small defensive force was too great. However, Peaslee did not want to abort while he still had some options open to him.

Meanwhile, the 40th Combat Wing had orbited according to procedure, and at 1220 hours led the 1st Division assembly line over the coast of England, 20,000 feet above Orford Ness. Further south, the 45th Combat Wing, with the 96th Bomb Group in the van, led the 3rd Division over the Naze. Behind the 45th Wing came the 4th Combat Wing consisting of the 94th and 385th Bomb Groups, followed by the 13th Combat Wing made up of the 95th, 100th and 390th Bomb Groups. Fifteen of the 164 aircraft in the 1st Division and eighteen aircraft of the 160 aircraft in the 3rd Division either turned back with mechanical problems or became lost in the cloudy conditions. The long and complicated assembly was also responsible for diminishing the Fortresses' vital fuel reserves, especially those carrying bombs externally to make up for the lack of internal tonnage taken up by the bomb bay fuel tanks. Many of these crews were forced to dump their wing-mounted bombs in the Channel or abort the mission.

Aborts had now reduced the 40th Combat Wing from fifty-three B-17s to forty-two, one third of a complete wing formation. Standing orders in the 8th prohibited bomber commanders to penetrate the enemy defences with less than a complete wing formation. In this situation the wing would have to abort. However, Peaslee reasoned that the loss of forty-two bombers would deprive the division of much needed fire-power and, most importantly, additional bombs. He called for a report from the tail gunner, a regular lieutenant co-pilot for the lead crew, who was acting as the eyes of the air commander by taking over the tail gun position. The lieutenant reported that the 1st Division was in excellent position and at full strength except for the missing 305th Bomb Group. (Seventeen B-17s in the 305th Bomb Group, led by Major C. G. Y. Normand, had taken off from Chelveston six minutes late and, after completing assembly, had been unable to find either the 92nd or 306th Groups. Normand led his group first to Daventry and then to Spalding without sighting the rest of the 40th Wing. He tried in vain to contact Peaslee by radio, but about thirty miles short of the enemy coast the 305th caught sight of the 351st and 91st Bomb Groups of the 1st Combat Wing. Normand's B-17s filled the still vacant low group spot provided by the absence of the 381st Bomb Group which had taken longer to assemble than anticipated due to a 10,000ft overcast which hung over Ridgwell. Eventually, Major George Shacklady's sixteen aircraft finally caught up with the 1st Combat wing over the Channel and moved in next to the 351st Bomb Group in the high position.)

Peaslee decided to continue to the target, moving the 92nd and 306th formations into the high slot just above and to the left of the 91st. In effect this would give the 1st Wing five groups. Peaslee retained air command but would relinquish the lead to Lt-Col Theodore Milton, CO of the 91st, flying at the head of the 1st Combat Wing in *The Bad Egg*, piloted by Capt. Harry Lay (subsequently killed on a second tour in fighters). The air commander broke radio silence long enough to advise Milton of the plan, at the same time advising the new leader that the 40th Combat Wing would join his formation in close support, thus grouping nearly 100 bombers in a mutually protective mass. Milton must have had mixed feelings because he had only taken off with eleven B-17s, now reduced to just seven because of aborts. Having the 305th along must have provided some relief. The news that the 91st was to take over the lead prompted Capt. David Williams, the lead navigator flying with Milton, to think back to that fateful day on 17 August when the 91st had led the first Schweinfurt raid. 'Mission 115 was my twenty-third combat mission and the second time that I would have the dubious honour of being in the very first B-17 over the target. It was an eerie feeling once

more to be the vanguard, striking out across the Channel towards a target which had dealt us so many devastating losses just a few months before, all the more so this time since four of our group had already aborted and we were setting course with just seven aircraft comprising the 91st effort. I kept thinking of the ten we had lost in August and somehow could not seem to reconcile the mathematics which were going through my mind. The navigational chore ahead left little time for such speculation.

Bringing up the rear of the 1st Division bomber stream was the 41st Combat Wing, the third and final wing. In the lead was the 379th Bomb Group led by Lt-Col Louis W. Rohr and Capt. Edwin Millson, with the 303rd in the high spot and the 384th, low, in 'Purple Heart Corner' led by Capt. Philip Algar, who had flown the first Schweinfurt mission with Major George W. Harris.

At mid-Channel the lieutenant tail gunner aboard Peaslee's ship reported, 'Fighters at seven o'clock climbing. They look like P-47s.' The delay in forming up over England had put the Fortresses ten minutes behind schedule and the forty-four P-47s of the 353rd Fighter Group, which were on schedule, had met the bombers in mid-Channel. The 1st Bomb Division crossed the mouth of the Scheldt at 1225 hours, the same time as the 3rd Division was leaving the coast of England. Olds' force was only five minutes behind schedule, having avoided the bad weather problems that had dogged the 1st Division assembly. At 1305 hours, forty-eight P-47s of the 56th Fighter Group rendezvoused with the 3rd Division. Of the 164 B-17s assigned to the 1st only 149 remained after mechanical failures resulted in fifteen aborts, and the 3rd was reduced from 160 B-17s to 142 for the same reason.

Over Walcheren Island more than twenty Me 109s and FW 190s, zooming in from over 34,000ft, attacked the 1st Division. The Thunderbolt pilots stood their ground and met the attacks at around 31,000ft, a height at which the Thunderbolt had the advantage over the enemy fighters. At 1330 hours, at a point between Aachen and Düren, the 353rd Fighter Group, at the limit of their range, was forced to break off and return to England. They had done their job well, beating off a succession of attacks and claiming ten fighters shot down and another five damaged or destroyed for the loss of one P-47 in combat and another which crashed in England on the return leg. As the 1st Division continued its south-easterly course, away from the heavily defended towns of Antwerp and Aachen, and as soon as the Thunderbolts had departed, the Luftwaffe sailed into the attack. Some 300 to 400 enemy fighters ripped through the unprotected Fortress formations, firing rockets and cannon into the wings and fuselages of the bombers amid fierce return fire from the B-17 gunners. Capt McLaughlin recalls: 'The first big jolt came when my co-pilot riding in the tail called out, 'A large formation approaching at five o'clock', which we believed to be the 40th Combat Wing and which thereafter proved to be a large gaggle of twin-engined Messerschmitts passing us on the starboard side, positioning themselves for head-on passes and firing large rockets into the midst of our formations. With no fighter protection we soon became easy targets for the German rockets, and as our damaged wingman fell behind we could see the FW 190s finishing them off with relative ease.'

Crews had guessed before take-off that the Luftwaffe would be up in force and the 306th lead ship, piloted by Capt. Charles Schoolfield and Capt. Charles Flannagan, was one of many which carried an extra 12,000 rounds of ammunition. Three B-17s in the 306th Group had already turned back with mechanical problems, the last leaving at 1320 hours just as the Luftwaffe were beginning their attack. The fifteen remaining B-17s fought off the persistent attacks with as much firepower as they could muster. At 1400 hours, 1/Lt Douglas H. White in the 367th Squadron was the first to be shot out of formation by the German rocket-firing fighters after taking hits in the horizontal stabiliser. White's Fortress, a new B-17G, went down and exploded. Only the radio operator survived. 1/Lt Willard H. Lockyear's B-17 was hit at about the same time by rockets, and three engines were set on fire. The radio room also erupted in flames and 2/Lt Paul N. Welton, the navigator, and 1/Lt Albert J. Nagy, the bombardier, were killed in the nose of the aircraft. The striken aircraft finally fell at Neuweld. The rest of the crew managed to bale out, but the ball turret gunner later died in hospital from internal injuries.

The fight reached a crescendo and 2/Lt McCallum's *Queen Jeannie* was shot down. McCallum was killed along with his co-pilot, 2/Lt Homer D. Fitzer, who was flying his first mission. 1/Lt Vernon K. Cole's B-17 in the 423rd Squadron

was also shot down, by a rocket-firing Ju 88, which set the bomb bay on fire. The radio operator and ball turret gunner were both killed by rocket fragments. One of the waist gunners failed to bale out and Cole, who elected to remain in the aircraft to allow the others to bale out, was blown out in the subsequent explosion and his body was found later, hanging in his parachute from a tree.

The 306th's gunners fought back. At 1410 hours S/Sgt William L. Threatt Jr, a waist gunner in 1/Lt Virgil H. Jeffries' B-17, lead ship of the first element in the 423rd Squadron, shot down a FW 190 and damaged another. T/Sgt James S. Porter, the top turret gunner, aimed at a gaggle of four Ju 88s and scored hits on one of the attackers just as it fired off two rockets. The Ju 88's right engine appeared to leave its mounting and the fighter spun away out of control. Porter himself was hit in the leg by a machine-gun bullet but he stuck to his task and hit another fighter which burst into flames. Henry C. Cordery, the co-pilot, recalls: 'We were under constant attack. I don't know how long the first attacks lasted but there was a lull. I left my position to get more ammo' from the radio room. Passing through the waist I found the right waist gunner, Michele, severely wounded. His leg was off. The left waist gunner was also wounded. I called Lt Moon, the bombardier. He came back and we both administered first aid. I took the protective covering off the needle of the morphine only to discover it was frozen. I must have had at least five uncovered and I put them all in my mouth to thaw them. I had considerable difficulty getting them out, as my hands were numb from the cold. Then I returned to my position and just about in time, as the attacks started again.'

At 1415 hours, a combination of flak and fighters shot down 1/Lt John D. Jackson's B-17 over Friesburg. Jackson went down with his aircraft and Bernard Bernstein, the navigator, was killed as he baled out. Two gunners were also killed but the rest of the crew landed safely. In the 369th Squadron, 1/Lt George C. Bettinger's B-17 and 1/Lt Gustave S. Holmstrom's *Piccadilly Commando*, had also been lost. *Piccadilly Commando* had lost its no.4 engine in one of the first attacks, but it had been feathered successfully and Holmstrom managed to maintain formation. Just past Frankfurt a large hole appeared in the left wing and fuel began streaming out. The pilot asked FO Philip D. Anderson, his navigator, for a heading to Switzerland, but just as Holmstrom pulled out of formation a German fighter followed and opened fire. *Piccadilly Commando* went into a climb and Holmstrom ordered the crew to bale out. Anderson and 1/Lt Jack A. Kelly, the bombardier, went out through the nose hatch and were never found. Holmstrom and five of the crew survived.

In the 367th Squadron, 1/Lt Richard Butler's B-17 erupted in flames on the bomb run between Wurzburg and Schweinfurt after being hit repeatedly by fighters in the first attack. All the crew baled out safely before the aircraft exploded and were captured. In the lead ship, one of Schoolfield's waist gunners, T/Sgt Robert J. Conley, was seriously wounded in the left hand by an exploding 20mm cannon shell. S/Sgt Bert Perlmutter, the other waist gunner, applied a tourniquet and Conley returned to his guns, shooting down a FW 190 at 150 yards. Conley passed out and after recovering returned to man his guns again. He later received the Distinguished Flying Cross for his action.

For a little over three hours, from 1333 to 1647 hours, exceptionally large numbers of enemy fighters had attacked the 1st Division. The worst of the attacks had taken place between Aachen and the Frankfurt area and the out-of-position 305th had suffered worst of all. Three B-17s from the Chelveston outfit had already turned back, one with a broken exhaust stack, one with an oxygen leak and a third which lost its way during forming up. Of the fifteen which remained, none came in for rougher treatment than Lt Douglas L. Murdock's crew, flying 'tail-end charlie'. Edwin L. Smith, the co-pilot, recalls: 'An explosion occurred between the number one and two engines, stunning both the pilot and myself. On coming to, we recovered control of the plane but realised both engines were out and that we were way out of formation. We also realised it was impossible to get back to the formation or to the deck in time to save the crew as six or eight FW 190s and Me 109s were chewing us up at close range. I ordered the crew out, flipped the auto-flight control on and baled out. Murdock was to follow but I never saw him again. The bombardier and navigator had already left when I checked their positions on the way past. Bill Menzies was the only crew member I ever saw again.' The 92nd was also badly hit, as Capt. McLaughlin recalls: 'Under the pressure of continued heavy attacks our ranks were soon greatly decimated. After three hours, as we closed

our formation for the target run, my group looked more like a squadron. We had but twelve airplanes left out of the twenty-one we took off with.' One of the 92nd crews which survived to the target was captained by Bill Rose. 'It was indescribable. This was the first time I had any thoughts that we were in for a fight. I will always remember the tail gunner reporting formations of B-17s flying into positions behind to protect our rear. We thought we weren't going to have the attacks on the tail like we had been getting on our last two missions. Then, all of a sudden, 'Oh my God!' The Germans were letting go air-to-air rockets, straight into our group. I was fortunate in that one went right past my window. The rocket landed right in the wing of the lead plane right by a gas tank. I watched it burn and it wasn't long before the entire wing was on fire. The pilot dropped back and the stricken crew baled out. Eventually, the B-17 blew up. It was a terrible sight to see.'

Capt. David Williams in the 91st continues: 'Our crew in *The Bad Egg* were extremely fortunate on this trip for I do not recall any casualties and very little, if any, battle damage to the aircraft. Nonetheless, we had a grandstand view of the entire frightening battle which once more was characterised by vicious frontal fighter attacks. They appeared to be concentrating their efforts on the low group rather than the lead group of aircraft. In any event we expended many thousands of rounds of .50 calibre ammo' against the attacking fighters on their way to the less fortunate Fortresses of our wing.'

The 3rd Division encountered some fighter opposition, but it was not as intense as that experienced by the 1st Division. Only two Fortresses were shot down before the Thunderbolt escort withdrew. Bob Hughes, flying in the 100th Bomb Group formation, recalls: 'We were a little south of our course and about four minutes late. We could hear chatter on the radio from units and their escorts ahead of us, who seemed to be drawing enemy fighters. We seemed to be getting much less action than the 95th and 390th Bomb Groups in our wing.' The 3rd Division had proceeded on a converging course with the 1st Division towards Aachen. At 1410 hours the 1st Division, now flying an almost parallel course to the 3rd Division, arrived at a point twenty-five miles north of Frankfurt where it was to change course and head south-south-east for the

River Main. This was designed to deceive the German defences into thinking that Augsburg or Munich was their destination. About ten miles south of the River Main, the 1st Division turned sharply onto a north-easterly heading for Schweinfurt.

Capt. David Williams in the 91st continues: 'Fortunately, the overcast had disappeared at the southern German border and the weather was absolutely clear for the remainder of the route to the target and withdrawal until just east of Paris. This provided us with an opportunity for precise navigation and excellent bombing, but also provided a field-day for the German fighters and anti-aircraft gunners.' By the time it entered the target area, the 1st Division had lost thirty-six bombers shot down and twenty had turned back, but the 3rd Division had come off surprisingly lightly, losing only two bombers to fighter attacks. This left a total of 224 Fortresses to win through to the target itself. Collectively, this seems a reasonable force but most of the groups in the 1st Division had been torn to shreds by the intense fighter attacks, and some were barely skeleton formations. By the time the 305th Bomb Group could see the city of Schweinfurt, twelve miles in the distance, it had lost its entire low squadron of five aircraft and parts of the high and lead squadrons. Only three of the original eighteen aircraft remained and they were joined by a Fortress from another group. It was not enough for effective bombing, so Major Normand, the group leader, decided to join the depleted 92nd and 306th formations for the bomb run. Of the thirty-seven Fortresses in the 40th Combat Wing that had crossed the Channel, only sixteen remained, and worse was to follow.

Crew members recall the dozens of great red flashes in the flak columns as they turned on the IP. Many called out that the enemy was using red flak, not realising that they were in fact witnessing the explosions of many B-17s in the groups ahead. The enemy pilots showed complete disregard for the tremendous flak barrage over the target and made almost suicidal attacks on the bombers. For the moment the lead bombardier aboard *The Bad Egg* had to try and ignore the attacks as he set up the Automatic Flight Control Equipment (AFCE) that linked the aircraft's controls to the bombsight. *The Bad Egg* led the 91st over the city and at 1439 hours they began unloading their deadly cargoes on the

streets, houses and factories of Schweinfurt. Budd J. Peaslee described it as 'a city about to die'.

The 91st was to claim the best overall bombing results for the 1st Division. However, the 351st Bomb Group, from the same wing, the 1st, was the most accurate, with Capt. H. D. Wallace, squadron bombardier in part of the group formation, placing all his bombs within 1,000 feet of the MPI. Excellent visibility allowed Lt J. Pellegrini, the lead bombardier in the 305th formation, to pick up the actual aiming point at the IP and instruct his pilot, Lt J. W. Kane, to turn onto the bomb run. Pellegrini's AFCE had been badly shot up on the run in and he was not sure if the pilots' directional instrument was working so he set up his own rate and dropped on it. Only three bombers in the 305th formation remained and the bombing of the briefed aiming point would have caused the three B-17s to become separated from the other groups, so they bombed the centre of the city instead. Immediately after 'bombs away' the 305th Bomb Group's thirteenth victim was claimed by fighters, leaving only Major Normand and another B-17 from the eighteen that had set out from Chelveston. The two survivors turned away from the target and followed the lead group home.

Then it was the turn of the 40th Combat Wing. McLaughlin and his bombardier, Edward T. O'Grady, conferred over the interphone, and as the bomber rolled out on a heading towards Schweinfurt, they hooked up to the AFCE. Ahead of them was the daunting sight of the 1st Wing almost blotted from sight by the concentrated flak barrage. Capt. McLaughlin recalls: 'Looking back now I have to admire the courage of Harry Hughes as I listened to him on the aircraft interphone coolly directing Edward O'Grady to the target amidst the constant rock and roll of the exploding flak shells and fighter attacks. We had to calm down one of our leaders whose anxiety overcame him and he began to interrupt the interphone conversation during the bomb run by muttering to himself and damning the Germans!'

Flying in the number five slot in the 92nd Bomb Group formation directly beneath Peaslee and McLaughlin was Bill Rose. 'I looked straight up when the bomb bay doors opened and I could see right into the bomb bay. If his bombs had fallen out prematurely, they would have fallen on us. Fortunately, I had told my bombardier to tell me one minute before 'bombs away' so I could cut the throttles and drop back to let the lead ship release his bombs right in front of the nose of our plane. When all his bombs had gone and he had closed his bomb bay doors, I pulled up again right underneath him. In my position the German pilots had a real hard time getting at us. The only way they could get to us was to come underneath. I think this was how we were able to survive; protected in every direction apart from underneath. We came home, the four of us, one right underneath another and one out on each side.'

The 306th Bomb group formation followed the 92nd Bomb Group and dropped its 1,000lb bombs. Sixteen of them landed within a 1,920-foot circle. Henry C. Cordery, the co-pilot in Lt Jeffries' B-17 recalls: 'We came off the target and re-grouped. I looked around at the group and there wasn't much of us left. In my squadron we started with six ships in two three-ship elements, and being in the lead ship I saw all five of them go down. Out of eighteen aircraft we had six left. I remember someone, I believe it was Lt Jeffries, saying, 'That's the government's half, now for ours.'' The 40th Combat Wing turned away from the target and headed in the direction of the 1st Combat Wing, now making for

B-17F-115-BO, 42-30727, piloted by Lt William C. Bissom in the 367th 'Clay Pigeons' Bomb Squadron, 306th Bomb Group, was lost on the Schweinfurt raid on 14 October 1943 when flak knocked out two engines and fighters riddled the rear fuselage, killing S/Sgt Thompson E. Wilson, the tail gunner. Only 2/Lt Charles R. Stafford, the co-pilot, who exited through the side cockpit window, and four crewmen in the aft section escaped death (Richards).

the French border. 1/Lt Ralph T. Peters' B-17 had arrived over the target with its no.2 engine out but had completed the bomb run. After 'bombs away' the group went into a climb from the 22,500ft bombing altitude and Peters' Fortress, suffering from the strain imposed on its damaged wings, gave up the ghost and he ordered the crew to bale out. All ten made it before the B-17 exploded. About twenty minutes after the target, 1/Lt William C. Bissom's B-17 in the 367th Bomb Squadron, 306th Bomb Group, was brought down by flak – which scored two direct hits on the engines – and fighters. S/Sgt Thompson E. Wilson, the tail gunner, was killed. Charles R. Stafford, the co-pilot, and four others managed to bale out safely. When the heat of battle eased a little the tail gunner and formation observer, Lt Curtis L. Dunlap, who had tried to keep abreast of what was happening, could only tell a shocked Schoolfield that just five ships were left. Schoolfield and his co-pilot, Capt. Charles Flannagan, nursed their ailing bomber home despite a fire in the no.3 engine and a failed attempt to bale out when the bale-out button refused to work. The withdrawal route, well away from the line of penetration, was devised by General Anderson to limit casualties and took the bombers south of Paris and then north towards England. Capt. McLaughlin spoke into his oxygen mask to his tired crew and Col Peaslee sitting beside him: 'We've flown this far for Uncle Sam, from here we fly for the US – us.'

The third and final wing, the 41st added its bombs to the conflagration and turned off the target to allow the 3rd Bomb Division, flying six minutes behind, to take its turn. First over the target was the 96th Bomb Group at the head of the 45th Combat

Crew of the *Eightball* in the 390th Bomb Group pose beneath their B-17 just before the second Schweinfurt mission. Lt Dick Perry, the pilot, is standing at the extreme right of the picture (Perry).

Wing. Its target was obscured by smoke from the preceding bomb runs, but crews had not flown this far to be thwarted by smoke from their own bombs and released them anyway. The second group in the wing was the 388th with sixteen aircraft. The lead bombardier was unable to identify either the Kugelfischer ball-bearing works or the marshalling yards located to the south, so he set his sight on the bridge over the River Main and released his bombs slightly to the right of the ball-bearing plant. The bombs cascaded down into the southern half of Schweinfurt and the western end of the marshalling yards.

The 13th Combat Wing was the last wing in the 3rd Division to cross Schweinfurt. Joey Poulin, the 19-year-old French-Canadian ball turret gunner

aboard *The Eightball* in the 390th Bomb Group flown by Bill Cabral and Dick Perry, had a lucky escape when a piece of flak ripped off his turret door. Only his slender lifebelt prevented him from falling 25,000 feet without a parachute (like almost all ball turret gunners, Poulin could not wear one in the close confines of his turret). Many gunners might have scrambled back into the belly of the aircraft, but if any Luftwaffe fighters spotted that the ball turret was out of action it would have been an open invitaton to attack. Poulin chose to stick it out, praying all the time that the lifebelt would hold. Close on the heels of the 390th Bomb Group were the 95th and 100th Bomb Groups, their crews eager to release their bombs and head for home as quickly as possible. Lt Bob Hughes, pilot of *Nine Little Yanks and a Jerk* in the latter group, recalls: 'We saw gas and oil fires dotting the countryside, attesting to the furiousness of the defence and the determination of the bomber crews to place their bombs squarely on the target and not be denied. From time to time, we had seen flak from a distance but as we neared the target area it took on a more personal feeling. Periodically, we could see the red hearts of the bursts of 'Big Stuff'. We could now see the target area. Lt Richard E. Elliott, our bombardier, and I, had attended a special briefing on the target even though we were scheduled to drop on the lead bombardier's release. This intense target study before take-off paid off handsomely because it allowed us to distinguish the target under the most unfavourable conditions. We had also been briefed about the smudge-pots marking a dummy target area. Elliott and I recognised them for the dummies they were. They were smoking like the whole town was on fire.

'Suddenly, our attention was diverted. The leader of the 95th was struck by flak just as we approached the IP for the final turn to the target. He descended rapidly from formation. Flak was intense and my co-pilot, Lt Donald S. Davis, yelled 'Move Bob!' I had felt the 'whump' from the burst which had lifted our wingman's plane, and was sending it directly into us. Lieutenant Howard Keel temporarily lost control of the craft. The Good Lord kicked left rudder, down stick, left aileron, then back-stick and rolled out of a well-executed diving split 'S'. It allowed Keel to pass through the space which we had occupied to execute a co-ordinated recovery. It also placed our ship on a direct course to the primary target. Dick Elliott picked up the target immediately and called 'Skipper, target dead ahead, set up and follow PDI!' *Nine Little Yanks and A Jerk* was now completely alone so Hughes questioned Elliott: 'Dick, I do not have the right to commit a man to this course of action against his will. It would have to be a 100 per cent volunteer.' Dick called for a vote starting with the lowest ranking man. One by one all agreed, and I said 'Gentlemen, we go!'

'We considered we had the element of surprise on our side and that we could maintain an appearance of a crippled aircraft by not opening our doors until just before 'bombs away'. We reinformed the crew that we were flying in a heavily defended area and the best information had it that the German planes would not penetrate the area. We also doubted that the flak guns would fire upon the one ship but would allow us to leave the area and become fighter bait. It was our best guess that they did not want to draw attention to the steam-plant and allied ball-bearing shops by firing on one ship. If we couldn't find it, they were not going to disclose it. Dick Elliott

opened the doors just long enough to release the bombs. We already had our strike camera running. It was on intervolometer but our bomb sight was not. Dick, knowing that he had the rate killed and the course was beautiful, set the selector switch on 'Salvo'. Bombs were away at 1454 hours. All fell in the MPI. The roar on the intercom was 'PICKLE BARREL!' *Nine Little Yanks and a Jerk* had just opened up the north segment of the target area and there were more bombs to follow. Our aircraft was strike photo aircraft for the 100th Bomb Group and we had picked up the 95th Bomb Group, which was still struggling, trying to get into formation. My wingmen joined me and we asked the new leader if we could be of assistance in re-forming the group, explaining that we had an experienced formation controller, Sgt Robert L. McKimmy, one of the finest formation critics in the business, riding the tail guns. The offer was graciously accepted. He lined them up for us in a hurry because we were running out of the defended area, and in a very short time the 95th was formed and the 100th flight took its proper position in the high squadron. We rejoined the 390th Bomb Group and we were once again the 13th Combat Wing.'

The city of Schweinfurt had soaked up over 483 tons of high explosives and incendiaries. The 3rd Division had dropped the most bombs on target and the 390th was the most successful. Despite the lead ship experiencing difficulty, all fifteen aircraft placed fifty per cent of their bombs within 1,000 feet of the MPI. The Fortresses turned off the target and flew an almost complete 180 degree circle around Schweinfurt. A group of FW 190s headed for the 1st Division formation and singled out the trailing 41st Combat Wing. The leading 379th Bomb Group lost three B-17s in the first pass and another bomber also hurtled to earth after a collision with one of the fighters, which also went down. Both divisions headed for their respective rally points and began forming into combat wings again for the return over Germany and France.

The surviving B-17s headed for the coast. At 1640 hours the 1st Division crossed the Channel coast and were followed, just five minutes later, by the 3rd Division. Approaching the French coast the two surviving aircraft in the 305th Bomb Group sighted the 92nd and 306th Bomb Groups for the first time on the mission. Luckily, the two B-17s had met little fighter opposition on the way home for they had

Capt. Nathaniel 'Gus' Mencow, navigator in Lt James R. Geary's crew aboard *Betty Boop*, *The Pistol Packin' Mama* in the 570th Bomb Squadron, 390th Bomb Group, pictured with the 14 October strike photo of Schweinfurt (Gus Mencow).

Massachusetts men with the 390th Bomb Group. *Left to right* Lt Hugh J. 'Mac' McCarthy, bombardier; Lt William F. Burke, navigator; Capt. Gus Mencow, navigator; Capt. Daniel Lenilian, chaplain; Lt John B. Mooney, navigator; Capt. Philip J. Dower, pilot. McCarthy and Mencow flew the 14 October mission to Schweinfurt in *Betty Boop, The Pistol Packin' Mama*, in the 570th Bomb Squadron, piloted by Lt Jim 'Rally' Geary, which led the high squadron that day (Gus Mencow).

used almost all their ammunition before the target. The Fortresses' return to England was hampered by the same soupy weather that had dogged their departure. Capt. McLaughlin recalls: 'This really topped it all off. Low ceilings and poor visibility loomed as an almost insurmountable problem because most of our remaining twelve aircraft were damaged and at least two had wounded on board who needed immediately attention [one of these landed in East Anglia while the other remained in formation]. Harry Hughes directed me to the landing end of our home runway at Podington, using for the first time an inter-setting 'Gee Box' line as an instrument approach system. With our wounded wingman, who, as I recall, was Lt 'Smoke' McKennon, we tracked into a descending approach to the runway and when we had it in sight, by pre-arrangement we pulled up and let him land. Then we led the other two remaining aircraft around and

General Maurice 'Mo' Preston, CO of 379th Bomb Group, listens to Major 'Rip' Rohr upon his return as leader of the group during the disastrous mission to Schweinfurt on 14 October 1943. Preston noted that Rohr 'looked harassed, shaken and more agitated than I had ever seen him' (Preston).

back to the final approach and landing. Five aircraft back in England and four back at home base out of a full group that morning; a long, tough, soul-searching day I'll not soon forget.'

In all, the 1st Division had lost forty-five Fortresses on the raid. At Chelveston the ground staff and crews left behind were devastated to learn that theirs had been the highest loss of the day. Of the eighteen B-17s which had taken off that morning, only two returned to base. There was not even the consolation that some crews might have put down at other bases. Second highest loss in the division went to the 306th Bomb Group with ten. The 92nd Bomb Group had lost six and a seventh was written-off in a crash landing at Aldermaston. The 379th and 384th Bomb Groups had each lost six B-17s in combat and three crews from the latter group had to abandon their aircraft over England, making nine in all. The 303rd Bomb Group lost two aircraft, including one which crash-landed after the crew had baled out near Risely. The 91st, 351st and 381st Bomb Groups each lost one B-17. The 3rd Division had lost fifteen aircraft. The 96th had lost seven, including Lt Silas Nettles' aircraft which was flying in the 100th Bomb Group formation. His air-craft had been the last B-17 over the target. The 94th

lost six Fortresses and the 95th and 390th each lost one B-17. The 100th, 385th and 388th Bomb Groups suffered no loss although few aircraft, if any, escaped scot-free. Of the bombers which returned to England, 142 in both divisions were blackened and charred by fighter attacks and holed by flak.

Bob Hughes, pilot of *Nine Little Yanks and a Jerk*, which put down safely at Thorpe Abbotts, concludes: 'After our strike photographs had been developed and the damage assessed by local intelligence, the results were called into division. Dick Elliott and I had been summoned to observe the strike photos. Later in the evening word was received that General LeMay wanted me to attend the critique the next day. This was to be an experience for me. I had never seen so many 'Eagles' in one room. I had never even been to a critique. In fact, I had never been out of formation over a target before. When all the representatives from all the groups were assembled the critique was called to order and we had just been seated when General LeMay asked, 'Will Lt Hughes from the 100th Bomb Group come forward.' When I stepped up onto the stage he said, 'Will you tell this group what you did yesterday?' I related how we had been forced to dive for our lives and that when we recovered, the target lay dead ahead; how all the men volunteered, that we had a perfect bomb run and that Elliott had 'pickle-barrelled' the target. General LeMay asked how I knew we had 'pickle-barrelled' the target. I informed him that I had studied the strike photos and that *Nine Little Yanks and a Jerk* was a designated strike photo aircraft for the 100th Bomb group. He responded, 'That's right gentlemen: ten bombs MPI'. Stepping up to the strike map he pulled the butcher paper away to reveal an enlarged strike photo showing the strike. His next comment was: 'The lieutenant should have a commendation', to which the reply from the back of the room, in clearly enunciated words, was 'The S.O.B. should be court-martialled for breaking formation!' Those words were spoken by my now good friend, Colonel Budd J. Peaslee. Having reached the age of twenty-five I had watched enough cards to know that in poker this is called a 'push'. If I didn't ask for a commendation, Col Peaslee wouldn't offer a court martial!'

Sixty Fortresses and 600 men were missing. Five B-17s had crashed in England as a result of their battle-damaged condition and twelve more were destroyed in crash-landings or so badly damaged that they had to be written-off. Of the returning bombers, 121 required repairs and another five fatal casualties and forty-three wounded crewmen were removed from the aircraft. The losses were softened by Press proclamations that 104 enemy fighters had been shot down. The actual figure was something like thirty-five but both the Press and the planners alike were carried away on a tidal wave of optimism. Even the British Chief of the Air Staff, Air Marshal Sir Charles Portal, said: 'The Schweinfurt raid may well go down in history as one of the decisive air actions of the war and it may prove to have saved countless lives by depriving the enemy of a great part of his means of resistance.' Later, Brigadier-General Orvil Anderson publicly stated: 'The entire works are now inactive. It may be possible for the Germans eventually to restore twenty-five per cent of normal capacity, but even that will require some time.' Unfortunately, only eighty-eight out of the 1,222 bombs dropped actually fell on the plants. Production at the Kugelfischer plant, largest of the five plants, was interrupted for only six weeks and the German war machine never lacked for ball-bearings throughout the remainder of the war. As in many other German industries, dispersal of factories ensured survival for the German ball-bearings industry, and careful husbanding of resources meant that some forms of machinery needed less or no ball-bearings at all.

Four days after the raid, General 'Hap' Arnold confidently told gathered pressmen: 'Now we have got Schweinfurt!' However, VIII Bomber Command had to return to Schweinfurt again and again before the end of hostilities. It was only when the city was finally overrun by US armoured divisions that America could at last confirm that it had 'got Schweinfurt'. In recognition of the 8th's heavy losses, and the 305th's in particular, the 'Rainbow Division' presented the German flag, captured flying over the Kugelfischer plant, to the group at Chelveston shortly before it returned stateside. The cruellest remark of Arnold's was that 'the loss of sixty American bombers was incidental'. Very few would agree with him and it could hardly have endeared the general to his crews. Many had lost buddies on the raid and for those who survived, life would never be the same again. Bill Rose, who put down at Bovingdon, recalls: 'My crew and I were now ten nervous wrecks and we didn't sleep much that night. In fact we slept fitfully for about the next year. Nightmares continued most nights until 1945. The battle has affected everyone, myself included, morally and in other ways, for the rest of our lives. Like the terrible battles of World War One, when 24,000 men could be, and were, lost on a single day, the nightmare would not and never will go away.'

CHAPTER 7
The Marianas 'Turkey Shoot'

While the great air battles raged in Europe in 1944, in the Pacific US forces were continually on the offensive, pushing back the Imperial Japanese tide, island by island. The offensive had begun after the Amerian success at the Battle of Midway in June 1942 and had continued in August when the US Navy boldly struggled for supremacy of the sea around Guadalcanal. With Japanese reinforcements and supplies cut off by the Navy, retreat became Japan's only option. Heavy losses at Guadalcanal so weakened the Japanese Navy that it could not stop the campaign to isolate

An Asashio class destroyer is obscured in smoke as a TBM Avenger passes overhead during the first raid on Truk, February 1944 (US Navy).

the important base at Rabaul. By April 1944 Rabaul no longer posed a threat.

Between late 1943 and mid-1944 the advance in the South Pacific, combined with a drive in the Central Pacific, breached the Japanese defensive perimeter and opened the way for the liberation of the Philippines. While General Douglas MacArthur advanced through the South Pacific along New Guinea the US Navy began the Central Pacific campaign, capturing bases in the Gilberts and the Marshall Islands. Carrier task groups shattered Japanese bases and intercepted their naval forces. The Gilberts were attacked and occupied in November 1943 and, in February 1944, the main atolls of the Marshalls were overrun. As part of the assault on Eniwetok, the most westerly of the

ABOVE
Douglas SBD-4 Dauntless *Push Push* wheels over Bougainville Island in the Solomons during the 'Cherry Blossom' operation in November 1943, as Navy destroyers shell Japanese installations before the US Marines landed (McDonnell Douglas).

LEFT
Grumman F6F Hellcat of VF-5 on hangar deck catapult of USS *Yorktown*, June 1943 (Grumman).

BELOW
Grumman Hellcat F6F-3 of VF-16 is flagged away from CV-16 USS *Lexington* during the 'Marshalls' campaign in November 1943 (Grumman).

Marshall chain, a huge two-day air strike on the Japanese navy base at Truk in the Carolines was carried out by the aircraft carriers in Admiral Raymond Spruance's 5th Fleet. Truk capitulated and the Japanese retreated, first to Palau, and finally, in March 1944, to Singapore.

New large 'Essex'-class CV and light 'Enterprise'-class CVL escort carriers, as well as amphibious landing craft, had helped make the American onslaught victorious. Newer, more powerful types of aircraft had also arrived late in 1943 onwards to replace the older fighter and torpedo bomber aircraft used in the early Pacific battles. The Grumman F6F Hellcat, which had first flown in prototype form shortly after the Battle of Midway on 26 June 1942, was now the standard fast carrier fighter in the US Navy. The Hellcat made its combat debut on 31 August 1943, being flown by VF-9 on *Essex* and VF-5 on *Yorktown* on strikes against Marcus Island. It was faster in level flight and the dive than the Mitsubishi A6M5 Zero. The Cyclone-engined FM-2 Wildcat, then in service aboard the small escort carriers, had benefited from experience gained by the Royal Navy. It had a better rate of climb than the earlier Wildcats and other improvements meant that it could hold its own against the A6M3 Zero and its descendants. The Grumman TBM/TBF

Avenger, meanwhile, was the standard torpedo bomber aboard American carriers, while the Curtiss SB2C-1C Helldiver was on the verge of replacing the Dauntless SBD-5 dive-bomber. The new dive-bomber had its drawbacks though. It required more maintenance than the Dauntless and carried only the same bomb load with no improvement in range. Although it soldiered on until the war's end, plans were considered for re-equipping with SBDs again in July 1944.

Despite the harrowing defeats of late 1943 and mid-1944, Japanese naval forces in the Pacific were still far from finished. The A6M Zero remained the standard carrier-borne fighter, for after attempts to bring the A7M Sam successor into service had failed, the A6M5 Model 52b, which was a cleaned-up version of the A6M3, was introduced at the end

Newer, more powerful American fighters arrived in the Pacific late in 1943. Two of the finest were the Grumman F6F Hellcat (left), which made its combat debut on 31 August 1943 and became the standard fast carrier fighter in the US Navy, and the Pratt & Whitney Double Wasp engined F4U Corsair (right), which was first used in action by the 'Cactus Air Force' during the defence of Guadalcanal in February 1943, and which fought in every major Pacific battle with the US Navy, flying 64,051 sorties and destroying 2,140 Japanese aircraft (Steve Jefferson).

US Marines watch as five TBF Grumman Avengers attack Japanese positions on the north end of Namur Island, Kwajalein Atoll, 1–2 February 1944 (Grumman).

of 1943. The Zeke 52 had a top speed of around 350 mph at 20,000 feet with more powerful 20mm cannon and a 13mm machine-gun complementing its other 7.7mm machine-gun in the fuselage. Numerically, Japan possessed a much larger carrier force than the United States, and their Navy could call upon 1,700 land-based fighters if the American

fleet could be lured to a suitable killing zone either in the Palaus or the Western Carolines where they were within air striking range from bases in the Netherlands East Indies, New Guinea, the Bismarcks, the Philippines and Singapore. Some 484 aircraft were based on Tinian, Guam and Saipan in the Marianas, while a further 114 were based in the Western Caroline Islands. With such air and naval forces at their disposal the Japanese admirals believed they could win a decisive sea battle and re-establish their naval supremacy in the Pacific.

The American admirals, however, had their own ideas. Plans had long been formulated for the invasion of the Marianas Islands and in June they were put into effect. On 6 June Task Force 58, a huge carrier strike force composed of four self-contained task groups each with its own escorts, and commanded by Vice-Admiral Marc 'Pete' A. Mitscher, left Majuro for Saipan. TG58-1 was composed of *Hornet*, commanded by Rear-Admiral J. J. Clark,

A pair of SBD-5s of VB-10 with arrester hooks down prepare to land on the deck of the USS *Enterprise* following a patrol during the Palau raids, 29–30 March 1944. Both aircraft carry Yagi radar antennae beneath the wings (US Navy).

Yorktown, Bataan and Belleau Wood, with a total of 265 aircraft. TG58-2 was made up of Bunker Hill, commanded by Rear-Admiral A. E. Montgomery, Cabot, Monterey and Wasp, with 242 aircraft. TG58-3 comprised the Enterprise, commanded by Rear-Admiral J. W. Reeves Jr, the new Lexington (Mitscher's flagship), Princeton and San Jacinto, with a total of 227 aircraft. TG58-4 was composed of the Essex, under the command of Rear-Admiral W. K. Harrill, Langley and Cowpens (affectionately known as the 'Mighty Moo'), with 162 aircraft. On 11 June Task Force 58 began 'softening up' the Marianas with heavy gunfire while a fighter sweep by 211 Hellcats and eight Avengers was sent in to gain fighter superiority over the islands. Zeke 52s tried to intercept the Hellcats over Guam but thirty were shot down and Hellcats of VF-28 from Monterey destroyed six Mitsubishi G4M2 Bettys over Tinian. By 14 June, after four days of fighting, the US Navy pilots had destroyed almost 150 Japanese aircraft.

Meanwhile, on 8 June, the US Northern Attack Force under the command of Vice-Admiral Richmond Turner, arrived at Eniwetok from Hawaii with 71,000 troops to capture Saipan, while the Southern Attack Forces, under Rear-Admiral R. L. Conolly, arrived with 56,500 troops from Guadalcanal and Tulagi to assault Guam. The

Grumman TBM-1C Avenger of VT-2 from USS Hornet with four HVAR rockets under each wing flies over the Saipan invasion fleet, June 1944 (US Navy).

massive invasion fleet, which included twelve escort carriers, seven battleships and ninety-one destroyers, set sail for Saipan, which was planned to be invaded by amphibious forces on 15 June. On 12 June, Saipan and Tinian were shelled heavily. Two groups remained in the area to establish total air supremacy while that evening TG58-1 and TG58-4 sped 650 miles north to attack Chichi Jima and Iwo Jima. On 15 and 16 June Hellcats from TG58-1 and TG58-4 brought down about ten Zeros in combat and destroyed sixty aircraft on the ground. The Japanese pipe-dream of engaging the American fleet on their terms was vanishing into a fog of self-delusion. Vice-Admiral K. Kukuda, who commanded naval aircraft in the Central Pacific from his base on Tinian, omitted to tell Admiral Jisaburo Ozawa, who commanded the Japanese Main or First Mobile Fleet, of the true losses. On 13 June Admiral Soemu Toyoda, the commander-in-chief, ordered Ozawa's force to set course for the Philippine Sea where it was to rendezvous with the huge battleships Yamato and Musashi and six other vessels in a detachment commanded by Vice-Admiral Ugaki,

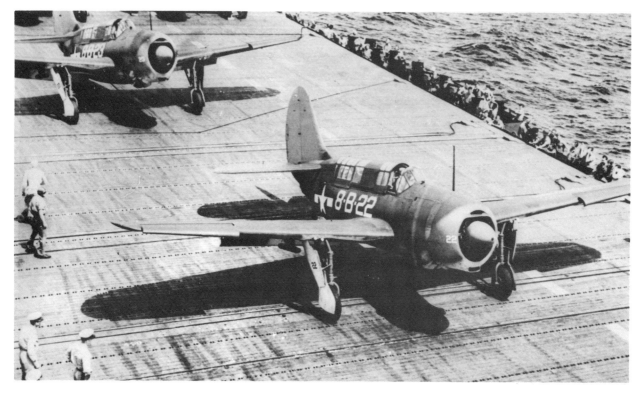

Curtiss SB2C-IC Helldivers aboard the USS *Bunker Hill* in June 1944 (US Navy).

who was told to abort an earlier mission to support Japanese forces fighting MacArthur's troops on Bataan in the Halmaheras. On 16 June Ozawa rendezvoused with Ugaki's detachment. Next day was spent refuelling before the huge force resumed its easterly course towards the Marianas. The vast armada was composed of three forces: 'A' Force, made up of three large fleet carriers, *Shokaku*, Ozawa's flagship *Taiho* and *Zuikaku* which had a total air strength of some 430 aircraft; 'B' Force, commanded by Rear-Admiral T. Joshima, comprising the fleet carriers, *Hiyo* and *Junyo* and the light carrier, *Ryuho*, which contained 135 aircraft; 'C' Force, commanded by Vice-Admiral Kurita whose three light carriers contained only eighty-eight aircraft but was employed as a diversionary force for the other two groups. All the carriers in the three forces were protected by a defensive screen of destroyers, cruisers and battleships.

On 17 June American shipping was attacked by Japanese aircraft based in the Carolines. Nakajima B5N Kate torpedo bombers from Truk attacked and sank an amphibious landing craft between Eniwetok and Saipan, and in the evening seventeen Yokosuka D4Y2 Judys and two Yokosuka P1Y1 Frances torpedo bombers, escorted by thirty-one Zeke 52s, made attacks on transports and escort carriers. Some forty-two FM-2 Wildcats were flown off the small escort carriers and steamed into the attack. The Fighter Direction Officers were inexperienced, and wrongly directed them to their targets. The Wildcats made fewer interceptions as a result although they did shoot down eight of the bombers. Seven more were shot down by anti-aircraft fire. Bombs fell close to two other light carriers; the *Fanshaw Bay* was hit and was forced to retire from the operation.

That same evening the US submarine *Cavalla* spotted part of the large Japanese force 780 miles to the west of Saipan, but the message did not reach Spruance until 0345 hours on 18 June. At this point he could have ordered TG58-2 and TG58-3 to steer towards the enemy and launch an air strike, but Spruance did not want to split his forces, Spruance, with his twelve light carriers and the rest of the invasion fleet, decided to stay within 100 miles of Saipan in order to meet any enemy attack that should threaten the amphibious landing by the Marines Corps and US Army assault troops. The four

American carrier groups rendezvoused at noon. Land-based reconnaissance aircraft and air searches from the US flat-tops failed to find the Japanese fleet, but enemy catapult-launched floatplanes succeeded in finding elements of Task Force 58 in the early afternoon. In 'C' Force, Rear-Admiral S. Obayashi ordered sixty-seven strike aircraft ready on deck, but the mission was cancelled on orders from Ozawa who wished to attack the next day.

Sixteen E13A Jake seaplanes were launched from the decks of the Japanese carriers in 'C' Force at 0445 hours on 19 June, followed by fourteen more from Obayashi's aircraft carriers half an hour later. At 0530 hours a D4Y1-C Judy reconnaissance plane from Guam, which discovered the American carrier groups, was promptly shot down by fighters of VF-28 from Monterey. The first group was intercepted by the combat air patrol from TG58-4 who shot down eight of the seaplanes. The second reconnaissance group turned back for their carriers after failing to sight the American fleet, but at 0730 hours on the way home one of the seaplanes spotted ships of TG58-4 and flashed the sighting report to Ozawa. Ozawa acted immediately and the order was given to assemble an air striking force on the decks of his carriers. By 0830 hours forty-five A6M2 Zero fighter bombers, eight Nakajima B6N2 Jill torpedo bombers and sixteen A6M5 Zero fighters from 'C' Force were in the air. Close behind came fifty-three D4Y Judy dive-bombers, twenty-seven Jills and forty-eight Zeros from 'A' Force, which began taking off around 0900 hours. At 0930 hours 'B' Force despatched twenty-five A6M2s, seven B6N2s and fifteen A6M5 Zeros. While the aircraft of 'A' Force were taking off, the US submarine Albacore, lurking in the depths beneath the enemy, fired six torpedoes at Ozawa's flagship, Taiho. One torpedo was exploded by a Japanese pilot who made a suicide dive on the tin fish before it could strike the carrier. Another torpedo struck the carrier and caused some damage to the forward elevator and some fuel lines, but the Taiho continued to launch her aircraft. At the same time the air strike force was fired on by nervous gunners in 'C' Force. Two aircraft were shot down and another eight were damaged before identification was correctly established.

Instructions for the attack were picked up by the R/T monitoring system on board the American flat-tops. It came as no surprise to the Hellcat pilots therefore, when the eight B6Ns broke away from the main formation at 18,000 feet and descended to sea-level to begin their torpedo attacks. The Jills were intercepted in their dives by six Hellcats of VF-25 from Cowpens but they were too fast for the American fighters and only one of the torpedo bombers was brought down. Meanwhile, eight Hellcats of VF-15 from the Essex attacked the covering Zeros at 25,000 feet and were soon joined by Hellcats of VF-2 from the Hornet and VF-27 from the Princeton. Japanese aircraft which managed to escape the Hellcats were met by VF-10 from the Enterprise, which shot down three aircraft before the anti-aircraft barrage opened up. By now the Japanese had abandoned any thoughts of attacking the carriers and the twenty survivors decided to hit the battleships of TG58-7 which were closer. One 550lb bomb hit the South Dakota, killing twenty-seven men in the explosion, but seventeen enemy aircraft were shot down by gunners on the ships. The fighters had had a field-day, shooting down forty-two of the enemy for the loss of only three Hellcats.

The second Japanese strike fared as badly as the first, although the dropping of 'chaff' (thin metal strips designed to 'snow' enemy radar) proved successful and American interceptors were sent to the wrong location to attack the fake blips. Once again the Japanese air leader took his planes into a circle and over the radio waves made his plans obvious to anyone listening. Some eighty-one Hellcats already airborne intercepted the real raid about fifty-five miles from the carriers, while thirty-three more followed closely behind after being flown off the carriers. First to attack was Commander David D. McCampbell's six Hellcats of VF-15, which went after the dive-bombers. Six minutes later VF-14 from Wasp joined the fight, followed by twenty-three Hellcats of VF-16 from the Lexington and eight more from VF-27. Altogether, the Hellcats destroyed seventy aircraft for the loss of only four Hellcats. Lieutenant Alexander Vraciu of VF-16 shot down six 'Judy' dive-bombers, making him the Navy's leading ace with eighteen 'kills'. David McCampbell, who was to finish the war as the US Navy's top-scoring fighter pilot with thirty-four victories and the Medal of Honor, shot down four enemy aircraft in this engagement and three more in a second action on 19 June. Only about twenty enemy aircraft managed to break through the fighter defences and reach the American

An F6F-3 Hellcat is prepared for take-off (Grumman).

destroyer screen; the majority were brought down by intense anti-aircraft fire. A few of the bombers dropped their bombs and torpedoes, but those that did hit only caused minor damage to the aircraft carriers *Bunker Hill* and *Wasp*. By 1200 hours it was all over and the thirty survivors began returning to their carriers.

Twenty minutes later the submarine *Cavalla* struck again; this time three of its torpedoes hit the *Shokaku*. Three hours later it caught fire and exploded, killing most of the 1,263-man crew. By coincidence, the *Taiho*, which had been hit earlier, blew up at almost the same instant the *Shokaku* was hit when vapour from its ruptured fuel tanks ignited, sending blasts throughout the carrier. Ozawa and his senior officers were taken off and transferred to a cruiser, but only 500 men from the 2,150 crew had been rescued when a further explosion signalled the end of the ship. The carrier capsized and sank beneath the waves.

At around 1300 hours the Avengers and Helldivers that had been orbiting to the east of the carriers were unleashed on Orote Field on Guam. The bombers blasted the airstrip with 500lb and

1,000lb bombs until it was so badly cratered that it was of no use to enemy aircraft damaged in action against the Hellcats. Meanwhile, the Japanese air strikes continued. The forty-seven aircraft in 'B' Force had been sent too far northward. About twenty bombers turned to search for the carriers, but Hellcats of VF-1 from the *Yorktown* and VF-2 from the *Hornet* destroyed seven of the enemy and the survivors dropped their bombs hastily and at random without hitting anything, although the *Essex* was missed by only thirty yards. The third strike, involving eighty-seven aircraft launched from *Zuikaku* and the three light carriers of 'B' Force, was also misdirected, and the force flew too far to the south of the American fleet. The eighteen Zeros from the *Zuikaku* turned for home. En route, three Zeros were shot down when ten tangled with two Avengers and a Hellcat on a search patrol. Only a few bombers found the southern carrier group and the bombing was weak and ineffectual. Nine D4Ys and six A6M5s which, unmolested, attacked the *Wasp* and *Bunker Hill* only to place their bombs well wide of the mark. Four of the dive-bombers were shot down by anti-aircraft fire. Meanwhile, the remaining forty-nine aircraft in the enemy strike force was heading for Guam. They were intercepted

Grumman F6F Hellcat of Air Group Two's VF-8 'Fighting 8' is manhandled into position for take-off from the 'Essex' class carrier USS *Bunker Hill* (CV-17), 12 October 1944 (Grumman).

by forty-one Hellcats who shot down thirty-eight aircraft in five minutes and damaged another nineteen beyond repair.

By 1600 hours the great air battles were over, although a skirmish between Hellcats of VF-15 and a dozen Zeros shortly before sunset resulted in the loss of the CO, Commander C. W. Brewer, and two of his wingmen. That night Hellcats sought further combat over Guam and Rota but the only successes went to two F6F-3Ns of VF(N)-77A from the *Essex* which shot down three enemy aircraft as they tried to take-off. A dawn raid on 20 June by Hellcats from *Essex*, *Cowpens* and *Langley*, destroyed or damaged a further thirty enemy aircraft. Clearly, the great battles on the 19th had revealed that the Japanese crews were not of the same calibre as those the US Navy pilots had confronted in the battles of the Coral Sea, Midway and the Solomons. Many who had completed their indoctrination were only half-trained and some were still under training when they flew from Japan to the battle zone. The same appears to have been true among the gunners and fighter controllers on board the carriers. Ozawa had lost 243 aircraft and over thirty damaged out of 373 which had been despatched against the American fleet, while other losses reduced the number of

survivors to just 102. Some fifty-eight land-based aircraft had also been shot down in the air and another fifty-two destroyed on the ground. Japan could not hope to replace the horrendous losses in pilots and crews, while American losses amounted to just twenty-three aircraft shot down (including fourteen Hellcats and one Dauntless) and six more lost operationally. Hellcat pilots had accounted for 250 of the enemy aircraft shot down on 19 June.

Once again in battle the opposing American and Japanese fleets, sailing 400 miles apart, never faced each other or fired their massive guns at each other. Air power had once more decided the outcome of a major battle at sea, and this time there would be no recovery for the Japanese. The US Navy had destroyed Japan's naval air power. All that remained was for Spruance to chase the Japanese carriers, narrow the 400-mile gap between them, and then, when in range, send off his bombers to destroy them too. Unfortunately, American reconnaissance aircraft could not locate the enemy fleet

Douglas SBD-5 Dauntlesses in flight. The SBD was phased out of carrier service in July 1944 but continued to see service with land-based USMC squadrons until the end of the war (McDonnell Douglas).

and Spruance was also duty-bound to protect the bridgehead on Saipan. At dawn on 20 June scouts were flown off the carriers to help aid the search, but they too drew a blank. Ozawa's force could have reached safety at this point by heading for Japan but the Japanese commander, now aboard the *Zuikaku*, believed that the majority of his missing aircraft had landed on Guam and would be ready for another strike on what was left of the American carrier force (returning crews had reported hundreds of American aircraft shot down and at least four carriers sunk). He decided to refuel and join the battle as soon as possible.

The time taken to refuel enabled Task Force 58 to close the distance sufficiently for an air strike on the enemy. At around 1600 hours an Avenger reconnaissance aircraft from the *Enterprise* sighted the Japanese fleet and radioed its position to Mitscher. They were 300 miles from the American carriers. If Mitscher sent off his aircraft immediately they could reach the seven remaining Japanese carriers, but it

would mean they would have to land back on their carriers in the dark. He pondered for a brief moment, then turned to his staff on the bridge of the *Lexington* and said, 'Launch 'em'. At about 1630 hours, fifty Helldivers, twenty-seven Dauntless dive-bombers and fifty-four Avengers, escorted by eighty-five Hellcats, took off from the carriers and headed westwards in gathering darkness.

Half-a-dozen fuel tankers were spotted first and a section of Dauntlesses from *Wasp* broke away to attack and sink two of them. The rest of the force pressed on until thirty miles ahead it sighted the Japanese fleet protected only by about forty Zero fighters. They fought well and succeeded in shooting down six Hellcats, four Avengers and ten Helldivers, but only about fifteen Zeros survived the frenetic twenty-minute air battle. Four TBM Avengers of Torpedo Squadron 24 from *Belleau Wood*, led by Ltjg George B. Brown, made runs on the *Hiyo* and two hits were thought to have been made. Brown's aircraft was so badly shot up during the low-level strike that he ordered the crew to bale out. Brown stayed with his aircraft and a wingmate tried in vain to lead him back to his carrier. Brown was last seen disappearing into cloud. The outnumbered but valiant Zero pilots could not prevent the dive-bombers causing several fires on board the *Zuikaku* either. The carrier *Chiyodan* was also ablaze and a cruiser and a battleship had also been damaged.

The American aircraft broke off their attacks and returned to their carriers, 300 miles distant. Few of the American pilots had ever made a night landing on a carrier before and hitting the rolling decks in the darkness would be well-nigh impossible. Mitscher threw caution to the wind and ordered all available lights on the carriers to be turned on to help guide the tired and over-anxious fighter and bomber pilots in. Low on fuel, they had but one chance to find the deck and land safely. Unfortunately, the assistance of searchlights, navigation lights and flight-deck floodlights and red masthead lights, was not enough and eighty aircraft either crashed on the decks or splashed into the sea. The thirsty Helldivers suffered particularly badly, and over twenty-five had to be ditched because of fuel starvation. Only five SBC2s landed back on board the carriers. The rescue services worked around the clock and managed to save the majority of pilots and crew. Overall, only forty-nine of the 209 aircrew were lost.

The Battle of The Philippine Sea, as it was officially called, ended in victory for the US Pacific Fleet in what was the last carrier battle of the Pacific War. Once again US Navy aviation had decided the outcome of the battle, which will forever be known as the 'Great Marianas Turkey Shoot'.

13,000 ton heavy cruiser *Nachi* under attack in Manila Bay on 5 November 1944. Avengers and Helldivers scored numerous hits causing 'Myoko'-class ship to sink stern first (Grumman).

A twin-engined Japanese Kamikaze aircraft narrowly misses an American carrier from CVE 71 during the Philippines campaign (Grumman).

CHAPTER 8

Battles of the Big League

The American strategic bombing offensive in the ETO (European Theatre of Operations) in World War Two was so great that the theatre became known as the 'Big League'. Many of the truly big battles took place in the ETO during 1944 when, in terms of men and machines, the US Strategic Air Forces, comprising the 8th Air Force in England and the 15th in Italy, were at their zenith. Even the names for these battles grew in stature. Now they were called 'Big Week' and 'Pointblank', while raids on Berlin became 'Big-B' or the 'Big City'.

The Luftwaffe, however, was still a force to be reckoned with, especially when one considers its highly effective night-fighter force, which in one night could destroy RAF bombers by the score, and the day-fighter Geschwaders of conventional and jet-powered fighters which could shoot down dozens of B-17s and B-24s on a single mission. Despite a highly effective fighter shield of long-range P-51 Mustangs which could accompany the bombers to their targets and back again, the USAAF was, on occasion, powerless to prevent German fighters causing carnage on a large scale as the bombers flew even deeper and in greater numbers to the far-flung targets of the Third Reich.

Operation 'Argument' was the first battle involving the mass use of bomb groups of the Strategic Air Forces. General Carl 'Tooey' Spaatz and his subordinate commanders, Major-General Jimmy Doolittle (8th Air Force) and Major-General Nathan F. Twining (15th Air Force), planned to make a series of co-ordinated raids on the German aircraft industry, supported by RAF night bombing, at the earliest possible date. Good weather finally permitted Operation 'Argument' to take place during the week 20–25 February, which quickly became known as 'Big Week'.

On 20 February 1,028 B-17s and B-24s and 832 fighters of the 8th Air Force attacked twelve aircraft plants in Germany for the loss of twenty-five bombers and four fighters. Three Medals of Honor (two posthumously) were awarded to B-17 crewmen. The 15th did not take part because it was committed to supporting the Anzio operation. Next day, 21 February, 924 bombers and 679 fighters of the 8th Air Force bombed aircraft factories at Brunswick and other targets. The 15th was grounded by bad weather. This time the 8th lost nineteen bombers and five fighters, but sixty German fighters were claimed shot down. On 22 February the 8th bombed targets in the Reich including Gotha and Schweinfurt for the loss of forty-one bombers. Meanwhile, 118 bombers in the 15th Air Force bombed the Messerschmitt assembly plant at Regensburg for the loss of fourteen aircraft. On 23 February bad weather kept the 8th Air Force heavies on the ground, but 102 bombers in the 15th Air Force destroyed twenty per cent of the ball-bearing works at Steyr, Austria. On 24 February, 114 B-17s and B-24s of the 15th Air Force returned to Steyr. Seventeen bombers failed to return. Meanwhile, 231 Fortresses in the 1st Division, 8th Air Force, attacked Schweinfurt, losing eleven B-17s, while 236 B-17s in the 3rd Division struck at targets on the Baltic coast without loss. Some 239 B-24s in the 2nd Bomb Division headed for the Messerschmitt 110 assembly plant at Gotha. Flak was heavy over Holland and the B-24s encountered repeated attacks by the Luftwaffe.

The arrival of three Thunderbolt groups just after 1200 hours was unable to beat off attacks by over 150 enemy fighters, and five of the 445th's twenty-eight Liberators were shot down in almost as many minutes. The enemy fighters continued to attack all the way to the target and four more 445th B-24s were shot down. P-51s and P-38s took over from the flagging Thunderbolts near Hannover and covered the Liberators as they neared the target. Major Myron H. Keilman, deputy lead pilot in the 392nd

Bomb Group, recalls: 'Luftwaffe fighters made attempts to penetrate our formations but our 'little friends' kept them at a distance and, when the opportunity prevailed, dove in for a 'kill'. Using our thick vapour trails as a screen, the Germans often struck from below and from behind to shoot up any lagging bomber. Bending south-eastwards towards Gotha, the white, snowy earth looked cold and lifeless; only the large communities, rail lines and an autobahn stood out in relief. Fighter attacks became more persistent. By the time we reached our IP (Initial Point) to start our bomb run, the sky about our three squadrons was full of busy P-38s and P-51s fending off the Germans. They dove past the lead ship in pursuit of Messerschmitts and Focke Wulfs making head-on attacks. Our gunners got in a lot of shooting, too. The staccato of the turrets' twin fifties vibrated throughout the airplane. It was real scary.'

Some confusion arose in the Liberators' ranks at the IP when the 389th lead navigator suffered oxygen failure and veered off course. The bombardier slumped over his bomb sight and accidentally tripped the bombs. Before the small 445th formation reached the target its tenth and eleventh victims fell to the German guns. By now the 445th consisted of only fourteen Liberators, three having

On 24 February 1944 Thunderbolt close escort fighters were unable to beat off attacks by over 150 enemy fighters, and losses among the Liberator groups en route to Gotha were high. P-47Ds like this one, *Angel Eyes*, from the 356th Fighter Group (tucked under the starboard wing of a 458th Bomb Group B-24 – which group made its bombing debut this day), covered the heavies until the longer-range P-51s and P-38s took over escort duty deeper into enemy territory (Author).

aborted before entering Germany. Another 445th B-24 was shot down just after leaving Eisenach. The thirteen remaining 445th B-24s, realizing that they had veered off course, continued alone. They arrived over the target at 1325 hours and executed an eight-minute bomb run. Some 180 500-pounders dropped from 12,000 feet inflicted heavy damage on the Me 110 plant. A further 171 B-24s dropped another 468 tons of assorted bombs from varying altitudes and directions. The 445th's thirteenth B-24 was shot down moments after 'bombs away!' The 392nd Bomb Group released ninety-eight per cent of its bombs within 2,000 feet of the aiming point. Intelligence sources later estimated that six to seven weeks' production of Me 110s was lost. Myron Keilman wrote: 'The bombs were smack 'on target' but the battle wasn't over. No sooner had the wing left the target's flak than we were accosted by

On the 24 February mission Lockheed P-38 Lightnings took over escort duties from P-47 Thunderbolts near Hannover and covered the Liberators as they flew on to the Messerschmitt 110 assembly plant at Gotha (via Mike Bailey).

German fighters again. Strung out and with some planes slowing down from flak damage, our three squadrons became vulnerable to vicious attacks. For the next hour and more, Messerschmitt, Focke Wulf and Junkers fighters worked us over until our fighters could fend them off.

'As deputy command pilot, I frequently changed off flying formation with the airplane commander to keep occupied and not to have to watch the Jerries press their blazing gun attacks. The interphone was alive with excited calls of enemy action. Head-on passes and tail attack – in singles and in 'gaggles' – rockets, 20mm cannon, and even some cables were thrown at us. Seven of our B-24s were shot down. Many of us were shot up, but it was not all one-sided. The gunners of the twenty-two airplanes that returned accounted for sixteen German fighters.' Only thirteen Liberators in the 445th returned to Tibenham and six 389th Liberators were also lost. Both the 445th and 392nd Bomb Groups were later awarded Presidential Unit Citations for their part in the raid.

On 25 February the USSTAF brought the curtain down on 'Big Week' when 1,300 8th and 15th Air Force bombers and 1,000 fighters were despatched

Two B-24 Liberators of the 445th Bomb Group in formation fly below a line of vapour trails left by a flight of seven friendly fighters flying high cover. Lack of close fighter support on 24 February led to nine 445th Liberators being shot down by enemy fighters before the target, and after veering off course the group lost three more B-24s to the German defences. Almost the same sequence of events, with even more catastrophic results, was to dog the 445th six months later on 27 September, when the group strayed from the briefed track to Kassel (USAF).

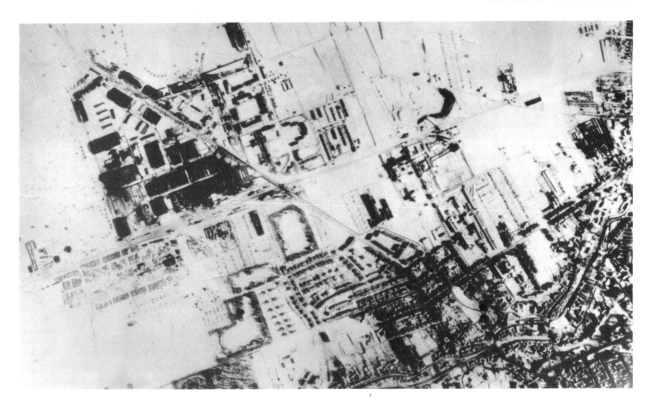

to aircraft plants, ball-bearing works and components factories throughout the Reich. The 1st Bomb Division caused heavy damage to the Messerschmitt plants at Augsburg, and the ball-bearing plants at Stuttgart were also bombed. The 2nd Bomb Division bombed the Me 110 components plant at Fürth and very considerable damage was caused to the Me 109 plants at Regensburg by the 3rd Bomb Division and 176 bombers of the 15th Air Force. The latter hit the aircraft plants an hour before the England-based force arrived over the city. Output at both Augsburg and Regensburg was severely reduced for four months following the raids. The 8th lost thirty-one bombers while the 15th Air Force lost thirty-three bombers. The intensity of the battles of 'Big Week' can be judged by total losses of some 226 bombers.

Less than a week later the USAAF launched its first attack on 'Big-B' – Berlin. The 3 March attack was aborted because of bad weather and the following day only the B-17s in the 95th and 100th Bomb Groups defied the elements. They dropped the first American bombs on the 'Big City'. On 6 March the 8th despatched 730 heavies and almost 800 escort fighters to targets in the suburbs of Berlin. American gunners claimed over 170 German

This dramatic photograph of the Messerschmitt Bf 110 assembly plant at Gotha standing out in the snow-covered terrain was taken shortly before bombs from Liberators of the 2nd Bomb Division tumbled down from 12,000 feet. Some 98 per cent of the bombs dropped by the 392nd Bomb Group landed within 2,000 feet of the MPI (Myron Keilman).

fighters destroyed but the 8th lost a record sixty-three bombers and eleven fighters, while 102 bombers were seriously damaged. On 8 March the 8th Air Force despatched 600 bombers and 200 escort fighters to the VKF ball-bearing plant at Erkner in the suburbs of Berlin. The leading 3rd Division lost thirty-seven Fortresses to fighter attacks. Altogether, the 8th Air Force attacked Berlin on five occasions in March 1944. On the 22 March raid on 'Big-B', 800 bombers were despatched.

From February to May almost all raids were in support of the Allied invasion of Europe, beginning on 1 May with a series of all-out attacks on the enemy's rail network in support of the Pointblank directive, when 1,328 8th Air Force bombers struck at targets in France and Belgium. After D-Day, 6 June, the USAAF continued to dominate the skies over Europe, but individual group losses mounted. On 7 August 1944 the 492nd Bomb Group in the 2nd

Bomb Division was withdrawn from combat having lost fifty-four aircraft between May and July 1944. This was the heaviest loss for any B-24 group for a three-month period. The 491st Bomb Group moved from the 45th Combat Wing to take the place of the 492nd in the 14th Combat Wing. By the autumn of 1944 oil targets had assumed top priority. The synthetic oil refineries at Merseberg in Leuna were attacked on at least eighteen occasions in 1944. On the final raid, on 30 November, twenty-nine American bombers and forty fighters were shot down. Between late August and early September, the Liberators transported supplies to the Allied ground forces in France and to the Allied airborne divisions involved in Operation 'Market Garden'. On 27 September the Liberators of the 2nd Bomb Division got back to the bombing war with sad results. The B-17s of the 1st and 3rd Bomb Divisions would head for oil targets and engineering centres at Cologne, Ludwigshaven and Mainz, while 315 B-24s went to the Henschel engine and vehicle assembly plants at Kassel in central Germany.

1/Lt Raphael E. Carrow, the pilot, poses in the cockpit of his B-24J 42-110022 *Patches* in the 700th Bomb Squadron, which was shot down on 27 September (via Mike Bailey).

The day began like many other days in England. Solid cloud overhead in the morning showed signs of probable rainfall but groups put up a mission as scheduled. The 445th Bomb Group was used to days like this. However, in a few hours the combat crews were to learn that this was not just another day. It would be one which would live forever as one of the most tragic and probably the most disastrous raid for a single group in the history of American air warfare. Some thirty-nine Liberators taxied out at Tibenham, but Lt Rene J. Schneider's B-24 ran off the perimeter track and cut a tyre and took no further part in the mission. Crews sat impatiently in their cramped Liberators on the runway, waiting for a long time for better weather before they got the green light. Then, at 30-second intervals, each roared down the runway, lights on, slowly climbing into the pre-dawn darkness.

At 15,000 feet the sun was shining brightly in the blue sky. Flares of red-green, at regular intervals, were fired from the Zebra ship – the gaudily painted, stripped-down old B-24 used as an assembly ship – as it continually circled to allow the 445th to form up on its tail. In the distance, other Zebras were firing green-green, green-red or red-red, as they too circled in their patch of the sky. The group formed into a whole and took its place at the head of the 2nd Combat Wing. The wing joined the rest of the 2nd Bomb Division assembly line, which stretched for sixty miles, and headed for Kassel. Lt McLelland in *Tahelenbak*, Lt Frost, and *Heavenly Body*, flown by Lt Wilkins, aborted with various mechanical problems and returned to England. The remaining thirty-three Liberators flew on and made landfall at the Dutch coast before proceeding uneventfully towards Kassel. Lt Raphael E. Carrow, the pilot of *Patches*, in the 700th, lead squadron, noted: 'The crew didn't talk much on the intercom. We were already old hands. This was our twenty-first mission. Only four more to finish the tour. Mostly, we were anticipating the leave which would be due to us before returning to the States for reassignment. Occasionally, we listened to the chatter on the receiver. A group of American fighters somewhere were engaging with the Germans. Our own fighter escort was comfortingly nearby.'

2/Lt George M. Collar, a bombardier, had finished twenty-eight missions and was supposed to leave on a three-day pass that fateful 27 September, but a young bombardier by the name of Aarvig, from Chicago, failed to return from his pass and Collar had to take his place aboard 2/Lt James W. Schaen's ship. He remembers: 'As we approached the IP, we could see the Kassel flak coming up in a blanket and bursting at our altitude. At the group IP we were to turn downwind in a more easterly direction. Suddenly, before we got to the IP, the lead plane in the lead squadron [flown by Capt. John H. Chilton with Major Donald W. McCoy, the 700th Squadron CO, aboard] made a left turn and the whole group followed. At this point, our navigator, Corman Bean, said over the intercom, 'That Mickey man in the lead ship has screwed up. We shouldn't have turned yet.' By the time the lead pilot discovered the mistake, it was too late to turn back on course, as all the other groups following us were in the way as they proceeded to the correct IP. At this point we would have been okay (in my judgement) if the lead pilot had circled 360 degrees and followed the last group in, but he made a snap judgement to continue on an easterly course, and bomb the town of Göttingen, which lies about twenty miles north-east of Kassel.

'We got to Göttingen and dropped the bombs, using PFF through solid cloud cover, but they fell in open fields half a mile short of the town. Unfortunately we lost our fighter escort. At this point our leader made another error in judgement (in my opinion). Instead of getting out of there and

Luftwaffe pilots of II/JG 300, one of three assault group or *Sturmgruppen* used against the Liberators on 27 September, discuss tactics (Heinz J. Nowarra).

making a beeline for England, his army-trained mind followed the original plan for Kassel, which was to bomb downwind from the north-west, hit the target, then turn south for about fifty miles, then turn west and cross the Rhine near Koblenz and head for friendly territory in France before proceeding back to England. He turned us south from Göttingen with the intention of flying south to a line which would bring us back towards Koblenz. Of course, by this time we were 100 miles behind everyone else, with no fighter escort.'

The 445th had flown into an area a few miles from Eisnach where three assault groups, or 'Sturmgruppen' (II/Jagdgeschwader 4, IV/Jagdgeschwader 3 'Udet' and II/Jagdgeschwader 300), each with a strength of around thirty FW 190s, were forming for an attack. The FW 190 A8/R

Focke Wulf 190-A8/Rs of II/JG 300. The 'Rammbock' (Rammer) or 'Sturmbock' (Battering Ram) fighter was heavily armed and fitted with heavy armour plate for combat with American bombers (Heinz J. Nowarra).

Staffelkapitän Oskar Romm of Sturm IV/JG 3 'Udet', who shot down three 445th Bomb Group Liberators in a single attack on the 27 September mission to Kassel (Heinz J. Nowarra).

fighters – also called 'Rammbock' (Rammer) or 'Sturmbock' (Battering Ram) – were specially equipped with two heavy MG 131 30mm cannon and four MG 151/20 20mm machine-guns and heavy armour plate which could deflect the American .50 calibre bullets with ease. In addition, three 'cover' groups – I, III/JG4 and I/JG300 – were equipped with Bf 109s and were to pick off any badly damaged stragglers left by the FW 190s. The fighters had been directed by radio by the 1st Fighter Division at Doeberitz, but, much to the chagrin of the ground commander, the Luftwaffe pilots at first failed to see any bombers. Then they did. The 'Sturmgruppen' attacked at about 1003 hours in three waves, each wave with fighters in line abreast, from the rear and with cannon and machine-guns blazing.

Leo P. Pouliot, co-pilot in Lt Jackson C. Mercer's B-24 in the 703rd Bomb Squadron, which was flying

Messerschmitt Bf 109G-6/R3, similar to ones which equipped I and II/JG 4 and I/JG 300 at the time of the air battle on 27 September 1944 (Heinz J. Nowarra).

low left, wrote: 'The tail gunner of Cecil J. Isom's ship [*Patty Girl*] to our right started to fire at something. Then I noticed that small white puffs were appearing throughout the formation, and realized that we were being jumped by enemy fighters.' The Liberators stood little chance from the Germans' cannon and heavy machine-guns at close range, and the explosive effects of their shells in the poorly armoured bombers were devastating. In less than five minutes the Luftwaffe fighters decimated the 445th Bomb Group, shooting down no fewer than twenty-two Liberators in the space of just three minutes, and three more in the following three minutes. Three of the bombers were shot down in one single attack by Staffelkapitän Oskar Romm of Sturm IV/JG 3 'Udet'. Attacks by Ernst Schröeder, a pilot in II JG/Sturm 300, were also successful, as he recalls: 'When we approached the bombers in a closed formation, suddenly some of these large aircraft started to catch fire, some even blew up. This

Three Mustang groups, including the 361st Fighter Group, seen here on an escort mission, tried valiantly to rescue the 445th Bomb Group during the Kassel battle, and in a brief fight they did shoot down a few enemy fighters. One of the 361st fighter pilots intercepted Ernst Schröeder's FW 190 at low altitude and duelled with the Luftwaffe pilot, and another, 2/Lt Leo H. Lamb, died when he collided with a FW 190 (Author).

led us to believe that other German fighter formations had attacked the Americans before us. But then it was very quickly our turn. My squadron leader and I had had a test gyro-sight installed in our aircraft. With the aid of this sighting mechanism I was able to down two B-24s within seconds. The [first] aircraft turned on its side and plunged. Also, the neighbouring machine was already smoking from a previous attack. Both left engines were burning. I only needed to change aim to shoot again then this one stood in bright flames. The new aiming device was functioning astonishingly. I was so surprised and fascinated that I flew alongside my victim and stared at the metre-high flames which were pouring out of this Liberator all the way back beyond the elevator. Then this great machine clumsily laid itself over on its back and went down.'

The B-24 pilots put out frantic calls for help on the Fighter Channel. Leo Pouliot started to call for some of the escort. 'I called Balanc 3-1, 3-2 and 3-3 and was answered immediately. I told them we were having trouble. They asked our position and I switched the jackbox to interphone to get our position from Milton Fandler, the navigator. Then our plane got several hits in the waist and the radio was knocked out.' Immediately, two Mustang groups covering the 3rd Division, seventy-five miles away near

U/Ofz Ernst Schröeder of II/JG 300 in the cockpit of his FW 190-8/R8 Kolle alaaf. Schröeder downed two B-24s of the 445th Bomb group on 27 September (Ernst Schröeder).

Frankfurt, and the 361st Fighter Group, escorting the 1st Division 100 miles distant, were speeding to the rescue. However, six precious minutes were to elapse before the 361st Fighter Group could reach the beleaguered 445th Bomb Group and the other two P-51 groups arrived after the enemy had departed. One of the 361st fighter pilots intercepted Ernst Schröeder's FW 190 at low altitude and duelled with the Luftwaffe pilot. Schröeder wrote: 'After passing each other, we both turned our aircraft around and headed at each other with blazing guns. During the first approach I received two hits in the tail unit. During the second approach, my guns failed. Evidently, I had used up all my ammunition when firing at the two bombers, or my guns were jamming – I no longer know exactly what happened. We made about four or five more frontal passes at each other, but all that was left for me to do in order not to get hit again was to take evasive action. After the last frontal approach of the American I finally 'hugged' the ground and was lucky enough to escape – most likely because of the camouflage paint on my aircraft, 'Red 19 – Kolle-alaaf!' [Cologne-aloft, because Schröeder was born in Cologne].'

Meanwhile, B-24 crews were fighting for their lives. The sky was filled with exploding shells and burning and exploding aircraft. Crews later estimated that there were between 100 and 150 attacking fighters. They ripped through the four squadrons in the 445th with ease. William R. Dewey, pilot of *Wallet A-Abel* in the 701st Squadron, wrote: 'Our tail gunner, Ruben Montanez, yelled: 'I see fighters, I see flak.' Then the entire plane began to shudder and shake with the guns in the rear of the plane firing simultaneously, and from the impact of 20mm and 30mm enemy shells. As our plane continued to shake, my co-pilot, Bill Boykin, pointed out of his side window at B-24s in the other squadrons going down on fire, and enemy fighters exploding. Our intercom went out to the waist and tail within seconds. Our top turret gunner, Charley Craig, reported that there were five enemy fighters on our tail for a few moments. I could see the tail gunner in our squadron and element lead motioning for us to tuck in closer so he could get better shots at the 109s and 190s.' Leo Pouliot, looking to the right, saw 'just plain Hell. Planes were going down – some in flames, others just exploding. The air was full of 20mm shells. I thought the whole

German Air Force was in the air at the same time.'

In the leading 700th Bomb Squadron formation, none of the ten aircraft made it back to England. 2/Lt William S. Bruce, pilot of *Bonnie Vee*, wrote: 'It was just unbelievable how many enemy fighters came at us in large groups, sitting at the back of us and below us, and shooting the living hell out of us. They had their wheels down, stayed in formation and raked us steadily with machine-gun fire and 30mm cannon. It was just a hopeless situation – there were just too many of them. I saw at least seven ships go down in flames: four of our group and several German ships. Our fighters were nowhere in sight. I could not understand where the hell they could be.'

The lead ship (a 703rd Squadron B-24) and five other Liberators were blasted out of the sky. Sergeant Tom G. Spera, the photo-observer aboard *Terrible Terry's Terror*, piloted by 1/Lt William F. Hunter, wrote: 'The leading Liberator, on fire from nose to tail, came swinging towards us like a severely wounded animal, then peeled away as if to pick a spot away from us to die. The next bomber moved up in its place. One Liberator with two engines on fire on the left wing came up from below us to explode when it had reached our level. A human form fell out of the orange-coloured ball of fire. As he fell through space without parachute or harness, he reached up as if to grasp at something.' William Bruce continues: 'Our ship, *Bonnie Vee*, had been hit several times – two engines were on fire and the interior of the plane was in a shambles. The gunners kept firing but finally they were all wounded or dead. At this time I knew we were in serious trouble with no hope of flying any longer. I finally gave the bale-out order because at this moment only one engine was running, and not too well at that. I asked my co-pilot to unbuckle my seat-belts before he baled out. Just as he stood up to do so a 30mm cannon shell cut him in half.

'I really knew it was the end of our flight. The right wing was rammed by a German fighter, tearing it off. Next, the left wing blew up and only the fuselage remained. We were then at 19,000 feet. It must have just exploded because the next thing I knew I was clear of the plane and hurting very, very much.' Bruce (only one other member of his crew survived) had broken his neck and his right pelvis and badly damaged his right shoulder. After capture, German officers fractured his jaw with a

pistol butt. Almost totally paralysed and black and blue all over, Bruce spent three days on a train which took captured airmen to Frankfurt interrogation centre, and then another week on a train before his severe injuries were at last treated by a German doctor. Bruce was finally sent to Stalag Luft III, Sagan.

Other lead squadron B-24s followed *Bonnie Vee* down. *Mairzy Doats*, flown by 2/Lt Edward T. Hautman, managed to crash-land near Bassenheim, while *Bugs Bunnie*, flown by Lt R. V. Heitz, made it to Belgium and crashed fifteen miles east of Brussels. *Patches*, flown by 1/Lt Raphael E. Carrow, was not as fortunate. Carrow explains: 'I noticed an unusual red glow in the sky around us. As I turned my head to the right, through my co-pilot's window, I saw a parachute floating down. Then the plane in front of us burst into flames. Other parachutes appeared on all sides. Suddenly, a FW 190 swooped in front of us from underneath and behind. At the same time my arm was being

B-24H 42-9810 *Terrible Terry's Terror* in the 700th Bomb Squadron, which was piloted by 1/Lt William F. Hunter on the Kassel raid and crash-landed near Lille after being badly shot up by enemy fighters (via Mike Bailey).

Sgts Knox (left) and Baldwin (right) pose in front of *Bugs Bunnie*, in the 700th Bomb Squadron, which was flown by Lt R. V. Heitz on the Kassel mission. The aircraft made it to Belgium and crashed fifteen miles east of Brussels (via Mike Bailey).

pounded by my co-pilot, Newell Brainard. One engine was on fire; while working to feather the prop, other German fighters came into view. All around us was on fire . . . black smoke . . . planes going down . . . more parachutes . . . machine-guns firing . . . the shudder of 20mm shells hitting . . . another engine gone . . . intercom out . . . plane out of control . . . a gripping fear – near panic . . . then, fire! The bomb bay was a roaring inferno. Our route of escape was blocked. On the flight-deck behind me the radio operator stood petrified, fascinated, staring into the flames. Brainard quickly got out of his seat. I never saw either again. [It is possible Brainard was one of at least nine airmen who landed in or near the village of Nentershausen who were murdered or executed by German civilians, and in one case, by a German soldier home on leave].

'Now I had to find a way out but I was frozen to the seat! The simple task of unbuckling the seat-belt, removing my flak vest and Mae West, became major problems. The plane was now completely out of control. All possible means of escape raced through my head. Each one presented an alternative death. There seemed to be no way out. Finally, free, I arose from my seat in the falling plane and as I faced the rear, instead of the expected inferno, I saw the blue sky. The plane had broken in two and the other half had taken the fire with it.' Carrow baled out and landed in a field near a group of buildings surrounded by a high fence. A German soldier who apprehended him, pointed a rifle at the American and asked, 'Jude?' Carrow landed near a slave labour camp.

Terrible Terry's Terror was also hit. Tom Spera wrote: 'A 20mm shell tore through the bomb bay, ripping off the doors and severing fuel lines. Two fires started simultaneously in the bay. What strange mystery of fate kept us from exploding, I'll never, never be able to fathom. The engineer, T/Sgt Robert Ratchford, threw off his parachute, grabbed a fire extinguisher and put both fires out before the 100 octane gas had been ignited. Then we attended to the gas leaks from which fuel was pouring out like water from a fire hydrant. Gasoline had saturated the three of us in the ship's waist and we all had a difficult time moving about. The two waist gunners were slipping and sliding as they sighted their guns. A large puddle of gasoline accumulated on the camera hatch, blown in by the slipstream outside.

'A bullet from a Focke Wulf probably saved my life. My oxygen mask had become disconnected and before I realized it I was losing consciousness. A 20mm shell came through the waist above the head of waist gunner S/Sgt Joseph K. Selser, and caused S/Sgt Robert J. Cannon, to look around from his position at the right waist gun, notice my trouble and connect the oxygen line again. I gained consciousness to find the battle continuing. One wave of enemy fighters followed another, until after six minutes the attacks ceased as suddenly as they had started. In spite of the loss of one engine, our ship managed to keep in contact with the others for a while. When the navigator, 2/Lt Robert M. Kaems, informed us that we had reached friendly lines, the sickening feeling relaxed its hold in the pit of my stomach, but a dry muddy taste remained in my mouth. It proved impossible to stay with the other bombers for long and an escort of P-51 Mustangs picked us up in answer to a call from the radio operator, T/Sgt Jake S. Monzingo. We were approaching a landing field in northern France [near Lille] when the second engine on our left wing cut out and a third engine spat and sputtered. Those of us in the waist rushed to crash-landing positions in the nick of time. Hunter cleared a clump of trees by inches, clipped a set of high-tension wires, and brought the ship down on a potato patch, skilfully jumping several ditches, only to have one wheel catch in a hole, buckle, and dig the right wing into the ground. We all took a severe bouncing but our only casualty was a cut hand for the bombardier, 2/Lt George E. Smith.' Hunter's crew, which had come down at Willems, near Lille, returned to England and the majority of them were killed on a raid on 9 March 1945.

The 702nd Bomb Squadron, which was flying high right, also contained ten ships. Aboard the PFF lead ship radar, Frank J. Bertram, the lead navigator, sat just behind Capt. Reginald R. Miner, the pilot, facing the rear of the aircraft and could see the battle through a small side window. He observed: 'After [the group] veered off course I immediately informed Miner, who passed the word on to the group leader. Shortly thereafter we were advised to 'keep it together' and stay with our lead squadron. It is my opinion – I'm not alone – that the lead ship deliberately ignored all calls from the rest of the group regarding the navigational error. The target was visible – not so much on the ground, but the intense flak clearly indicated where we should have been heading. It is just hard to believe that two radar ships could be off. The third radar ship (which was ours) had no such trouble. The city of Kassel made a much larger blip on radar than the town of Göttingen – which we also missed.'

The prescribed turns scattered the 702nd Squadron all over the sky, and they were easy prey for the enemy fighters. Frank Bertram looked out his side window and saw 'little puffs of black about the size of basketballs'. He thought it was a new kind of flak. FW 190s then 'rained destruction upon all our ships practically at once'. Only Lt Stanley E. Krivik's B-24 made it back to England, where it crash-landed in Norfolk. The rest, including *Roughhouse Kate*, flown by 2/Lt Howard A. Jones, *Our Gal*, flown by 2/Lt Leslie E. Warman, *Eileen*, piloted by Lt Donald E. Brent, *Fort Worth Maid*, flown by 1/Lt Carl J. Sollien and *King Kong*, flown by Lt James C. Baynham, were shot down in fierce fighter attacks. Three members of Baynham's crew were murdered by German civilians. Bertram continues: 'Our ship was hit, and hit badly. Why it didn't blow up is a mystery. We took severe blows with shells going through the ship, explosions, fire, direct hits on vital parts . . . Virgil China, the co-pilot, and Joseph H.

Guilfoil, the radio operator, were killed. The rest of us baled out. As I floated down, the sky looked like a paratroop invasion, with 'chutes all over the place.

Aboard 1/Lt James W. Schaen's ship, the bombardier, 2/Lt George M. Collar, who had originally flown in Miner's crew, describes their same sad demise: 'A wolf pack of FW 190s came out of the high clouds behind us, and hit us so fast that our tail gunner never got to call them. He and the two waist gunners must have been hit almost immediately. The top gunner, Eppley, got in a few shots as he watched the 20mm shells hitting the top of the fuselage and crawling towards him. I was in the front turret and wondered what those small flak bursts directly in front of us were. I soon found out as there was an explosion directly under the turret, which blew out all the controls for the turret and the guns.

Capt. Reginald Miner's original crew, 702nd Bomb Squadron, 445th Bomb Group. Front row, *left to right:* Frank Bertram; Virgil China (KIA 27 September); Reg Miner; George M. Collar (who flew with Lt Jim Schaen's crew on 27 September). Back row, *left to right:* Art Lambesson; Larry Bowers; R. M. Ault; James E. Weddel (who after being wounded on a previous mission was sent home and replaced by Joe Gilfoil – KIA 27 September); M. C. Thornton; Alvin O. Hitchens (Frank Bertram).

I was helpless as the FW 190 streaked past. He couldn't have cleared us by more than six feet. We were in the high right squadron and I could see the fighters attacking the lead squadron like a swarm of bees. At this time I heard the bale-out bell ringing, so I got out of the turret and found Corman Bean, the navigator, putting on his 'chute. The whole nose compartment looked like a sieve. Those exploding 20mm shells had blown up right between us but neither of us were hit. By this time we were nosing down and the whole left wing was on fire. We opened the nose wheel door and baled out.

'In the meantime, Sgt Eppley was still firing from the Martin turret and failed to hear the bale-out bell. He happened to look down and saw the pilot coming out of the cockpit and starting across the flight-deck, so he decided it was time to leave. He followed the pilot down into the bomb bay. Imagine his surprise when he found the bomb bay doors closed. Schaen was going up the tunnel towards the nose following the radioman and the co-pilot. Eppley automatically reached for the bomb door handle and to his surprise, the doors opened, so he went out there. He was no sooner out than the ship blew up. We learned later that the radioman, Sgt Collins, and the co-pilot, Bobby McGough, got out, but were wounded. Unfortunately, Jim Schaen never made it. He left a wife and baby. We never found out why the men didn't go out of the bomb bay as they were supposed to. Perhaps the first one down pulled the handle the wrong way and thought the doors were stuck.' Schaen's B-24 went down 800 metres south of Forstgut Berlitzgrube, and Collar was among five of the crew who were captured.

The 701st Bomb Squadron, which was flying high-high right, had also started out with ten B-24s. Bill Dewey wrote: 'As suddenly as it started, it was all over – maybe three to five minutes in all. Only seven planes remained at that moment to form on the one surviving PFF plane, so our squadron leader became the group leader.' *Heavenly Body*, piloted by Lt Wilkins, and *Ole Baldy*, flown by 2/Lt William F. Golden, were shot out of the sky. *Little Audrey*, piloted by 2/Lt Donald N. Reynolds, was badly shot up and crash-landed south-west of Koblenz, while Lt Edgar N. Walther's ship exploded in the air. Walther, who was wearing a back-pack, was thrown clear and awoke in a German prison hospital suffering from leg and arm wounds, concussion and amnesia. He was the only survivor. *Sweetest Rose of Texas*, piloted by Lt Swofford, and another ship, flown by Lt D. W. Smith, made it back to Tibenham.

Bill Dewey's ship was in trouble too. 'Our nose gunner, Les Medlock, reported more fighters coming at us from eleven o'clock low. Thank God, they were ours. Since the intercom was out, I sent the co-pilot back to the waist to report on damage. When he came back, Boykin, a tough ex-football player and former cavalryman, was shaken. The tail turret had caught fire from direct hits by 20mm cannon. Both waist gunners and the tail gunner were wounded and bloody. There was a huge hole in the right waist ahead of the window and the left waist window was shattered. Control cables to the tail were partially damaged and the twin vertical rudders were frayed and appeared to be disintegrating. Looking out of the co-pilot's window, we could see a three-foot hole in the upper surface of the wing behind the no.3 engine, where 100 octane gasoline was splashing out. The hydraulic fluid fire in the tail turret was quickly extinguished. There was no oxygen and the electric flying suits were inoperative at the waist positions. The navigator, Herb Bailey, took over the nose turret, while Medlock made numerous trips, carrying portable oxygen bottles, from the front of the ship to the two wounded waist gunners and slightly wounded tail gunner. He covered them with his jacket and applied first aid. Fortunately, our VHF radio performed perfectly. I made several calls to the new group leader, asking him to slow to 160 mph, because our ship was shaking and shuddering like it was about to break apart.' Dewey and Boykin nursed their ailing B-24 to Manston and landed safely.

The 703rd and fourth Squadron, which was flying low left in the formation, had reached the target with nine ships but the German fighters attacked again in line abreast. Leo P. Pouliot, in Lt. Mercer's ship, observed that 'the first pass that they made took most of the squadron with them'. Six ships, including *Fridget Bridget*, piloted by Lt Joseph E. Johnson, were shot down.

One of the first four or five to be lost was *Hot Rock*, piloted by Lt William J. Mowat. Theodore J. Myers, the top turret gunner, looked into the bomb bay and saw several large streams of fuel shooting down into the bomb bay doors. Myers wrote: 'A mist of gasoline was floating forward onto the flight deck.

B-24H 42-51105 *Sweetest Rose of Texas* in the 701st Bomb Squadron, which survived the Kassel battle and returned safely to Tibenham with Lt Swofford's crew (Author).

The first thing that entered my mind was to try to stop the gas flow. If those shells ever entered the ship, the ship would explode. So I climbed down into the bomb bay to look at the holes in the gasoline tanks, hoping they would seal themselves. The holes were too large to seal up, so I decided to open the bomb bay doors to let the slipstream blow it out of the ship. During that time I got soaked from head to foot with gas. The slipstream started to clear up the inside. I turned around to get on the flight-deck (all of this took less than a minute) to tell the pilot we had been hit bad and were losing gas fast. Before I could move one or more 20mm shells went off under my feet, wounding me in the right foot and both legs. The blow lifted me up and hurt my back as I fell on my back on the catwalk. Then I saw a blinding flash and I was on fire from head to foot. I felt my face burning and that was all I remembered was I thought I was dying.' Myers regained consciousness to find himself hanging in his parachute. 'The slipstream had blown out the fire. My face was so badly burned that I could only see out of my left eye. I saw a big streaming mass go by me about 200 or 300 feet away. I am sure the ship exploded about that time.' Myers and Frank T. Plesa, the tail gunner, who was also badly wounded

and burned and blown out of the B-24, were reunited in a German hospital.

Leo Pouliot, in Lt Mercer's B-24, noted: 'In the 703rd only Isom's and our ship was left. There was no-one to protect us from the rear. Enemy fighters were all over the sky. Our plane was shaking like a leaf in a good blizzard from the guns, all firing at the same time. On the right a B-24 with its number three tank on fire blew up and three of the men got out of the waist. The air was full of the debris of burning planes and 'chutes. Some of the boys pulled their 'chutes too quickly and the silk caught on fire. They went plummeting to the earth.

'The enemy was having a time of it also. On my right, where the fight was occurring, I saw a FW 190 going down. It flew into another in a death spin that crashed into yet a third. The whole scene was unreal and unbelievable. Meanwhile, our nose gunner, Ted Hoite, was frantically busy keeping the fighters off Isom's tail. His plane was slightly higher than ours and a little to the right. FW 190s were coming up from beneath and trying to get him from the belly.

One of them stalled out in front of us and immediately Hoite was upon him with his guns blazing and the turret shaking from the long burst that he was giving the Boche. The enemy plane just hung there trying to pump Isom's ship with 20mm shells. But Hoite was the better man with his .50s. The fighter caught fire, fell over on its back and went down to disappear in the clouds. Another fighter came up under the tail of Isom's ship but could not get to him. So he swung around hard to his left and came in at us at two o'clock with all his guns going. It seemed that his whole wing was on fire. I thought at that moment that we had had it. But our top turret man, Kenneth Kribs, turned his turret around in a violent manoeuvre and took on the attacking plane. Our plane shook from the long burst that Kribs was pulling. The Nazi plane kept on coming closer and closer and Kribs kept on shooting. Then suddenly the fighter disappeared in a cloud of debris.

'An attack came in from the left waist and I could feel several hits, which destroyed our controls, shot off our rudder, hit our hydraulic reservoir, and hit several of the oxygen bottles in the waist. Jack switched on the C-I Automatic Pilot and we got in with what was left of the formation. There were only four of us. We waited for another attack but none came.' Mercer's crew and Isom's ship both made it back to England; *Patty Girl* landing at Tibenham and Mercer making it to Manston. Even the intervention of the 361st Fighter Group's P-51 Mustangs was not enough to prevent the destruction of the 445th, although, in a brief battle, they did manage to shoot down a few enemy fighters. One 361st pilot, 2/Lt Leo H. Lamb, died when he collided with a FW 190. Altogether, twenty-nine enemy fighters were shot down by the American fighters and bombers and eighteen German pilots were killed.

The 445th had lost twenty-five bombers shot down and five more had crashed over France and England. Only five made it back to England. It proved the highest group loss in 8th Air Force history. There were 236 empty seats in the mess halls at Tibenham that evening. Altogether, the 445th lost 117 men killed and forty-five officers and thirty-six enlisted men had been made prisoners of war. Some, like Eppley, Lt Somers and George Collar, were first ordered by the Germans to collect the burnt and charred remains of their colleagues from the crashed aircraft. Collar had landed close to the village of Lauchroeden near Eisenach and had been forced to run the gauntlet of a lynch mob determined to beat the 'Americanishe Terrorflieger' to death. A irate farmer broke Collar's nose and blackened both his eyes and a younger man kicked him before he was finally rescued by the village Burgomeister and a policeman. Collar wrote: 'In an orchard, there lying on the ground, was the body of one of our fliers. The victim had obviously been blown out of the plane as he landed without a 'chute. Every bone in his body was broken. His name was Lt Bateman, a member of the crew of Lt Johnson in the 703rd Bomb Squadron. We travelled up and down the hills and forests all day, picking up approximately a dozen bodies, some of them horribly mangled. In the middle of an open field, we came across a radioman named Joe Guilfoil, who was a friend of Sgt Eppley. He had a bad leg wound but came down in his 'chute. He was lying in a pool of blood and was dead. One of the bodies we picked up was Lt Martin Geiszler. After the war I had the painful duty of confirming his death to his parents. Unfortunately, some of the men we picked up were not wearing their tags so their loved ones never knew for sure. In one of the burning wrecks we saw several more bodies but we couldn't recover them. That night when we returned to the village, we left the wagons containing the bodies at the cemetery, unhitched the horses, and walked to the village pump. We hadn't had anything to eat or drink since we left England about dawn. We were taken back to the jail and brought a loaf of bread and some ersatz coffee. It was the last white bread we were to eat until we were liberated in May 1945.'

Meanwhile, in England at 2nd Bomb Division headquarters, a plan to bring in twenty-eight crews from other groups was considered but by nightfall it had been shelved and the decision taken that all new replacement crews coming into the division would be diverted to the 445th. Ten crews were scraped together for the mission the following day, ironically to Kassel again. *Patty Girl*, flown by another crew, was the only Liberator from the previous day's mission to fly. All ten crews returned safely to Tibenham on this occasion.

The mutilated remains of a B-24 Liberator crew lies strewn around in a field. This was the grim sight which confronted George Collar when the Germans ordered 445th airmen to pick up the remains of their buddies killed in the air battle near Kassel on 27 September 1944 (Author).

CHAPTER 9
Misburg

At 1550 the long wait was almost over. M/Sgt John T. Keene and other ground crews gathered at the hardstands. At the end of the runway ambulances stood by. The wreckers near the tower were waiting for accidents. The sky remained empty. All eyes turned. Someone called, 'There they are!' At 1600 a squadron and a half came over the field but none were from Keene's squadron. He watched. The *Angel* will come home . . . she always has . . . maybe she had landed somewhere else. He wandered aimlessly over the oil stained concrete where he had worked on her so many days. 'Yeah, Bennett was a good guy . . . the *Angel* was a good ship . . . I bet she gave those damn Germans a run for their money . . . Damn! Damn! Damn!

It was Sunday 26 November, one month after the tragic raid on Kassel. The day before, at 1516, the daily operations conference in the 8th Air Force War Room had reached the moment of decision. The Commanding General studied the wall map with targets for the 26th marked with red ribbon. He turned to the Weather Officer. 'You say 1/10 to 5/10 cloud cover with ground haze at Bielfeld. Can you do any better at Misburg?'

'Yes Sir, 1/10 to 2/10 cloud cover.'

'Well, let's go.'

At 0150 hours on 26 November a chill wind blew across the base at North Pickenham, Norfolk. A moment later the teletype at 491st Bomb Group Operations began to clatter. It was 0430 when Keene, crew chief of *Ark Angel*, swung out of bed. This was no time to get up, but like a hundred other mornings, he dressed and was off to the mess hall. Out on the hardstand *Ark Angel* was being loaded with 500 pound bombs and 2,780 gallons of fuel. Lt Box's crew had flown a tour in her already and now Lt David N. Bennett was working on his. He would fly the *Angel* today. Late that morning, Fortresses of the 1st Bomb Division and Liberators of the 2nd

Bomb Division took off for a raid on the synthetic oil refineries at Misburg, a target they had partially destroyed three weeks before. The Fortresses took off first and led the raid, followed by nine squadrons of B-24s from the 389th and 445th Bomb Groups of the Second Combat Wing and the 491st Bomb Group from the 14th Combat Wing.

Don E. Ferguson, 2/Lt navigator in Lt James K. Wenzel's crew in the 854th Bomb Squadron in the 491st Bomb Group, which took off from North Pickenham, Norfolk, recalls: 'It was a beautiful, clear flying day and the stage was set for a great sky battle. Our crew was flying deputy lead and the usual nine men aboard. This was our fifteenth mission and the crew had become rather 'flak happy' at this stage of combat. We'd flown the fourteenth mission just the day before, to Bingen, west of Frankfurt on the Rhine.' Altogether, thirty Liberators took off from North Pickenham and rendezvoused above East Anglia at the usual 7,000 to 10,000 feet level for group assembly before joining the wing formation. The 855th flew lead squadron, and the lead plane, *Ragged But Right*, piloted by Capt. Joseph R. Metcalf, had Lt-Col Charles C. Parmele, CO of the 854th Bomb Squadron, flying as air commander. Close behind flew a stream of twin-tailed B-24s in the 854th (Low) and 853th (High) Squadrons, all jockeying their controls to remain in a tight, defensive formation behind the leading 855th. Formed up, the bombers left the British Isles behind and climbed to their bombing altitudes of 20,000 feet and above.

Don Ferguson: 'One plane encountered trouble and had to leave the group, leaving twenty-nine to go on the mission. Crossing the Dutch coast the bad word was received that 'bandits were in the area' and we were in for a rough time. It was then that a second B-24 notified the group that it was aborting the mission. This left twenty-eight B-24s to fly on into Germany and face the inevitable flak and

fighters.' Timing began to go awry and ultimately affected the outcome of the mission for the 491st Bomb Group, which was flying 'tail-end charlies', or last group in the divisional bomber stream. Over the North Sea both the 389th and 445th Bomb Groups turned late, which placed them four and five minutes behind schedule respectively when they crossed the enemy coast. The subsequent Misburg mission report stated that 'the B-24s lost more time en route to the target and were eleven minutes late at bombs away'. The 1st Division arrived at Misburg six minutes before ordered time. This increased the time spread between divisions and assisted the enemy in intercepting the 2nd Division. The planned shield of 1st Division escorting fighters, combined with escorting fighters of the 2nd Division, was thus rendered ineffectual as twenty-eight minutes, instead of twelve as briefed, separated the two [1st and 2nd Division] forces.

The 1st Division formation was spread over forty miles instead of twenty as briefed, and the three escorting groups could not hope to protect all the B-17s. The P-51 Mustangs engaged the Luftwaffe fighters, but forty slipped through and shot down four B-17s. The Liberators flew the remaining thirty

When this photograph was taken of 491st Bomb Group crews at briefing for their first mission on 2 June 1944, Lt Col Charles C. Parmele, CO, 854th Bomb Squadron (sitting second row, left) was a major. Parmele led the ill-fated raid on Misburg on Sunday 26 November 1944 when sixteen 491st Liberators failed to return (USAF).

minutes to the target alone. At around 1155 hours three Me 262 jet fighters were observed over the Dummer Lake area flying parallel to the 491st formation and 2,000 yards to the left. They were thought to be charting the strength, route and speed of the Liberators. As the 491st BG approached the IP at 1226 hours between 150 and 200 fighters were spotted high above the bombers but they made no attempt to attack the Liberators. Instead, the 197 Mustang and 48 P-47 escorts were lured away to dog fight with the enemy at 30,000 ft and half a mile to the south east. Don Ferguson adds: 'Continuing into Germany from Holland, one began to detect an atmosphere of trouble. The P-51 fighter escorts had been and gone. However, more were expected to arrive in our area of flight, up, over and north of the Ruhr. In the meantime, we began to hear of more enemy fighters, mainly Fw 190s, beginning to attack the bombers up ahead.'

On 26 November the planned shield of 1st and 2nd Division escorting fighters was rendered ineffectual by missed bomber and fighter arrival times and the fighters could not protect all the heavies. The P-51 Mustangs engaged the Luftwaffe fighters but forty slipped through and shot down four B-17s. The Liberators flew the remaining thirty minutes to Misburg alone, with disastrous results (via Mike Bailey).

The Luftwaffe, in anticipation of a deeper penetration, had prepared another striking force at the Muritz Sea. By the time the bombers had reached Steinhuder Lake, this concentration was in the process of assembling. However, as the Fortresses swung west to bomb Misburg, the 'out-foxed' enemy hurried his forces west. More than 350 fighters converged on the IP for Misburg at about the same time that the 2nd Division reached that point. Up to 80 fighters from III *Gruppe*, 1 *Geschwader*, attacked the tightly packed boxes of bombers on a wide front between Uelzen and Perleberg. Three escorting groups of P-51s battled with the enemy for about twenty minutes. II *Gruppe*, 1 *Geschwader*, alone lost five fighters to the P-51s.

At this point the Liberators, now over Wittenberge, changed direction and turned south. They flew west past Stendal and headed for the target. All three *Gruppen* of 301 *Jagdgeschwader* had taken off from their bases and they converged on the bombers just as the leading elements were approaching Hannover. Some 150 enemy fighters broke through and carried out mass wave tail attacks on the Liberators out of the sun in waves of three and five. The Mustang's pilots and the B-24 gunners replied to the onslaught with heavy machine-gun fire. At times the enemy fighter pilots had to ward off fighter attacks while trying to attack the B-24s. Three FW 190s were shot down and their pilots killed, while over Rethen 1st Lt Vollert, 5 *Staffel* leader, was intercepted by two Mustangs while hard on the tail of a Liberator and was downed after a tense dogfight. Altogether, 301 *Jagdgeschwader* lost 26 pilots killed and 13 wounded. Don Ferguson 'looked out of the north window and saw flak bursts, a B-24 on fire and losing altitude, and many parachues opening up and floating to earth. By this time, we were approaching the south-eastward turn towards Magdeburg and the IP. A comment over the intercom telling us of our 'little friends' coming into the battle area was welcome news, as more and more enemy fighters were being seen. Once we came to the IP and made the turn to the west-south-west for the Misburg target, the battle was on. Dense, heavy, black flak was seen straight ahead and the intercom was full of comments from the entire crew. I was taking notes like mad and trying to log anything of importance.'

Without fighter escort the 491st, which was the last over the target, was extremely vulnerable. The German anti-aircraft guns ceased firing and over a hundred fighters bore in for the kill. Don E. Ferguson continues: 'This was the beginning of the bomb run. Each squadron, with their radio-controlled bomb sights, was assigned a frequency whereby the lead bombardier's 'flick of the switch' automatically released all the bombs in every plane in the squadron to blanket the target. Through some fault of the lead bombardier, or malfunction, a premature release of all the 854th Squadron's bombs occurred some fifteen miles before the target was reached. Our bombardier was horrified at such a result and disgustingly announced the 'bombs away' message. One plane [Lanning] over the right side and slightly behind us did not have its bomb bay doors open in time and the bombs fell through the doors leaving them flapping in the breeze and causing the plane to fall behind.' Charles Parmele, the 854th Squadron Commander, decided at this point to miss the flak ridden target area and ordered a sudden left turn to the south and thence to the west to reach the original Rally Point with the rest of the bombers in formation. This may have been a mistake, as the fighter attacks from the south and east appeared to be on the increase.'

Parmele's decision effectively split the group and placed the 854th about 1,500 yards behind the leading 855th Squadron and off to the left by itself. At 1240, two minutes after bombs away, the 491st was attacked by approximately 75 single-engined enemy fighters of 27 *Jagdgeschwader* and IV Gruppe, 54 *Geschwader*. The FW 190s dived through the 854th Squadron, flying low-left, breaking up the squadron formation and attacking again, alone, or in pairs. They singled out stragglers and made their attack from 5 to 7 o'clock, a little high. Lloyd Murff, pilot of *Big 'Un* in the 855th Squadron, who survived the mission, recalls: 'We were left to fend for ourselves. The high right [853rd] was hit first from the rear. They were picked off one by one until they were all gone. The enemy attacked in waves of five or six abreast from six o'clock high and level, followed by individual attacks. One Liberator was seen to be hit by a single FW 190 which flew straight up and appeared to stand on its tail while firing into the bomber. The B-24 was observed to go down immediately afterwards.'

Lt Charles W. Stevens was flying his first mission since bringing his B-24 back to England on 20 June with the nose shot off and navigator and bombardier dead in the mangled front section. He could have gone home after this but elected to stay and fight because 'that's what I'd joined for'. The decision cost him his life. B-24 and Lt Daniel C. Budd's *Firebird* were shot down in the second pass. Stevens' engineer, Joe Boyer, was hit by a 20mm shell and fell through the open bomb bay doors. Nearing the release point Lt Warren Moore's *The Moose* and Lt Wayne E. Stewart's *Idiot's Delight* (whose crew were on their thirtieth mission) were hit but managed to make it over the target before falling out of the formation. Lt John P. Hite in *Problem Child*, Lt Robert E. Cloughley and Lt Charles J. Ecklund, whose entire crew survived, were also shot down. The two 853rd survivors, Lt Ralph J. Butler, flying *Dorty Treek*, and Lt David N. Bennett, in *Ark Angel*, which was badly damaged with a large hole in the right wing and its upper turret missing, tried to tack onto the lead squadron. Butler never made it and Bennett's B-24 gradually lost altitude and finally disappeared from view.

Don Ferguson adds: 'Our squadron began taking a beating from the FW 190s with some starting to shoot down our stragglers, namely [Lanning's]. Our gunners were firing by this time at the enemy fighters that were seemingly coming from out of the south-east and low – four and five o'clock low – as the intercom chatter stated. Things seemed in a bedlam with planes all over, in and out of formation, taking evasive action.'

Seven Liberators in the 854th Squadron were shot down. S/Sgt Carl W. Groshell, tail gunner in 1/Lt John S. Warczak's crew, recalls: 'My pilot was never able to get into his spot in the formation. (This was not my regular crew. I had missed two missions with my regular crew while sick and they had finished up, awaiting shipment back to the States.) There was a definite lack of training and combat experience in this replacement crew. We were hit flying far behind the rest of the formation. Two Me 109s, which came in from the left side and to the front, blasted us, their cannon fire sweeping the ship from front to rear. There was no warning over the intercom and the first I knew of the attack was the sound of their shells ripping through our ship. The first 109 finished his run at us and I was able to get a short burst off at him but it was an impossible shot. As far as I could determine, it was the only return

115

GREAT AMERICAN AIR BATTLES OF WORLD WAR II

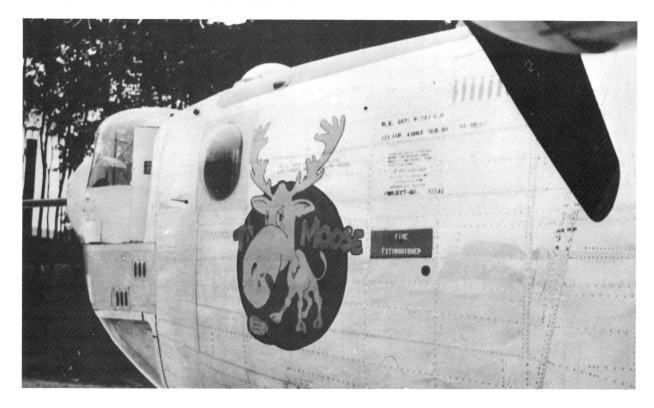

Lt Warren Moore's B-24J-150-CO *The Moose*, 44-40205 T8-G, of the 853rd Squadron, which was hit near the release point but managed to make it over the target before falling out of the formation (via Mike Bailey).

fire by our ship. By then the second 109 made his run and our ship went into a shallow dive to the right and the inside filled with smoke. I climbed out of my turret, snapped on my parachute and then made a near fatal mistake. In my haste I forgot to plug in my walk-around oxygen bottle. There was a plywood door between the tail position and the escape hatch.

It was jammed shut and I had to force it open. I saw one of the crew members bail out and then the hatch cover fell shut. It was almost impossible to see due to the intense smoke but I seemed to be aware of one other crew member near the hatch. Then a lack of oxygen caught up with me and I passed out.' Grosshell came to falling through the air. 'I told myself that I had better pull the ripcord. When my 'chute opened I looked for other parachutes and they were all tiny specks above me. One of the 109s flew past me at about fifty yards distant. The pilot took a good look at me and flew on.' Lt Warczak was thrown clear, the second time in two months that this had happened to him.

Wave after wave of fighters tore through the Low Squadron. Coming directly out of the sun, at ten o'clock high, the Luftwaffe attacked in waves of up to eight abreast, breaking away below the bombers. About ten waves attacked, followed by simultaneous attacks from three and nine o'clock by German fighters four abreast or in echelon. A few moments

Lt Robert W. Simons' B-24 *Grease Ball* 44-40172 6X-H, in the 854th Squadron was brought down by 20mm cannon fire which set the bomb bay on fire. Only three of the crew managed to bale out before it exploded (Dan Winston).

later Lt James A. Wynn's *Scarface* went down. Three of the ten-man crew were killed in the aircraft and six more were murdered by German civilians after they touched down. Kenneth M. Peiffer, the tail gunner and only survivor, was saved by a Frenchman who talked a farmer out of killing him. Peiffer spent nine weeks in hospital and six months as a PoW.

Lt Matthew Vukovich's Liberator fell off in a deadly spin from which it never recovered. There were no survivors. Lt Robert W. Simons' *Grease Ball* was brought down by 20mm cannon fire which set the bomb bay on fire. Only three of the crew managed to bale out before it exploded. *House of Rumor*, flown by Lt George A. Meuse, was also set on fire. Three gunners ignored the bale-out bell and went down with the ship, firing their guns to the end. The rest of the crew survived and were taken prisoner. Lt Floyd I. Weitz's *Hare Power* also went down on fire.

The Reluctant Dragon, piloted by Harold E. Lanning, was also in trouble. The bombardier,

Lt Floyd I. Weitz' B-24 *Hare Power*, 44-40107, 3Q-J of the 852nd Squadron, which went down on fire (Dan Winston).

B-24J-155-CO *House of Rumor*, 44-40271, 6X-K, in the 854th Squadron, flown by Lt George A. Meuse was set on fire. Three gunners ignored the bale out bell and went down with the ship, firing their guns to the end. The rest of the crew survived and were taken prisoner (via Mike Bailey).

Henry J. Latimore, recalls: 'Our aircraft was severely damaged with both right engines dead and we were losing altitude and unable to keep up with the remainder of the group. Our two waist gunners had been hit by enemy fire. I had no further duties in the nose and went to the rear compartment to help the

Harold E. Lanning's crew in the 854th Squadron, pictured during training in the USA. *Top row, left to right:* Lanning, pilot; Stephen Guzak, co-pilot; Henry J. Latimore, bombardier; George Wischeith, navigator. *Bottom row, left to right:* Gerald Burbank, engineer; Lee Taylor, waist gunner (KIA 26 November 1944); Arthur Ruppel, radio operator (killed in a crash on 11 October 1944); Desmond Clark, nose gunner (did not fly the Misburg mission); Adolph Carbone, waist gunner; Clement Dapra, tail gunner (Henry J. Latimore).

tail gunner give first aid to them. Taylor had received a bullet in his stomach and another in his buttocks and was in a bad condition. Carbone was wounded in the shoulder but was complaining about hurting in the groin area (the bullet passed from his shoulder to his groin). I inspected it but could not see any wound. We placed bandages over the wounds to try to slow the loss of blood. Meanwhile, Lanning was able to maintain control of the plane by gradually losing altitude, and as Taylor would not survive the opening shock of the parachute, we decided to try and reach friendly territory and land at an airfield in Belgium.'

'We were at about 10,000 feet when we crossed the front lines, as there was a barrage of enemy fire in the area. Lanning decided we would have to bale out

because he did not have sufficient control to make a safe landing [two engines were out on one side and Lanning could only maintain a straight course by applying full strength to the rudder]. The tail gunner and I got the injured men out of the rear compartment lower escape hatch and followed them. By the time I made my exit the aircraft was at about 8,000 feet.' All but Lee Taylor (who landed on a roof and was killed) in Lanning's crew were picked up by a British patrol and taken to Brussels, where Carbone was treated at a British field hospital.

Only three 854th Liberators survived the attacks. Don Ferguson adds: 'Our aircraft had only four small hits, all about the size of a fifty-cent piece. We were just plain lucky or divinely favoured and were thankful for that.' When the attacks subsided, no less than sixteen Liberators in the 853rd and 854th Squadrons had been blasted out of the sky – in the space of just fifteen minutes. Only the 855th Squadron had reached the target without being attacked. They bombed with 'good results'. Further losses were prevented by the timely arrival of eight P-51 Mustang Weather Scouts led by Bob Whitlow, which held the FW 190s at bay until reinforcements could arrive to save the dozen remaining B-24s. Then an orderly retreat back to England began by

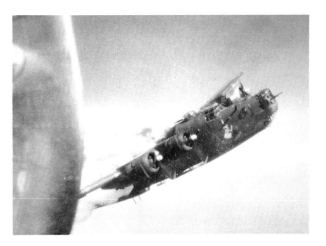

Although the majority of the Liberators featured in this dramatic sequence of photographs are not 491st aircraft, they are shown here to represent the events that unfolded and to convey the horror that took place when the group lost sixteen Liberators in rapid succession. (*Bottom right*) B-24J-145 CO *Ark Angel* – 44-40073, flown by Lt David N. Bennett and crew, was one of nine 853rd Squadron Liberators shot down on the mission (David Bennett). The Martin upper turret was knocked out and a large hole put in the right wing before the B-24 went down. There were no survivors. The other fifteen B-24s suffered much the same fate (Dan Winston).

B-24J 42-95610 *Reluctant Dragon* of the 854th Squadron, 491st Bomb Group, which was shot down on the Misburg mission, 26 November 1944 (Harold E. Lanning).

regrouping the B-24s into one formation. The 491st's only consolation was that the Luftwaffe had suffered even more heavily; all Gruppen losing approximately 90 fighters.

Lloyd Murff looked around for survivors from the other squadrons. 'The remainder joined us. We really closed ranks and returned blistering fire from about seventy .50s. I saw only a couple of FW 190s which passed about thirty yards to my left, peeling to the left. Oliver L. Hicks, my engineer top turret gunner, bounced tracer or 'fireball' ammo' off the belly of one. My crew was credited with one kill. The left waist gunner, a bombardier from another crew on his last mission, got the credit (when we returned he hit the ground, kissing it).'

M/Sgt John Keene, waiting forlornly at *Ark Angel's* revetment, picked up his tool box and put it in his shack (bomb crate box) by the hardstand. He then rode his bicycle back to the 853rd. Forty years were to elapse before he discovered that the *Angel* had crashed and burned about 15 km northwest of Hildesheim, 20 km south of Misburg, between the towns of Jeinsen and Oerie. Villagers ran to the Liberator and found all the crew members still strapped into their seats but they had burned to death.

Command acted quickly to replace the losses. The control tower log entries for that day said: 'Sixteen replacement B-24s arrived from Stansted, Shades of Dawn Patrol.'

491st Bomb Group gunners, still in their heavy flying clothes and Mae Wests, show the strain and fatigue during de-briefing after their first mission in June 1944. Exactly the same scene was performed at North Pickenham following the Misburg mission on 26 November (USAF).

CHAPTER 10

The Big Day

High losses sustained on raids such as Kassel and Misburg were very hard to take at group and command level, but they did not prevent the USSTAF from mounting more raids in even greater intensity than before. On Christmas Eve 1944, a record 2,034 8th Air Force bombers took part in the largest single strike flown by the Allied Air Forces in World War Two, in support of the Allied armies in the Ardennes. The Luftwaffe failed to turn back the Allied Air Forces and seemed to offer little opposition as the US bombing offensive struck at oil targets in January 1945.

The Jagdverbande had made a few concerted attempts at turning back the bombers late in 1944, but on each occasion they had been beaten off with heavy losses inflicted by escorting P-51 Mustangs and P-47 Thunderbolts of the 8th Air Force. On 2 November the defending 8th Air Force Mustangs routed their German attackers, and the 352nd Fighter Group established a record thirty-eight kills on that occasion. Despite these losses the German Air Force could still be relied upon to make a major effort against the 8th Air Force heavies on occasions.

On 14 January 1945 the 8th Air Force sent 600 bombers from the 2nd and 3rd Air Divisions to oil targets in north-western Germany again. The Fortresses were well-protected by escorting Mustangs, including red- and yellow-nosed P-51s of

P-51 Mustang *Bobby Jeanne* which was flown by Col. Irwin H. Dregne (Merle C. Olmsted).

Col Irwin H. Dregne, the 357th Fighter Group CO (Merle C. Olmsted).

the 357th Fighter Group based at Leiston, Suffolk. In the past eleven months the veteran group had flown 252 missions (most of which were bomber escort), and its pilots had been credited with 517 victories. No less than thirty-nine pilots had attained ace status. Col Irwin H. Dregne, the CO, in *Bobby Jeanne*, and his wingman were first to take off, at 1010 hours. The remaining sixty-four fighters followed them into the cold grey sky over Suffolk. Despite a slight haze, visibility was excellent but three P-51s landed again with mechanical problems. Seven others, including Lt 'Dittie' Jenkins, who was flying White Two in the 362nd Squadron, who had a rough engine, and White Three who escorted him home, turned back before the group rendezvoused with the leading bombers north of Cuxhaven at 1150 hours. Lt-Col Andrew J. Evans, the Deputy Group Commander, flying as a spare, took over. Capt. Chuck Yeager (later the first man to exceed the speed of sound in level flight) and Clarence Anderson, the Operations Officer, both took off as spares. It was their last mission. If they were not needed to fill in on the mission, they would go off on their own sight-seeing. They wandered around the south of France and to Switzerland, where they

dropped their tanks on a lake and strafed it just for the hell of it. Upon returning home, they learned that they had missed the biggest dog-fight of the war!

The 3rd Bomb Division Fortresses made a feint towards Berlin in an effort to split the enemy fighter force, entering Schleswig-Holstein airspace andthen heading south-east towards the German capital where the combat wings split to bomb their respective targets. The leading groups turned for their target at Derben to the west of Berlin, while the following groups flew on to Magdeburg and Stendal further to the west. The leading Fortresses were at about 24,000 feet, protected by the 363rd (Cement) Squadron on high cover at about 30,000 feet, and the 362nd (Dollar) and 364th (Greenhouse) Squadrons providing close escort at about 26,000 feet. At 1245 hours, while some twenty miles north-west of Brandenburg, Dregne spotted a large formation of enemy single-engined fighters at one o'clock heading towards the lead box of bombers. The enemy fighters, about 130 in total, were from JG 300 and included seventy-plus FW 190s at 28,000 feet and about 100 Bf 109s flying top cover at around 32,000 feet. The heavily armoured FW 190s were in line abreast, or 'company front' formation, in waves of eight aircraft each.

Dregne led Greenhouse Squadron intending to intercept the high force but as soon as he noticed the FW 190s, he ordered Greenhouse Squadron to drop tanks and peeled off. Dregne led the 364th and 362nd Squadrons down towards the FW 190s and instructed Major Robert Foy's 363rd Squadron to intercept the high flying Messerschmitts. Dregne recounts: 'I told Greenhouse Squadron to drop tanks and we turned into the 190s. They broke formation and scattered, some of them rolling, some split-essing, but the majority broke right and then going into a Lufberry. I got my sights on a 190 and started firing, observing strikes on the fuselage and tail. He broke left and then went into a spin. I broke left and continued turning, finding myself in a Lufberry with eight or ten FW 190s. I started a tight climbing spiral, the 190s following, but I was able to outclimb them. My flight was broken on initial attack by enemy aircraft flying through us.' Lt-Col William C. Clark, the no.2 in Dregne's flight, gave a FW 190 a short burst but did not see any hits. Clark wrote: 'For a second I lost sight of [Dregne]; his plane was faster than mine and he had pulled away.

A 190 came up from underneath and I fired a burst at him. His right wheel fell down and he stalled. I overran him and pulled up to make another pass. The 190 was going into a spin with the right wheel still down and it looked to me like the pilot fell out. I saw two 'chutes. Two 190s came in on my tail and I turned so sharp that I spun in. I recovered at 10,000ft and several 109s shot at me as they came down. I climbed up to about 30,000ft but saw no more enemy aircraft.'

1/Lt Raymond M. Bank, in *Fire Ball*, was flying 'Greenhouse Green' no.3, led by Capt. Chester K. Maxwell. 'Lt Karger called in a jet [Me 262] was bouncing our flight, and that he was firing at the no.2 man. The enemy aircraft overshot and made a slight turn to the left. I turned on my gun switches and pulled my nose up and fired at the Me 262 before rejoining my flight. The 262 disappeared from sight. Maxwell got on the tail of some twenty-five to thirty FW 190s and a Lufberry to the left began. Two 190s got on my tail and one fired at me. I closed to about 100 feet and set him on fire and then shot the other down in flames. I bounced a third 190 and he dived and came up into a loop. At the top of it he kicked it into a hammerhead to make a head-on pass. He was going fairly slow and gave me a perfect target. I fired until he burst into flames.' Maxwell, flying in *Tangerine*, had just shot down three FW 190s and was about to engage a fourth when he looked back to check his tail and discovered a yellow-nosed P-51 there. Safe in the knowledge that he was covered, Maxwell turned back onto the FW 190 only to feel the thump, thump of cannon shells on his own aircraft, and his canopy flew off. The yellow-nosed Mustang closed in, realised his mistake, and flew off, leaving Maxwell with badly damaged controls, no radio, coolant problems and belts of ammunition trailing from one wing. Maxwell cut the overheated engine and glided down to 8,000 feet where he levelled off and cut it back in again using 1,900 rpm and twenty-two inches of mercury. Incredibly, Maxwell nursed *Tangerine* the one-and-a-half hours back to friendly territory where he bellied-in near Antwerp. In the heat of the battle with hundreds of fighters milling around it is surprising more 'friendly' aircraft were not attacked by their own comrades. A 357th pilot fired on a 20th Fighter Group P-51 and strikes were observed on the wing, but the black-nosed Mustang headed back to England apparently undamaged.

1/Lt Raymond M. Bank in the cockpit of his Mustang *Fire Ball*. Crew chief Paul Slentz stands behind him (Merle C. Olmsted).

Altogether, the 364th Squadron accounted for twenty-one and a half enemy fighters, the half being a 109 shared by Robert Winks and a 361st Fighter Group pilot. Dregne radioed the 363rd Squadron to harry the FW 190s and make sure that they did not reform and attempt another attack on the heavies. Major Robert W. Foy, who was leading 'Cement' Squadron, the 363rd call-sign, in *Little Shrimp*, wrote: 'The 190s broke their company front formation and headed in every direction imaginable. I turned to the right and lined up with a FW 190 closing in to good firing range, giving him short bursts while in a shallow turn at about a thirty-degree deflection. Strikes were observed on both wings of the enemy aircraft and he immediately straightened out and flew level for a second or two. Suddenly, the pilot jettisoned his canopy and baled out. I pulled up sharply to avoid colliding with him.

'I observed another FW 190 flying ninety degrees to my path of flight and directly beneath me at about 3,000 feet. I did a quick wingover and split-essed onto his tail. The pilot apparently saw me closing in and did a split-ess towards the deck. I followed him, giving him short bursts and observing strikes on his

Major Robert Foy, CO, 363rd Fighter Squadron, 357th Fighter Group, in the cockpit of *Little Shrimp* (Merle C. Olmsted).

left wing. He continued his dive and must have been indicating well over 553 mph as I was following closely behind and was indicating better than 550. He made no move to pull out of his dive so I started a gradual pull-out at about 4,000 feet but kept his ship in view off to one side. The enemy aircraft dived straight into the ground and I made a 360 degree turn diving to get a picture of his ship burning on the ground. I levelled off and made climbing turns towards the bombers and giving my flight an opportunity to pull up into formation. My no.2 man, Ralph Mann, pulled up somewhere en route and during the fun I apparently lost my second element. I rejoined the bombers and proceeded around the target and out, breaking escort just west of Steinhurder Lake as my fuel supply was low and my oxygen almost nil. I took up a heading for base and dropped to about 10,000 feet altitude.'

Ralph Mann continues: 'Just east of Nienburg, Captain Foy spotted a locomotive. I dropped in trail and we went down and destroyed it. Again we started for home when just east of Nienburg we saw a small airfield with a FW 190 sitting on one end of the runway. I circled the field and Captain Foy went in to strafe it. He got strikes all over the plane and it burst into flames.' Mann rejoined Foy and they flew back to their Suffolk base alone. Foy, who was on his second tour after returning to the USA in the late summer of 1944, finished the war with a score of seventeen victories and three strafing victims. Tragically, he was killed in a post-war flying accident.

1/Lt John R. Stern, another pilot in the 363rd Squadron, who was leading 'Cement White' flight, claimed three 109s destroyed. He wrote: 'As three Me 109s crossed from my right to left I broke into them, picking out the tail-end charlies. I fired several bursts observing hits near the cockpit and wing roots. We made a couple of turns. Then he began to snap and spin. Smoke, flames and coolant could be seen – his wheels also dropped partially down. He pulled up, went over on his back and spun in.' Stern's wingman, Lt George Rice, saw the enemy aircraft spin in. He wrote: 'Just as Stern's FW 190 spun out I noticed a Jerry pulling deflection on me so I broke into him and in about 360 degrees got in a snap shot. He split-essed and I rolled over and followed. I fired another burst and saw a few strikes. Finally, I got into a good position, and with small deflection fired a long burst. I saw many strikes in the wing roots and cockpit area. He started streaming smoke and coolant, rolled over and jettisoned his canopy. Last I saw of him he was headed straight for the ground out of control.'

Stern meanwhile, had problems. 'My radio went out. I got on the tail of a single Me 109. The action here was practically the same as the first; many hits were observed around the cockpit and wing roots. His wheels dropped partially. He started spinning and snapping violently. I fired another burst and observed hits. Pieces came off the plane. Thinking he might be just taking evasive action I followed him down until he crashed and exploded. It is my belief that the pilot was killed before the crash. I located my number three and four men. I saw two Me 109s in a slight dive for the deck at nine o'clock. They were flying line abreast. I attacked from dead astern, closing rapidly, too rapidly. I overshot one and called one of the other boys to take him, which he did. I fired several bursts at the other, which was out of range. No hits observed. As I closed, hits were seen around the bottom of the fuselage, cockpit and wing roots. Coolant and smoke could be seen issuing from the enemy aircraft. I overran him and pulled up to one side. He crashed into a wood, tearing off both wings. The plane slid a short way through the trees and caught fire. I think he was trying to belly-in to a small field but he overshot.'

Altogether, the 363rd Squadron downed a dozen enemy fighters but Lieutenant Jim Sloan, who was on his 43rd mission, and William Dunlop, who was leading Blue flight, had miraculous escapes when their Mustangs were brought down. Sloan's flight was unable to keep up with Dunlop, who dived into a mêlée of about thirty enemy fighters. Sloan shot down one Me 109 and then broke right into another before his canopy was shot away and his fuselage was severed behind the cockpit, possibly as a result of a mid-air collision with the enemy fighter. Sloan baled out and passed out. He fell face up and after failing three times to right himself, he pulled the ripcord and floated safely down. Dunlop, meanwhile, shot down one of the 109s and saw the pilot exit from the side of the cockpit before his Mustang was badly hit and caught fire. It zoomed to earth and the G-force held Dunlop so firmly in the cockpit that he could not raise his hand to release the canopy. A few seconds later the Mustang blew up

and Dunlop was catapulted through the sky. He had no time to pull the ripcord of his parachute, but incredibly he landed 'still in the bucket seat with armour attached and shoulder straps neatly in place.' It was a very narrow escape. The wreckage of his P-51 lay strewn around about fifty feet from where he landed, and pieces were still falling. The wrecked 109 had crashed 100 yards away, its ammunition still 'popping'. Dunlop and Sloan were captured later but both escaped from a forced march some months later and returned to the Allied lines.

Meanwhile, the 362nd Squadron, call-sign 'Potent Dollar', shot down twenty-one enemy fighters in almost as many minutes. Major John B. England, the CO, flying in *Missouri Armada*, wrote: 'The enemy aircraft seemed to hesitate in making an initial attack [on the bombers]; they made several orbits as though they were sizing the situation up. This was to our advantage. While they were 'debating', I placed my squadron in the proper position and at the same time headed towards the enemy aircraft, hoping to break up the gaggle before they could attack the bombers. They did start an attack before I could get to them, but we interfered slightly and engaged the Krauts in individual dog-fights. I caught one Me 109 which slipped through and started towards the bombers. I got on his tail but was out of firing range. The pilot displayed a little judgement by looking around, then he put his ship in a ninety-degree vertical dive from 32,000 feet. I followed him down. At about every 5,000 feet during the descent he would roll and do some very violent manoeuvres. I just did a tight spiral around him. At 8,000 feet he made a very tight pull-out and levelled off. Evidently, the pilot thought he had lost me for he began flying straight and level. Maybe he didn't realise the speed of the .50 calibre bullet and decided to take time out for a decision. I made a little tighter pull-out and started firing at 200 yards, closing to fifty yards. I got strikes all over the left side of the fuselage and left wing. Just before I released the trigger, about four feet of the left wing ripped off. The pilot did not get out as his ship went into the ground, making a big explosion. The pilot had been very fair but he had made the usual mistake which prevents fair pilots from becoming

Major John B. England, CO, 362nd Fighter Squadron (Merle C. Olmsted).

Major Joseph 'Bob' Broadhead (Merle C. Olmsted).

good pilots.' England finished the war with a score of seventeen-and-a-half victories but, sadly, was killed in a flying accident in France on 17 November 1954.

Major England had just destroyed the fighter and was circling for altitude when his flight was joined by two more P-51s. A lone FW 190 got onto the tail of Major Joseph 'Bob' Broadhead, the leader of 'Dollar White' flight. As the FW 190 passed by, 2/Lt Donald W. Cheever slipped in behind and fired from about 100 feet, hitting the tail, wings and fuselage. The FW 190 snap-rolled and dived for the ground where it exploded on impact. Lt Hyman, who followed him down, reported that the pilot never baled out. The flight had just reformed again when Broadhead spotted a lone Me 109. He attacked the German from the rear and pumped shells into the tail, fuselage and wings. The canopy came off and the pilot baled out.

Lt-John L. Sublett (right) and Pete Pelon after the 14 January mission. Sublett shot down two enemy aircraft (Merle C. Olmsted).

Several pilots in the 362nd Squadron knocked down two enemy aircraft apiece. Lt John L. Sublett, who achieved this feat, wrote: 'There was a long line of Me 109s, in no particular formation, except a sort of long column containing six to ten abreast. To my right and above were several Jerries doing snaps, rolls and spins. I called my wingman, Lt William W. Gruber, and told him that when they finally got through passing by we would tack onto their rear and start shooting. It seemed an endless procession but finally they passed by and I tacked onto their tail end. The last four Me 109s then broke into us. We started a honey of a Lufberry which went about six turns. I finally cut the butter and got a short burst into one of them. I was going straight down when I fired from about 100 yards, seeing many strikes go right into the pilot through the top of his canopy. The plane went out of control and crashed into the ground. The pilot, who I am sure was dead from my bullets, did not bale out. I reefed upwards and went after another Me 109 who was at the tail end. He flicked over and started down. I followed and opened fire from about 700 yards but I saw no strikes. He hit the ground and exploded. The pilot did not get out.'

Capt. Leonard 'Kit' Carson, the 'Blue Flight' leader, who on 27 November 1944 had become an ace by shooting down five FW 190s, added three more kills to his score at the controls of *Nooky Booky IV*. He wrote: 'I closed to about 400 yards on a Fw 190 at the rear of a gaggle, firing a good burst and getting strikes all over his fuselage. I believe the pilot was killed. I went back up to the bombers, looked around for a couple of minutes and saw a formation of about forty to fifty FW 190s coming up about 1,000 yards behind. There were a couple of P-51s near and they broke with me. We met the enemy planes head-on. They didn't fire but we did.' One of the wingmen was 2/Lt John F. Duncan. 'I opened fire from 600 yards, closing to 200 yards, getting strikes on both wings. The Jerry split-essed for the deck and I followed him down, firing some more and getting additional strikes. At about 18,000 feet the pilot baled out and I watched his 'chute open. Shortly thereafter, Duncan shot down his second FW 190. This time the pilot did not get out of the exploding fighter. Carson, meanwhile, fired a burst from 350 to 400 yards at a Fw 190, getting strikes. He did a couple of snaps to the right with his belly tank on, and wound up on his back. I fired again, getting more hits on the fuselage. Pieces came off the enemy ship and he began smoking. He split-essed and headed for the deck. I followed him down

Capt. Leonard 'Kit' Carson, who shot down three enemy aircraft on the 14 January 1944 mission (Merle C. Olmsted).

P-51 Mustang *Nooky Booky IV*, with Capt. Leonard 'Kit' Carson at the controls, warms up on the steel matting runway at Leiston, Suffolk (Merle C. Olmsted).

until he hit, bounced and crashed. The pilot did not get out.

'I climbed back up to about 14,000 feet where two Me 109s came tooling by about 2,000 feet below. I dropped down and fired at one in the rear, getting

no hits. They dropped flaps and broke violently. I zoomed back up while they circled in a Lufberry. I made another ill-timed pass and pulled up again, getting no hits. The leader broke off and headed for the deck. I dropped down to tail-end charlie as he started down. He pulled up, losing speed. I kept my excessive speed, fire-walled it and started firing at about 300 yards, closing down to about twenty yards, getting hits all over the fuselage. His coolant blew as I pulled over him. Then he went into a sort of tumbling spiral and crashed.' Carson's three kills were confirmed and he finished the war as the top ace in the 357th with a total score of eighteen-and-a-half aerial victories and three-and-a-half strafing victims.

The 362nd Squadron pilots ripped through the enemy fighter formations, sending the enemy fighters down in flames. Lt George A. Behling, who was flying his 42nd mission, was on the receiving end and he spun earthwards pursued by his quarry, a FW 190. At 20,000 feet Behling levelled out, but the enemy pilot was still on his tail. He tried to outspin him down to 10,000 feet but the tenacious German pilot was still locked onto his tail. Behling dived for the deck at a ten-degree angle and finally outpaced his pursuer, but his engine began spluttering and belching out white smoke. Too low to bale out, the twenty-year-old American made a dead-stick belly landing in a field and stopped fifty feet short of a line of trees. Behling made a run for it but was apprehended by four elderly Volksturm members and sent to a PoW camp.

At times the aerial battle was waged from close quarters. Harold W. Wyatt, and Behling's wingman, James A. Gasser, flying *Muddy*, each destroyed a FW 190 after firing at them from 300 to 500 yards. Gasser had blacked out in a dive and when he recovered had discovered that his G-suit rubber hose connection had come loose. He had radioed Behling to tell him his tail was not covered but had received no reply. Meanwhile, 1/Lt Jesse R. Frey called 1/Lt Herman H. Delager to cover him while he went after two Bf 109s. Frey shot down one of the enemy aircraft with a three-second burst. The pilot went down with the aircraft, which exploded on impact.

1/Lt Charles E. Weaver, who was already an ace, sought out his sixth kill. It happened to be an olive, drab Me 109 with black and white 'invasion' stripes.

1/Lt Charles E. Weaver and his crew chief beside his P-51 Mustang at Leiston (Merle C. Olmsted).

'The pilot of the Jerry aircraft was definitely experienced. He was making a pass on a silver P-51. I immediately took chase, turning on his tail and giving him a short burst at 800 yards. The Me 109 went into a steep turn to the left. I cut the dive short and fired a burst in the semi-inverted position. I must have done something besides scaring the hell out of him, however, for he made no attempt to recover from his dive. He dove straight into the ground and exploded.' Weaver had followed the enemy fighter down to the deck and at treetop level he spotted a lone locomotive directly ahead of him. Weaver fired at 1,200 feet range and the locomotive blew up in a cloud of white smoke. 'Pulling off the loco, I was astonished to see a FW 190 doing barrel-rolls at 200 feet off to my left. I pulled up and came in for a seventy-degree deflection when he attempted another barrel-roll. He must have seen me preparing to attack for he suddenly tried to break to the left, stalled and crashed into the ground.' Weaver finished the war with eight aerial victories.

The two highest scoring pilots in the 362nd Squadron that day were Andy Evans and 1/Lt 'Big John' Kirla, who each shot down four enemy fighters. Kirla wrote: 'We dropped tanks and engaged the Jerries at about 27,000 feet. I picked out a FW 190 and clobbered him all over. I believe I killed the pilot. He dived inverted to the ground and exploded. My second FW 190 was in a dog-fight. I started to fire at him from about 400 yards, closing to fifty yards. He began to tumble and I watched him go into the ground. I looked around for another target and saw an Me 109 shooting down a bomber. I went after him, got on his tail and closed to about thirty yards. He went into a very tight barrel-roll going straight down. I fired a short burst then really gave him the works, clobbering him all over. He flipped over on his back and started to burn. Pieces fell off until, finally, just the framework remained. I laughed and commented to myself on the crazy contraptions they were sending up these days. There wasn't enough of the ship left to crash into the ground. Looking around again I observed two Me 109s flying 180 degrees to the bombers and a P-51 chasing them. The P-51 closed in and got the first Jerry but the second one was sliding onto the Mustang's tail. The Mustang was shot down. I was at close enough range by this time to get some revenge. I began firing at about 200 yards and

Lt-Col Andrew J. Evans, Deputy Group Commander, 357th Fighter Group, who shot down four enemy fighters on 14 January (Merle C. Olmsted).

played with him awhile. He was badly scared. I got tired of that and adjusted my K-14 and opened up at about fifty yards. I filled that 109 full of holes. Pieces started to fly off him and he went down like a falling leaf.'

Lt-Col Evans wrote: 'I took a FW 190 who was diving down on our aircraft below (we were top cover). Flames enveloped the entire aircraft as it spun earthwards. I pulled up and called to my wingman to see if he was still there but it seems that he had engaged an Me 109 that had come between us while I was hot on the Kraut's tail and had lost me entirely. It didn't require any searching to spot an Me 109 slightly above. Up I went and round and round, firing when I thought it was worth it. Knowing my tail wasn't covered I kept looking around. Seeing a bogie approaching from behind, I fired a quick and final burst and pulled up and away, watching the pilot bale out as I turned into

Col Dregne adds up the final score on the blackboard at Leiston. Watching are (left to right) Robert Foy, John Storch and Andrew Evans (Merle C. Olmsted).

what was a P-51. I started after the pilot in the 'chute to take a picture when two FW 190s closed in from the side. Throwing down ten degrees of flaps I turned like hell into them and started climbing; they ignored me. Then I spotted a formation of what I thought was about twelve P-51s, but I was quite chagrined when I pulled into formation from the rear to see that the damn things were Me 109s.

'Noticing that one of the Krauts didn't seem to know whether or not he was part of that formation, I made a diving pass. He saw me and broke, but, thank God, the others had something else on their mind. I thought I had him when, as I looked around to see if my tail was clear, he chopped throttle and dropped flaps; zoom . . . I cut back too late. Seeing his golden opportunity, he kicked rudder and our positions were reversed. I started thinking that today was Sunday and I should have been in church. He poured out the lead while I did my best to talk him out of it, to no avail. As a final 'parting gesture', I pulled up and kicked myself into a violent spin. Each time I started to pull out I looked

around at those flashing guns and changed my mind. I'll never understand why he didn't hit me. I finally had to come out a thousand feet. He didn't know, evidently, and went in with a big bang. Going around the deck I ran into another FW 190. He poured the coal to it and upstairs we went. I reckon he decided to fight it out, for at 15,000 feet he levelled out and went into a Lufberry. I couldn't line him up but I was trying like hell when all of a sudden he collided with somebody. I can't say whether it was friendly or not. It was all I could do to avoid the explosion as I went by. I came around, thoroughly shaken up by now, paused only long enough to take a picture of the explosion and climbed towards the bombers. There, at 31,000 feet, I joined another P-51 and escorted the 'Big Friends' almost to the Dummer Lake. When gas was low I set course for home, along with Lt-Col Dregne.'

On the way home Dregne spotted a lone Me 109 at about 20,000 feet. The colonel chopped his throttle, slid in behind him and started firing. Evans watched as Dregne poured shells into the cockpit, sending the 109 down spinning and burning. By 1445 hours all the 357th Fighter Group Mustangs had landed and pilots were soon telling their mission accounts to amazed interrogation officers at

Leiston. As the story went up the line to 66th Fighter Wing and Higher headquarters, re-counts were ordered. However, the score remained the same. Altogether, the 357th had shot down sixty-and-a-half enemy aircraft, a record for any 8th Air Force fighter group which still stood by the end of hostilities in Europe, for the Luftwaffe never again met the American fighters on equal terms. The 20th Fighter Group claimed nineteen-and-a-half victories and the 353rd Fighter Group claimed nine enemy aircraft shot down. In all, 161 enemy aircraft were destroyed. Only thirteen P-51s and three Thunderbolts were lost during the great air battle of 14 January. JG 300 reported twenty-seven pilots killed and six wounded, and JG 301 had twenty-two pilots killed and eight wounded.

General Jimmy Doolittle sent a message of congratulations to Col Dregne. In part it read: 'You gave the Hun the most humiliating beating he has ever taken in the air. Extend my personal admiration and congratulations to each member of your command, both ground and air, for a superb victory.' The 357th Fighter Group, which was to finish the war with no less than thirty-eight aces, was awarded a Distinguished Unit Citation for its impressive part in the battle.

The last major air battles between fighter groups of the 8th Air Force and the Luftwaffe took place on 18 April, when 1,211 heavies escorted by more than 1,200 fighters were sent to attack Berlin. Forty Me 262s from Jagdgeschwader 7 'Hindenburg' shot down twenty-five bombers with rockets. It was the final challenge by a dying enemy. The Luftwaffe was finished, destroyed in the air and starved of fuel on the ground.

Now only Japan remained to be defeated.

CHAPTER 11
The Shooting Down of Vice-Admiral Yamagata

Around dusk on Wednesday 14 March 1945, a Kawanishi four-engined H8K2-L Emily transport, a converted patrol flying-boat, arrived at the Second Southern Expeditionary Fleet HQ in Surabaya Naval Anchorage on Java from Ambon (Amboina), an island near New Guinea. On board the secret flight was fifty-four-year-old Chujo (Vice-Admiral) Seigo Yamagata, Commander of the Fourth Southern Expeditionary Fleet, eleven crew and twenty-two passengers, comprising six officers, eleven non-commissioned officers and five civilians. Their final destination was the Yokosuka Naval base in Japan. The Vice-Admiral had recently been relieved of his command following the Japanese defeat in the region. American forces had liberated Manila on 3 February and Corregidor on 27 February. By 1 March, Clark Field on Luzon in the Philippines was filled with US Army Air Corps and Navy aircraft. At sea, Admiral 'Bull' Halsey's 3rd Fleet, Spruance's 5th Fleet and Kincaid's 7th Fleet were sweeping all before them. From 16 February to 1 March 1945, Admiral Marc Mitscher's Task Force 58 had accounted for 648 Japanese aircraft destroyed and over 300,000 tons of Japanese shipping sunk. Yamagata and his staff knew there were no fighters left that could be spared to escort the Emily to their destination. The Vice-Admiral had been nominated for promotion to Kaigun Tasisho (full Admiral) and an appointment to become the next Under-Secretary of the Imperial Japanese Navy. Yamagata was looking forward to a fleeting family reunion with his wife Aiko and their daughter Akiko in Sakurayama, Zushi before his audience with Emperor Hirohito in the Imperial Palace in Tokyo.

American and Allied air and fleet units were even then patrolling the East China Sea and the Vice-Admiral and his staff were very worried about the large numbers of B-24s in the area. However, the Emily was at that time still one of the fastest and most outstanding patrol seaplanes in the world. Powered by four 1,850hp Mitsubishi 14-cylinder radials, a cruising speed of 184 mph at 13,125ft and a maximum speed of 290 mph at 16,400ft, the Vice-Admiral hoped that they could outrun any American aircraft. His H8K2-L was a 'Fat Cat', with two decks and some of the guns and

Vice-Admiral Seigo Yamagata, HIJN, Commander-in-Chief, Fourth Southern Expeditionary Fleet (via Paul Stevens).

V-Adm Seigo Yamagata, most likely taken when first selected for R-Adm and then promoted to VAdm. On 17 March 1945 he was en route to Tokyo for an audience with the Emperor, to be promoted to Full Admiral and become the Under-Secretary of the Imperial Japanese Navy (via Paul Stevens).

he was honoured to be chosen as the pilot to transfer Yamagata back to Japan.

On the morning of 15 March the Emily took off from Surabaya. The first leg of the journey to Japan was an 875-mile flight to Singapore. After an overnight stop in the former British colony to enable the crew to rest and allow refuelling of the aircraft, the Emily took off again next morning and headed for Saigon. Yamagata and his staff spent the night in Saigon and on the sixteenth the Emily flew out towards Hong Kong intending to reach Shanghai. However, bad weather or an engine malfunction caused the Emily to return to Sanya (Ya Xian) in Hainan Dao. Yasuda landed on the water and hit a reef, damaging the underside of the hull. Water was baled out of the Emily and it was refuelled all night long.

Next day, Yamagata had first decided to resume the journey to Japan in a conventional aircraft, but one was not available so he decided to use the

armour removed to cut down on weight and make room for the officials and their baggage. Only the bow and tail guns, armed with one and two 20mm cannon respectively, and two 7.7mm machine-guns, had been retained. It would have to make several refuelling stops en route. At each stop Yamagata's staff would gather intelligence information about American times and routes of possible patrols and choose the least dangerous time to fly. The departure time would therefore vary each time. On the evening of the fourteenth, the main pilot, Johiso (Chief Flight Petty Officer) Yoshikazu Yasuda, and twenty-four-year-old Nobuyuki Taniguchi, a Chief Flight Petty Officer in the crew, who had been classmates from the reserve pilot trainee programme, and both of whom came from Kyoto, had drinks together. Yasuda confided in Taniguchi that his superiors recognized his excellent flying skills as a pilot, and

Nobuyuki Taniguchi (taken at the age of 22 in 1943), Chief Flight Petty Officer assigned to the 'Emily' on 14–17 March 1945. As a survivor from V-Adm Yamagata's 'Emily', he was interviewed by Mihoko Yamagata in Japan while assisting in the preparation of the story of V-Adm Yamagata's demise (via Paul Stevens).

flying-boat as soon as it was repaired. On the morning of the seventeenth the party boarded the Emily again. Yamagata wished to stop at Taipei in Formosa where there was a seaplane facility. The waves there are usually high but they subside from time to time. If the waves were not too high, they would land there. If it was not possible, they would fly to Kyushu.

The Emily departed at around 1000 hours. They saw Formosa (Taiwan) and flew along the coast. Soon they found Tan Shui. While they were circling two or three times to decide what to do, the communication officer on board delivered a radio message to Yamagata. An air-raid alarm was sounding in Formosa and the Japanese were being attacked from an aircraft carrier. The Vice-Admiral thought for a while and then asked the captain how

Scene at one of the two Navy secret intercept stations in the Far East. Operators are busy intercepting, recording and taking RDF bearings on Orange (Japanese) naval, air, ground and ship movements. After the fall of the Philippines, the Corregidor tunnel intercept section and sixty-five intelligence operatives were secretly evacuated by two US submarines to Melbourne, Australia, where they resumed operations throughout the Pacific War (Naval Security Group Command).

much fuel remained. He replied that there was enough for one hour and twenty minutes flying time. Yamagata calculated the distance and ordered Yasuda to fly to Shanghai. Immediately, the pilot turned westwards and headed towards Shanghai at 160 mph at 13,200ft.

Yamagata thanked the crew for its good work and told his staff to distribute some snacks. The weather was getting worse. Clouds were hanging low and the captain ordered Yasuda to reduce the seaplane's altitude. Yasuda quickly finished eating and took over control of the aircraft and relieved the co-pilot, since they were entering a danger zone. The Emily descended and the crew saw the Chinese mainland. Yamagata and his staff smiled with relief. Had they known that their plans for this 'secret' flight had been intercepted by US Navy cryptologists before leaving Java and decrypted, they would have been less than relieved. Thanks to the unceasing work of Radio Intercept Unit, known as the 'On-The-Roof-Gang', due to their having been trained in a classified area, US Naval Intelligence knew the Vice-Admiral's schedule and plans had already been set in motion to shoot down Yamagata's plane.

At Clark Field US Navy crews – the 'Buccaneers of Screaming 104' – were tumbled from their tents

US Navy PB4Y-1 Liberator similar to the type flown by Lt Paul Stevens in the Pacific (Navy Dept).

late that Saturday morning. VPB 104, flying PB4Y-1s, VPB-119, equipped with PB4Y-2s, and VPB 146, equipped with PV-1 Harpoons, formed the Navy Search Group attached to the US 7th Fleet. Lt Paul F. Stevens, the 'Buccaneers' Squadron Executive, takes up the story: 'The morning of 17 March was different from the usual activities for Armed Reconnaissance Missions. Usually, we arose at 0200 hours, but this morning I rolled out of my cot and left the tent about 0700 hours. After breakfast, our briefing at Wing HQ was routine and brief. It consisted mainly of search sector assignments, issuing code books, and weather reports. Since we were to search our sectors, regardless of the weather, the weather briefing received little attention. However, of considerable importance and very much out of the ordinary, was our primary mission of the day. This was to intercept and shoot down an Emily reportedly carrying high-ranking Japanese officials. It would be a tremendous feat to accomplish this intercept. All crews flying this day were elated with the prospect. My own feelings were somewhat dampened by two factors. One, our search sectors where the Emily was most likely to be found, were assigned to crews from another squadron, VB-119. This irritated me very much as our squadron's crews of VB-104 and my own crew in particular

were far more combat-experienced than those of VB-119. We were approaching the end of our combat tour, whereas VB-119 was still in the early stages of their tour. However, the VB-119 crews were flying the PB4Y-2 Privateer, the single-tail development from the PB4Y-1 (or B-24). The Privateer was faster and more heavily armed than our older aircraft. My second feeling of detraction was my growing apprehension concerning the return portion of the flight, which would be conducted during hours of darkness, adding to the operational hazards of flying in the forward areas.

'Departure from Clark Field was made at 0915 hours. Our patrol was up the eastern side of Formosa (now Taiwan), between Formosa and Sakishima Gunto into the East China Sea, then southwards along the China Coast searching for Japanese shipping, aircraft, and any targets of opportunity. After passing Formosa and when descending through some clouds, for one of those rare times in the South Pacific, we collected a little ice on the airplane. We proceeded in towards the China coast just above the water. We felt this was our best offensive, as well as defensive tactic when

En route to his rendezvous with an 'Emily', Stevens sights and surprises this 3,000 ton AGS-2 *Koshu*, a Japanese freighter. He sinks it after two bombing and strafing runs at mast-head level (Paul Stevens).

deep in enemy territory. We could then both fight off Japanese fighters and achieve the element of surprise when attacking Japanese shipping. However, there was a fog bank lying on the water and I could go into the coastline only so far. I was then concerned about running into a hill or mountain along the coast, as my forward visibility was virtually nil. We then turned south-westwards and proceeded down the Chinese coast.

'This portion of the patrol was flown about 100 feet above the water and about three to five miles offshore. We were enjoying a relatively strong tail wind, when about 150 miles south-west of Hangchow Bay, I sighted a Japanese freighter leaving a harbour. Further out to sea a Japanese destroyer was obviously conducting an anti-submarine search. I judged him to be far enough away to be just outside effective gun range. I immediately applied full power and started running in on the freighter. The Japanese destroyer then opened fire on us, but was ineffective. As we closed on the Japanese freighter, my top and bow turrets, manned by Allen Anania and David Gleason, opened fire. When firing forward, the muzzles of the top turret, twin .50 calibres, were just behind the pilot's head. Believe me, the muzzle blasts from these fifties

Lt Paul Stevens' crew: *Back row, left to right:* Allen Anania, radio operator/top turret gunner; David Gleason, mechanic/bow turret gunner; Lee Webber, bombardier (wounded in previous actions and not present on 17 March); Lee Little, ordnance/port waist gunner; Adrian Fox, radioman/gunner; Arvid Rasmussen, mechanic/tail gunner. *Front row, left to right:* Marx Stephan, ordnance/belly gunner; ENS John McKinley, co-pilot; Lt Paul Stevens, Plane Commander; Ltjg Edwin Streit, navigator; Derral Pedigo, mechanic/gunner (wounded in previous actions and not present on 17 March). Present on 17 March but not in the photo were Thomas Yoakum (bombardier, and starboard waist gunner). Duffey McKenzie (radarman) and William Mathisen (Paul Stevens).

nearly drove one out of the cockpit! The noise was deafening. Running in closer against the Japanese freighter, our gunners generated a beautiful sight. The bow and top turrets appeared to be hitting with every tracer. And, more importantly, we caught him by surprise and there was no return fire. With the engines set at forty-five inches of manifold pressure and 2,500 rpm, and assisted by the tail wind, our attack speed was about 235 knots.

'The bomb load this day was ten 100lb bombs. These bombs were equipped with a five-second delay fuse. This permitted us to make a masthead

3,000 ton AGS-2 *Koshu*, a Japanese freighter, after the first firing and bombing pass (Paul Stevens).

bombing attack and then get clear before the bombs exploded. With a load of ten 100lb bombs we were thus equipped to attack large shipping, dropping the entire string of bombs and assuring hits, as well as attacking small shipping and dropping one bomb at a time in order to sink as many ships as possible. In attacks of this type, the bombardier released the bombs utilising the 'seaman's eye' method. That is, simply, a visual judgement of when to release. At masthead level and dropping a string of bombs, by an experienced bombardier, it was virtually impossible to miss. If we had surprise on our side, which we strived for, a bombing run of this nature with the B-24 pitted against a Japanese merchant ship was really not all that hazardous. However, if the element of surprise was not on our side, such a masthead attack could be fatal for the attacking aircraft.

'Just after the bombs had been released and a pull-up made, by laying my head up in the bubbleside-window, I could see the explosions of the ship, though several bombs had overshot. With the destroyer still out of gun range, I circled back, flew up-wind and came in for a high-speed strafing pass to ensure that we obtained a good photograph. The ship was burning and had made a 180 degree turn. As we passed by the ship, I observed crew men jumping over the side. (The following day one of our planes patrolling this area found conclusive evidence that this ship had been sunk, and we were credited with this kill. It was identified as the 3,000 ton *Fox Tare Baker*, AGS-2 *Koshu*).

'Shortly after pulling up from this second strafing and photo run, we sighted two Aichi E13A Jakes. They were slightly above and on an opposite course from us, in a formation, right echelon. They apparently did not see us and, staying low on the water, we turned and pulled up to join in as number three man in their formation. As was my practice, when assured that we had surprise, our aircraft would be flown to a position behind and slightly to the right of the enemy aircraft. Our gunners were not permitted to fire until we were at point-blank range. As we slid into the number three slot we were very nearly lapping wings. I was impressed with the sleekness, and as with most Japanese aircraft, the very smooth finish. [At Morotai in October 1944, while en route to join 'Screaming 104', Stevens and his crew had spent four days sanding and waxing

THE SHOOTING DOWN OF VICE-ADMIRAL YAMAGATA

down their PB4Y-1 with two gallons of floor wax to add 5–10 knots to their speed]. I noted that this aircraft was equipped with radar. It had the 'clothes line' antenna wiring all around the fuselage and wings. The rear seat man was seated aft and performed the classic 'double take'. As we joined in, he first glanced over at us, turned his head back then quickly turned back to look at us again. He made no attempt to use his 20mm gun. At that time we opened fire and very quickly the Jake started down. Following him down, we observed him crashing into the water.

'So far it had been a good day, and as we pulled up from shooting down the first Jake, my thought was to take on the other Jake. However, the pilot of that aircraft used his head and flew directly to the Japanese destroyer and began circling overhead. Japanese destroyers were greatly respected by us. Their gunnery was excellent and we rarely caught them by surprise. We, therefore, turned southward and resumed patrol. The Jake remained in a safe haven over the destroyer.

'Twenty to thirty minutes after the attack on the Jake, while travelling southwards along the China coast and continuing just off the water, I looked up and about five to eight miles ahead and

Painting of Paul F. Stevens' PB4Y-1 attacking and sinking the 3,000 ton AGS-2 *Koshu* on 17 March 1945 by Abrams, on display at the US Naval Air Museum in Pensacola, Florida (Paul Stevens).

approximately 3,000 to 4,000ft above, I spotted the aircraft we had been sent out to find – the Japanese Emily! It was a very slicked up airplane and a pretty sight. There was no question but that we had found what we had come for. Immediately upon sighting, I put on full power and told my crew to stand by to attack. My first thought was to pull directly head-on into the aircraft for no-deflection shooting. This is what I should have done. However, I discarded that idea and decided to climb in on a beam attack and, hoping to stay with the aircraft, to ensure bringing it down. With full power on we began a climbing approach and, as yet, they had not seen us.'

Aboard the Emily Nobuyuki Taniguchi was keeping watch next to Yasuda and he spotted the Liberator. 'I immediately informed Yasuda and the captain, who reported this to Yamagata. The Vice-Admiral asked how far we were from Shanghai. The captain answered, 'Twenty minutes'. Yamagata entrusted the captain with the task of taking evasive action to avoid attack.'

Stevens continues: 'A zoom-climbing 180 degree turn was made into the aircraft at point-blank range. The Emily put on power, increasing speed but attempted no evasive manoeuvres. We opened fire and both the top and bow turrets were shooting well. There were numerous tracer flashes on the deep fuselage indicating hits.' Nobuyuki Taniguchi says: 'The shooting by the enemy plane was fierce and I saw bullets coming through the fuselage. The chief engineer, a Taisa (Captain) in the Fourth Southern Expeditionary Fleet, died instantly from a round that went through his chest. He died with bubbles of blood coming out of his mouth. The Vice-Admiral sat in his seat, holding his sword with both hands. He asked me how many bullets remained for the 20mm gun. I answered that there were ninety bullets remaining, and 400 bullets for the 7.7mm gun. He encouraged me to do my best. The young gunner was having a problem changing a magazine. This was his first aerial warfare. I took over from him and started to shoot. When the enemy plane came within 100 metres (330 feet) I fired heavily. After a while, the Vice-Admiral asked about the

remaining number of bullets. The Vice-Admiral patted me on the shoulder and was pleased with my performance. At one point during the attack the distance between the two planes was only 100 to 150 metres and I could clearly see an American pilot's face.'

The PB4Y was not hit. Stevens, though, regretted his method of attack. 'I did not direct my gunners to shoot out an engine. Had we shot out an engine, it would have slowed him sufficiently to ensure a kill. With the zoom climb and turn into the Emily, a loss of air speed resulted and temporarily stalled our aircraft. The altitude difference was more than we could make and still maintain our flying speed. After recovering from our stall, the Emily was seen flying northbound, slowly descending, but apparently still in flying condition. We pursued the Emily but were only gaining slowly. Ensign John McKinley, my co-pilot, then asked me how far I intended to chase him. I was alleged to have replied 'All the way to Tokyo if necessary!' His query reminded me that we were at the end of our patrol sector, had already engaged in combat, and used a good deal of full power 'fuel-eating' settings. I continued the chase for approximately fifteen to twenty minutes when I sighted tidal mud flats off the China

H8K2-L 'Emily' patrol flying-boat under attack from PB4Y-1 (National Archives).

Coast south of Haimen and Tai-chou wan (bay). It now became a question of whether to break off the attack and head home, or continue the chase and face the certainty of running out of fuel and ditching at night. With a very sick feeling and great reluctance, I broke off the chase and set course for Clark Field.'

The joy on board the Emily was short-lived. Nobuyuki Taniguchi recalls: 'The pilot informed us that we had only enough fuel left for five minutes' flying time.' During the encounter with Stevens' PB4Y, the Emily had executed several full power speeds and turns southwards to escape its pursuer. This, aided by a brisk thirty-knot north-east wind on the surface (and upwards of forty to forty-five knots at the higher altitude) pushed them further south than they realized. By the time the Emily regained its northern track, and following the fire-fight with Stevens' PB4Y, they had consumed an exorbitant amount of fuel. Thus, the Emily could not reach Shanghai, another 240 statute miles north of Haimen. Taniguchi recalls: 'We tried to determine our location and a possible landing site. We saw what we believed was the Huangpu River [actually the upper north-west reaches of the Chien Tong River, north of Wenchow] and decided to land there. After landing on the water we feathered two engines to save fuel. We taxied on the water using the two engines, looking for a good site to dock the flying-boat. We realized it would be near a village on the right bank of the river, facing the ocean. All the engines were shut down.'

As Stevens turned homeward, much of the joy in shooting down one of the 'Jakes' and sinking a Japanese freighter became dulled. He then believed he had missed the chance of a lifetime. 'Our homeward trip was uneventful, except for the apprehension of insufficient fuel and a very dark night. Finding the airstrip at night with no navigational aids was an additional concern. And, of course, the tropical weather was always a factor. Thanks to a very strong tailwind, we arrived back at Clark Field at 2239 hours with 350 gallons of fuel remaining – about one hour and thirty minutes' more flying time, a reasonable reserve.

'Two days later, while having lunch in our mess hall, I noticed our Wing Commander, Capt. Carroll B. Jones, USN, with his staff at the head table having a rather gleeful conversation among themselves. They were laughing and patting one another on the

A smiling Lt Paul F. Stevens, USN, Executive Officer 'Screaming 104', the day after he bagged V-Adm Yamagata – hence the big smile (Paul Stevens).

back. I soon sensed that I was the topic of conversation, as they kept glancing my way. They finally waved me over to their table. I could hardly believe the words, when they said: 'You got him, yes, you got him!' Needless to say, I was thrilled with the news. I returned to my table and informed my two co-pilots, even though the nature of the mission was still very classified and was to be closely restricted.'

Nobuyuki Taniguchi relates the events after landing: 'No additional personnel were killed or injured as a result of the forced landing. It was dusk and the high tide was rapidly running out, and soon the flying-boat ended up sitting on the mud-flat beach. Hatsuji Nakano, the Taisa Gunicho, or Captain and Senior Medical Officer, of the Fourth Southern Expeditionary Fleet HQ, was aboard. He had served as the director of a hospital near Shanghai during the China Incident. He spoke Chinese. He asked a Chinese fisherman where we were. The doctor told the crew that it was near Lin-hai, based on the fisherman's answer. High officials on board said there was a possibility that Japanese Army Units were stationed in this area. Some people were going to be sent out as scouts. Two of the Vice-Admiral's staff and two crew members left to ask the Chinese location of the nearest Japanese unit. Just as the men jumped off the main wing to start their search, about 200 Chinese soldiers appeared on the bank about 3,300 metres (990 feet) ahead. They opened fire immediately and our search teams could not move from that point. They threw themselves to the ground and returned the fire.'

Although the Japanese held military control over Shanghai, and some major Chinese cities, there existed a well-organised network of Sino-American espionage agents and saboteurs. Unfortunately for the complement of the Emily, they had force-landed in SACO's (Sino-American Co-operative Organization) Camp no.8 sector, and near the Guerilla Raiders Group at Haimen in Chekian (Zhejiang) Province. The first guerilla columns on the scene belonged to the Haimen Raiders Group which had been alerted by SACO's coastal watchers, which had reported the Emily heading inland. Nobuyuki Taniguchi continues: 'We saw more Chinese guerillas on several junks on the river. They were approaching and taking us under fire at the same time. We were now being attacked on all sides. I removed the 20mm machine-gun from the stern turret and placed it at the door of the plane to respond to the enemy fire. We fired about 200 rounds sporadically to make it appear we had plenty of firepower.

'A staff member announced that a suicide squad was being organised and everybody, except those manning machine-guns, should gather. Everyone, except the Vice-Admiral, five of his staff members and three gunners, jumped onto the ground from the wing carrying guns and Japanese swords. The man who organised the suicide squad (I believe it was Cdr Sado Ashiwara) was shot in the head as soon as he climbed out of the plane. He died instantly and fell to the ground. Half of the people died on the wing. Only a few made it to the ground. I was firing the machine-gun and did not know what happened to them. I was told later that four of

them hid in a village, but were found by Chinese guerillas. They put up a struggle with guns but all of them were shot to death. I kept shooting until we ran out of ammunition. I then moved to the 7.7mm gun, but it was broken. I did not see the crew anywhere. As I walked through the passenger section of the plane my left arm was hit and injured in three places by bullets from small-arms fire from one of the junks. I fell and remember the Vice-Admiral holding me, saying, 'Be strong', but I lost consciousness.

When I came around, I heard people down in the lower level talking. [The flying-boat had two decks and the lower section was where the fuel tank/baggage storage area was located.] I was still alive. I tore my scarf in half, tied it around my wounds, and went to the deck below. The Vice-Admiral then called for the crew, and as I was nearby I answered 'yes'. He said: 'This is the end; destroy all classified documents and material, and then burn the flying-boat!' A Taii (Lt) from the Ambon Seaplane Corps was looking for a container for fuel to start a fire to burn the flying-boat. I brought him a container. The Vice-Admiral asked me to send a radio message before starting the fire. I operated the transmitter and sent the message in plain language. It was sent to Surabaya, Saigon, Sanya (Ya Xian Hainan), Shanghai and Taiwan, and it read: 'We engaged in battle with an enemy plane and made an emergency landing due to the fuel shortage. The location is the shore of Huangpu River, near Lin-hai. We will make an attack as a marauding unit. Long live the Emperor: 1630 hours.' I shut off the power to the transmitter without waiting for an acknowledgement from those bases. I confirmed to the Vice-Admiral that the message had been sent, then threw the crystal and code-book into the ocean.

'I then rushed to the fuel room, removed my scarf and soaked it in gasoline, lit it with my lighter and threw it under the fuel tank and left the area. Fire soon started to burn the front portion of the flying-boat. The main wing then began to burn. At that moment there was a huge ball of fire and it even engulfed me. In astonishment I rolled on the deck two or three times and finally extinguished my flaming clothes.

'As I climbed the stairs to the second deck where the other people were, I suddenly felt the pain from my wounds and fainted near the entrance. When I again regained consciousness, the left wing was almost completely burned and heavy; thick smoke filled the inside of the flying-boat. Breathing was getting difficult. I sensed someone was there and raised my head. I saw the Vice-Admiral holding his Japanese sword in his right hand and sitting with his legs crossed.

'In front of the Vice-Admiral were three or four staff members. The Vice-Admiral was composed and said gently: 'All of you have assisted me well so that I could serve the Emperor and our country. I deeply appreciate your support. You are still very young and have a future. Escape this situation and serve the Emperor. Thank you! 'The four officers listened silently with bowed heads. The Vice-Admiral then pulled his sword from the pinkish-brown sheath and without hesitation performed seppuku (suicide).'

Taniguchi and four others, including Capt. Nakano, the doctor, were captured and held as PoWs in China. Taniguchi was sent to Kunming and interrogated by the Americans. 'On the way to Chongqing, where I was detained in jail as a PoW, I was interrogated by a Chinese who was fluent in Japanese. He showed me a few photographs. One photo showed about twenty bodies on the bank beside the destroyed flying-boat. He asked me which one was the Admiral. I answered that the Admiral's remains were not there, since of course he must have been burned in the aircraft after committing seppuku. Vice-Admiral Seigo Yamagata was the only one aboard the aircraft who committed seppuku.'

The day following the Emily landing, 18 March at 1000 hours, two Japanese gunboats and a 4,000-ton transport came from the south and attempted to recover the plane and passengers. Barges were lowered from the transport and sailed up the river. The Chinese mustered about 2,000 troops and gave them considerable small-arms opposition from shore. Four Japanese planes joined in the search but neither the ships nor the planes were able to find the seaplane as it had been sunk and covered with earth and straw by the Chinese. In the evening an American plane came on the scene and the Japs withdrew. The transport was sunk by an American plane near Do Chen Island at about 1700 hours that evening.

Stevens was awarded the Silver Star for his successful patrol and mission. His cititation read, in part: 'By employing continued vigilance, he sighted another hostile aircraft which he destroyed, thereby depriving the enemy of the services of a group of its highest ranking officers and officials.' Stevens was awarded the Navy Cross, two Silver Stars, the Presidential Citation, and other awards for many combat actions against the Japanese forces. Post-war, his duties included command of squadrons, an air wing, and an auxiliary ship. In 1963 – as Capt. Paul Stevens, the CO of the USS *Procyon*, a Naval Auxiliary Refrigerator Ship – he hosted a luncheon for a group of Japanese businessmen during a port visit at the Yokosuka Naval base, Japan. During the course of the luncheon conversation, one of the Japanese guests stated that he had been a Navy Captain in the Imperial Japanese Navy. Further conversation revealed that he had served as the Engineering Officer on Vice-Admiral Yamagata's staff in Java and, on 15 March 1945, had been assigned to remain behind to close down the base operations. Stevens related his role in shooting down the Admiral's plane. The Japanese then confirmed the details that Stevens had essentially learned from the SACO unit's briefings.

Postscript: Paul Stevens retired as a Captain, USN, in 1965 after a very successful career, including in 1962–63, as Air Wing Commander at NAS Miramar (Top Gun). He resides with his wife in Nashville, Tennessee, now retired from a civilian career in corporate aviation and aircraft sales. Cdr Briggs has had a brilliant career in Naval Intelligence. It was he who actually intercepted and recorded the 'Winds Message' just prior to the Japanese attack upon Pearl Harbor. Mihoko Yamagata, granddaughter of Admiral Yamagata, now lives in California with her husband, a lawyer.

CHAPTER 12
The Battle of Kagoshima Bay

Ltjg Ronald 'Slim' Somerville of Chillicote, Missouri, a pilot of a Curtiss SB2C Helldiver bomber from the USS *Hancock*, successfully dropped his 1,000lb bomb on the Japanese Naval Air Station at Kagoshima Bay on the island of Kyushu, and was only concerned with returning safely to his carrier off Okinawa. The mouth of the bay was believed to be heavily mined. Two airfields were strategically located to defend its many installations. The largest city on the island sprawled midway on the bay's western shore with numerous smaller settlements fanning out and around it. The early morning raid on 29 March 1945, which had also included wharves, warehouses, factories and barracks, had been successful

Curtiss SB2C Helldiver, similar to the one Ltjg Ronald 'Slim' Somerville was flying when he was shot down on 29 March 1945 (US Navy).

with heavy damage to the air station and two tankers being set on fire.

For several days now the US fast carrier force commanded by Admiral Marc Mitscher had been off Okinawa to begin softening up the Japanese defenders before the Army and Marine landing scheduled for 1 April. Invariably, the carrier pilots' targets were deep in enemy territory. Large airfields had to be knocked out by ground-level strafing and rocket attacks, and factories bombed from low altitude by dive bombers. Twice a day the Hellcat and Helldiver crews of Fighting Squadron Six (VB-6) converged on the *Hancock*'s wardroom to get the latest information on the operation. 'Hank' Miller closed the meetings with 'Gents, this is the time now. We've got a whale of a job to do. When we head back to the States there's not going to be any Jap airforce left!'

Day after day strikes had been mounted up and

ABOVE
Grumman F6F Hellcat, similar to ones flown by Fighting Squadron Six from the USS *Hancock* (Grumman).

BELOW
Close-up of the famous 'cat with a bomb' insignia of Fighting Squadron Six (VF-6) painted on a restored Hellcat previously flown by Lt Alexander Vraciu, fourth ranking Hellcat ace in WW2 with nineteen aerial victories, nine of which were achieved flying with VF-6 (Author).

down the Nansei Islands and US Naval warplanes had attacked and destroyed airfields, aircraft, military installations and sunk Japanese shipping whenever they could be found. While sweeps and strikes were hitting land targets, combat air patrols in the air fended off Japanese 'kamikaze' attacks which dropped out of the skies on a one-way trip packed with explosives. Sweeps had been made on Sakashima Gunto and Minami Daito Jima, but on the 29 March mission the strike against Kagoshima Bay had meant a return to the Japanese mainland itself. The flight of Helldivers gunned their powerful Wright-Cyclone engines for the long overwater journey to their waiting carriers. The flight entered cloud, and at about 1100 hours at 2,000 feet Somerville suddenly felt a terrific jolt. The tail of the heavy Curtiss aircraft had been cut off in a mid-air collision with one of the other Helldivers. Frantically, 'Slim' Somerville tried to contact Aviation Radioman Louis F. Jakubec, his rear seat gunner. There was no reply. The impact threw the aircraft onto its back and then into a vicious spin. It dived uncontrollably until, at 800 feet, Somerville knew he must bale out before it was too late.

In his haste to leave the striken aircraft, Somerville's feet became tangled in the parachute's risers and he fell into the middle of Kagoshima Bay head first. Something slammed his head forward against his chest with tremendous force, filling his eyes and mouth with cold salt water. Struggling frantically in his tightly strapped parachute harness, he managed to free his sheath knife and began hacking away at his chest and leg straps. His head bobbed up for an instant and he sucked air into his burning lungs ('I needed that air to pray', 'Slim' said later). Releasing his death grip on the knife he inflated his life-jacket and fumbled with his life-raft. The hungry waters closed over his head again. He had forgotten about his feet being entangled in the shrouds and the parachute with its heavy canopy was sinking, pulling him down again despite the inflated life-jacket. Lungs pulsating in agony, he peeled off his right glove and managed to dig a small penknife out of his chest pocket. Doubling up under water he commenced hacking away at the

lines around his feet. When they finally parted he had lost both hope and feeling. The inflated life jacket carried him to the surface with a rush and he bobbed up for the second time utterly exhausted and ready to give up.

Spying the life-raft floating an arm's length away, 'Slim' made an effort to recover it and clung to it, dazed and nauseated. An inflated life-raft is difficult to climb into, and for a man in Somerville's condition it was well-nigh impossible. However, 'Slim' managed it in fifteen minutes and he slumped inside face-down in the water-filled dinghy unaware of his position just a mile and a half from the docks at Kagoshima.

Air-Sea rescue missions in the Pacific had become almost routine procedure for Navy airmen, but what followed is probably the most spectacular rescue attempt ever mounted in the whole Pacific war, and one which required the retrieval of a fallen airman from the very jaws of the enemy. Overhead, Commander Henry 'Hank' L. Miller, USN, Somerville's air group commander, in a Corsair fighter, had seen the collision and had watched a single 'chute leave the stricken Helldiver. He waited until he saw a life-raft blossom. Picking up his microphone, he radioed the downed pilot's position

Ensign Roland H. 'Bake' Baker of Fighting Squadron Six following his return to the USS *Hancock* after his water landing in a Hellcat alongside the destroyer *Stemble* (R. H. Baker).

Ensign Roland H. Baker.

twice and requested immediate help in the shape of a seaplane rescue bid. His message was picked up by F6F Hellcat pilot and division leader Lt Robert L. 'Cherry' Klingler – so-called because of his blushing cheeks when he smiled – who was flying a combat air patrol with three other Hellcats. 'Cherry' was a veteran of the Marcus to Truk series of Pacific battles and had downed two 'Bettys' along the line as well as helping to stop a heavy cruiser at Truk.

Ensign Roland H. 'Bake' Baker Jr, one of the F6F Hellcat pilots, recalls: 'That's where we came in. Our division, 'Speedy II', consisted of four F6F Hellcat fighters then on combat air patrol over the force about seventy miles from the scene. Apart from Klingler, our division consisted of his wingman, Ensign 'Willi' H. Moeller, Ltjg Louis Davis (section leader) and myself. We were ordered to proceed to Kagoshima Bay at 'Buster', which meant full speed. The plan was to protect 'Slim' until a rescue could be mounted. We knew we were in for trouble.' Meanwhile, twelve Hellcats from the *Hancock* and eight from another ship were launched within ten minutes and rendezvoused over two OS2U Kingfisher seaplanes from the cruiser *Astoria*. The

four Hellcats sped in over the bay under an overcast and relieved the lone Navy fighter that was on station. Klingler split his division into two parts. Davis and Baker were sent above the broken cloud layer to watch for enemy aircraft while he and Moeller flew a slow circle around the life-raft. Light anti-aircraft fire from three sides of the bay burst around them spasmodically, forcing them to maintain evasive action at all times. Of the four, Klingler was the only one who had been in action before.

After pulling his aching body into the life-raft, 'Slim' Somerville had collapsed, too exhausted to worry about his position. He thought his chances of being picked up were nil. He was through. The struggle to keep from drowning had weakened him so much that he couldn't raise his little finger. Then he sat up and looked at the shore. 'I could see a lot of Japs standing there near a dock watching me and waiting for me to drift in. In twenty seconds I had my paddles out and was rowing like a champ. It took forty-five minutes to get out to the centre of the bay again. I just forgot about being tired I guess.'

Roland Baker continues: 'We immediately searched for 'Slim'. We spotted him in his raft and he waved to us.' Somerville wrote: 'I saw four Hellcats overhead. I knew they were there to help me. Two of them were flying low over me and two more were higher up.' Klingler realised they were asking for trouble. The Japanese knew there was a pilot down in a raft and they also had reason to know that there were only four American fighters in the area. Somewhere inland there were many Japanese fighters waiting for an opportunity such as this and it was even odds who would reach them first, the rescue group or the Japanese fighters. As it turned out, the Japanese fighters won. Roland Baker continues: 'We hadn't been there long before being intercepted by eight Japanese Navy Zeros (code-name Zeke). All hell broke loose. Almost at once I was firing a deflection shot and observed pieces breaking off the Zeke but I could not follow through at such close quarters. I checked instinctively over my shoulder and saw a Zeke diving on me. I pulled around and climbed to meet him. We were then in a head-on match; both firing. The Jap passed directly under me, which was a relief as I was concerned he might elect to join his honourable ancestors by ramming me. I then made a tight turn to follow him. He never pulled out of the dive and hit the water.

'I levelled out (now at low altitude) and for a minute flew straight and level looking for the others. I observed one of our planes go straight in (I learned later that it was Louis Davis). That awful sight fixed my attention for that split moment but I came to quickly as tracers shot past my port wing followed by several hits opening up holes in the wing. I made a tight left turn pulling Gs with the help of my G-suit and thought I had lost him. Later, I learned that Klingler had shot him off my tail.'

In lightning response to Davis's call for help, Klingler and his wingman had poured on full power and climbed through the low hanging clouds. The battle was on in earnest. The surviving Zeros came in from all angles, singly and in pairs, firing long streams of tracers and then using their speed to zoom to altitude. A single Zeke slipped in behind Klingler's violently twisting fighter and began firing. Moeller, evidently unseen by the Japanese pilot against the clouds, raised his nose for a 'dream' shot and the third Japanese fighter erupted in flames and veered away. Turning to pick up his wingman, Klingler spotted a Zeke in the process of making a run on the trailing Hellcat. He fired and the Japanese pilot dived for the clouds.

Somerville watched the aerial battle from his bobbing life-raft. He wrote: 'One of [the Zeros] must have spotted my dye marker in the water, for he peeled off and started towards me. I got out of the last tough spot, but maybe this is the real one. But before the Zeke could even get a second look, the two Hellcat pilots, Davis and Baker, attacked the Japanese fighter and were soon joined by Klingler and Moeller. Then I saw a real fight. They milled all over the sky. It seemed unreal to me, somehow, sitting in that little raft. The Jap that had dropped down to look me over went out early. I saw one Hellcat chasing a Zeke, firing at him, with another Jap on his tail.' Klingler confirmed later that it was Davis's Hellcat: 'Later, I saw two splashes and two oil slicks in the water as I went for a Zeke on Baker's tail.' After Klingler had opened fire and shot down the Zero on Baker's tail he shot down one on Moeller's tail. 'That made five Japs in just a couple minutes, but the next thing I knew was one of the Japs that had parachuted from one of the planes shot down was coming down right on top of me. I figured this would beat it all; a naval engagement, rubber raft to raft, with a Jap in Kagoshima Bay, but I never saw him after he splashed into the water.'

By now Baker's Hellcat was badly shot up and limping at slow speed away from the bay area. Klingler sent Moeller to cover Baker's withdrawal and then began a search for Davis and the four remaining Zeros. Breaking through the overcast he saw a burning oil slick at the mouth of the bay. Spiralling down trailing smoke was what appeared to be a Hellcat fighter. A parachute billowed out in the air and then collapsed as the occupant hit the water. Klingler could not tell if the man was an American or a Japanese. As he zoomed low over the water to investigate he saw a burning Zero roll over on its back and crash on the shore. Sweeping the scene he failed to uncover any survivors and he headed back to check on 'Slim'. A lone fighter tore up the bay towards Somerville, staying close to the water. It was Klingler looking for his wingman. Coming towards him was a tremendous force of weaving fighters, blocking any chance he might have had for making a run on his base. Baker adds: 'As the three of us joined up we saw a large group of planes entering the bay and prayed they were friendly! It was the rescue group escorting two OS2U seaplanes that had been fired off our cruisers.' The rescue flight had arrived five minutes too

OS2U Kingfisher floatplane of the type which rescued Ltjg Somerville from the jaws of the Japanese in Kagoshima Bay on 29 March 1945, now on display at the Smithsonian Institute in Washington DC (Author).

late to get in on the fight. Thinking them to be the enemy Klingler headed straight for the formation with the intention of blasting his way through in one last attempt to take as many as he could with him. Lt-Cmdr R. I. Copeland, in the lead Hellcat, observing one of his fighters coming straight at him, called out over the air 'Take it easy Mac! We're friendly!'

The immense fighter cover fanned out and swarmed over the inner shores of the bay area, beating down any signs of Japanese resistance. The seaplane base at Kagoshima and the adjoining docks were destroyed by strafing runs by the Hellcats. Two small boats which attempted to strike out for the downed Somerville were burned and sunk. As the Hellcats circled, two more Japanese aircraft were sighted. One, a twin-engined machine, was shot down by Ltjg Clifford N. Seaver, and the other, a Zero, was shot down by Lt Hovland.

A division of fighters wove steadily over the circling OS2U Kingfisher seaplane which dropped a smoke bomb for wind direction and then landed skilfully to pick up the waiting Somerville. Baker

adds: 'The other picked up an F6F escorting pilot who was forced to ditch when his plane was hit by anti-aircraft fire from shore. Then everybody got the hell out of there. I was forced to ditch on the way back and had to make a no-flap landing in heavy seas. I was rescued by the destroyer Stemble.

'Slim' Somerville was landed aboard the USS Astoria while the force was under Japanese attack and the sky full of anti-aircraft fire. Somerville and Baker were returned to the Hancock at the same time a few days later. 'Cherry' Klingler and Louis Davis each received the Navy Cross for their actions on 29 March, while Roland Baker and Willi Moeller each received the Distinguished Flying Cross. Next day, and again on 31 March, Okinawa was again hit by all squadrons in the Fighting Squadron Six. On 6 April Baker was shot up again, over an airfield on Kikai, part of the Amami O Shima Islands, when the

Ensign Roland H. 'Bake' Baker (far left) describes his version of a dogfight with seven Japanese fighters to (left to right) Lt Robert L. 'Cherry' Klingler, Ltjg 'Slim' Somerville and Ensign Willis 'Willi' H. Moeller. Five Zeros were shot down by this division on 29 March (R. H. Baker).

drop tank was set on fire. The Hellcat took a lot of punishment but made it back to the *Hancock*.

Five months later the war in the Far East was over without an air battle but with destruction on a massive scale when an atomic bomb was dropped on Hiroshima on 6 August, and three days later another was exploded over Nagasaki. The Japanese government surrendered five days later, on 14 August. The official surrender ceremony took place aboard the USS *Missouri* in Tokyo Bay on 2 September. World War Two was finally at an end.

INDEX